Trust you
will enjoy

Missilema

11/10/18

MISSILEMAN

MISSILEMAN

The Secret Life of
Cold War Engineer **WALLACE CLAUSON**

JOHN CLAUSON

with Alice Sullivan

 WND Books

MISSILEMAN

Published by WND Books, Washington, D.C. WND Books is a registered trademark of WorldNetDaily.com, Inc. ("WND")

Book designed by Mark Karis

WND Books are available at special discounts for bulk purchases. WND Books also publishes books in electronic formats. For more information call (541) 474-1776, e-mail orders@wndbooks.com or visit www.wndbooks.com.

Unless otherwise indicated, Scripture quotations are from the Holy Bible, King James Version (public domain). Scripture quotations marked MEV are taken from The Holy Bible, Modern English Version. Copyright © 2014 by Military Bible Association. Published and distributed by Charisma House.

Hardcover ISBN: 978-1-944229-66-5
eBook ISBN: 978-1-944229-67-2

Library of Congress Cataloging-in-Publication Data
Names: Clauson, John, 1954- author. | Sullivan, Alice, 1979- author.
Title: Missileman : the secret life of Cold War engineer Wallace Clauson /
    John Clauson with Alice Sullivan.
Other titles: Secret life of Cold War engineer Wallace Clauson
Description: Washington, D.C. : WND Books, [2017] | Includes index. |
    Identifiers: LCCN 2017009438 (print) | LCCN 2017019350 (ebook) | ISBN
    9781944229672 (e-book) | ISBN 9781944229665 (hardcover)
Subjects: LCSH: Clauson, Wallace, 1922-1991. | Military research--United
    States--Biography. | Mathematicians--United States--Biography. |
    Engineers--United States--Biography. | International Business Machines
    Corporation--Employees--Biography. | Guided missiles--United States. |
    Swedish Americans--Biography. | Clawson family. | Crawford County
    (Iowa)--Biography. | Cold War--Biography.
Classification: LCC U393.5 (ebook) | LCC U393.5 .C53 2017 (print) | DDC
    623.4/51092 [B] --dc23
LC record available at https://lccn.loc.gov/2017009438

Printed in the United States of America
17 18 19 20 21 22 LBM 9 8 7 6 5 4 3 2 1

CONTENTS

Introduction: Four Days That Changed My Life 1

1 The Admission 7
2 Moving to Jersey 10
3 Building the Fence 17
4 Second Chances and a Gift from God 20
5 The Problem Solver 29
6 An Invitation from the NDRC 35
7 A Real Education 41
8 Hidden Genius 46
9 The Setup 51
10 Bombs Away 54
11 The Problem with Pearl Harbor 58
12 In the Navy 67
13 The Rise of Radar 71
14 Love and Marriage 76
15 The Farmer with an Engineering Degree 81
16 The Windmill 89
17 Albin Smells a Rat 94
18 The Greatest Living Room Debates 101
19 The Math Tutor 106
20 An Unlikely Cover 114
21 Hired by IBM 119
22 Fear and a False Alarm 126
23 NASA 132
24 Dangerous Technology and Safe Sundays 136

25   Making Time to Be a Dad 142

26   Jack-of-All-Trades 149

27   The Perfect Saturday 154

28   The Cuban Missile Crisis 159

29   The Six-Day War 165

30   The Curious Case of the Water Dam 169

31   No Attention to Detail 173

32   Moving to Switzerland 179

33   An American Teenager in Zurich 186

34   Secret Meetings and Broken Promises 196

35   The Invalid Valedictorian 206

36   The Yom Kippur War 210

37   The World's Greatest Hot Plate 218

38   Moving to England 222

39   The Evil Empire 229

40   Able Archer 236

41   The Deadly Diagnosis 243

42   Searching for a Miracle Cure 250

43   The Last Goodbye 254

44   The Funeral 258

45   The Fifteen-Year Refusal 261

46   Game On 264

47   A Woman's Faith 269

48   A Love Reunited 273

*Appendix: Yom Kippur Cease Fire Sequence
of Documents Between Kremlin and the White House* 277

Notes 298

Index 306

INTRODUCTION

Four Days That Changed My Life

IF AMERICAN NOVELIST ALAN FURST had set his historical tales of intrigue at the dawn of the Cold War instead of World War II, one of the characters hurtling toward an unexpected destiny could have been my father, Wallace Clauson. By mundane chance (or was it divinely guided?)—an eighth-grade math test—propelled him from an Iowa farm to a world of high-tech military secrecy. For nearly fifty years, he kept it all hidden from his family and concealed his double life behind a fog of vague excuses, bland diary entries, hammer-and-nail work projects that he attacked with an obsessive fury, and a refusal to form social friendships.

We moved often, much to the displeasure of my mother, Marilyn, and he seemed to always be traveling for work—sometimes months at a time with no contact or details of his whereabouts—because of his sales job with IBM, selling computers. At least that's what he told my mother, my siblings, and me. Yes, his paychecks came with an IBM logo on the upper-right-hand corner. Yes, he was in IBM company photos and he received IBM employee Christmas gifts.

But his real job was with IBM's clandestine Federal Systems Group, which meant that he was really taking orders from the Department of Defense. As such, he was one of the genius mathematicians behind the most important developments in twentieth-century military technology. From radar systems to nuclear warheads, he was there to provide mathematical brainpower, and to make sure American nuclear missiles hit their targets if they were ever fired.

I learned this just two years before he died. Several years into retirement, my father called me to say he was coming across the country from Seattle to help me build a fence, one of his typical home-improvement projects, for the new three-acre home I had purchased for my family near Princeton, New Jersey. I soon found out his visit over those four days was less about the fence and more about finally telling the truth about his career.

At first glance, when he got off the plane in Philadelphia wearing his Mister Rogers cardigan, he was the same father I'd always known. But during the drive home from the airport, as we drove through Philadelphia and Titusville, New Jersey, where I lived with my family in a fenceless house, he saw things—interstate signs and old houses—that triggered memories, and he believed some explanations were in order. He began to open up, pointing out places he remembered, their importance to national security, his role in the matter, and the other people involved. *Dad and national security? What is he talking about?* My dad had been a salesman his entire career—or so I thought.

While I loved my father dearly, we had never been that close, mostly due to his frequent travels and his closed-off personality. So his unsolicited and rather surprising revelation rendered me speechless. In fact, I barely slept that night, replaying his voice over and over and wondering, *Could it be true?*

The next morning, we began to dig the holes for the fence posts. Once the tap opened, his story gushed forth, and he began downloading decades of details, spurred on by hours of manual labor. As the last of four children, and the second son, I wondered if he'd told my older brother—or anyone else in the family, for that matter. *Did my mother know any of this? What about my sisters?* On the other hand, I felt a sense of pride that he was entrusting me with his secrets—if they were, in fact, secrets. He'd been diagnosed with cancer a few years before, and I couldn't help but wonder if it had returned, destructive cells somehow concocting a highly detailed fantasy world in Dad's mind.

What my dad told me that weekend was shocking on many levels. Not only did I discover that he was one of the key men responsible for the development and installation of nuclear weapons, and that he'd been living a lie for fifty years; it also put a new perspective on my childhood and teenage years. It made me realize that the reason we moved so often was because we were accompanying him around the United States and Europe on secret missions, not because he was switching sales territories. I now knew why he and my mother had few friends, and how necessary it was for him to find solace at church as he did every Sunday. And it accounted for the fact that he always seemed to know so much about my day-to-day activities even though he wasn't present—because at times there was a government detail following me everywhere I went.

Moreover, the stories my father told me revealed the secret operations of the U.S. government, and gave me an inside view on the politics, alliances, and personalities of the Cold War period. I marveled at his associations, legends such as Einstein and Fermi and von Neumann and Atanasoff.

I was now privy to the fact that in 1962, the Cuban missile crisis was much more serious than the American public was originally led to believe. And in the mid-1980s, the United States had come extremely close to nuclear war with the Soviet Union and that we were saved from that fate by a random but timely stroke of *very* good luck.

I now understood why he had paced through our home on countless sleepless nights under unbelievable stress; he knew that one missed calculation could lead to total disaster for the human race.

It explained why he was often reluctant to become involved in my life, whether that meant holding back on coaching Little League teams or avoiding school performances—because no stranger could ever be trusted.

Finally, Dad's revelation explained why he felt his life was ending at the right time. The cancer had, in fact, returned. He would fight it valiantly, but I believe, in some ways, he was ready to meet his Maker. With the death of the Cold War, the purpose of his life had come to an end too.

The man I delivered back to the airport several days later was different from the one who had arrived. My father seemed at peace, a heavy weight finally lifted from his conscious.

I was different too.

My house had a magnificent fence now, strong enough to stand up to any storm. As for me, this deluge of information had left me completely discombobulated. *How will I even begin to process this news?*

A month after his visit to Princeton, Dad's health went into rapid decline. He died nineteen months later, on May 2, 1991, at the age of sixty-eight, outlasting his doctor's prediction by one month.

After Dad passed away, the family was divvying up the assets to go to the various kids, and Mom requested that I receive Dad's prized workbench desk. When Dad was on his way out, he told Mom to make sure I got it. I was both thrilled and honored to receive it. It was a work of art, of course. He'd made it himself.

When I set it up in my garage, I noticed that one of the drawers wouldn't close completely. *That is strange*, I thought. It couldn't possibly be a design flaw. When I took the drawer out to investigate, I saw the culprit. Attached to the drawer's bottom by rubber bands was a stack of nearly ninety business cards, wrapped in an intricate maze of rubber bands and wire. The placement was clearly intentional, as if Dad was giving me a nudge from beyond the grave.

I realized the cards appeared to be from the early 1960s, many of the addresses along Wilshire Boulevard in Los Angeles. The company names spoke of nascent space and technology companies. I had no idea what to make of them, but I knew *Dad had left them for me on purpose.*

Still, I sat on the story for fifteen years, wrestling with my own inner turmoil and wondering if Dad had been telling the truth. I did nothing about the stack of business cards he'd left me, apart from an initial flip-through to read some of the names and a quick online search to confirm the validity of some of the businesses. In fact, I didn't reveal anything at all to my mother or my siblings, or to anyone else, except for the short snippets I told my wife, Celeste.

Of course, that doesn't mean I didn't think about Dad's tale. In fact, when he first told me the truth in 1989, I dwelled on it extensively. When I look back at my job performance that year, I can see a definite glitch. For someone who knew what he was doing, I made a whole lot of bad decisions. I was just simply too distracted by what I was told. But for whatever reason, I'd never taken the initiative to engage Dad in another conversation about his past. I somehow felt that he'd said everything he was going to say over that mid-week visit.

And then he died. I could never ask another question—even if I wanted to.

It took me those fifteen years to get over the shock of it all, and to accept that Dad had good reasons for keeping me (and our entire family) in the dark. I finally accepted that I shouldn't be hurt, that I should take the story for what it was—and him for who and what he was. Most of all, I understood why he wasn't able to be the father—or probably the husband—he wanted to be. It didn't make things right; but as an adult with a family of my own, I was able to empathize with the struggle he experienced because of his top-secret career—the trade-off of being a largely absentee parent, but quite literally saving the world from nuclear holocaust.

In 2005, I told the story to my family, and filtered snippets of it to my mother. I didn't think she'd understand what he'd really done and why he'd kept it from her—his wife and life partner—for more than fifty years. My only regret is that I didn't tell her more about Dad's life. I think she would have been very proud of his accomplishments and his determination to use his gift for the good of humankind.

I wasn't surprised that the first reaction for *most* members of my family was disbelief. They simply could not fathom that Dad had been living a lie. In a sense it was more difficult for them because they couldn't turn to him for clarification, nor could they hear him recount his life in such detail, as I had. However, with each passing year, my siblings, as they reflected on their own lives and childhood and adolescent memories, were able to see more and more that his story might just be possible. A few of them could even pinpoint exact conversations or instances where they *knew* there was more to the story, and that Dad was likely keeping something from the rest of us.

I accepted an early retirement package from my company and threw myself into conducting intensive research to confirm—or deny—the details he'd shared with me during the fence-building project. Time and time again, I found that Dad had been telling me the truth—it was *all true*.

I knew I finally had to tell his story—a story of the military-technology complex and the brains behind it, the Cold War that came within a hair of going hot in 1983, and the unacknowledged role of IBM's Federal Systems Group in the tensest moments of that war.

But it's our family's story too.

In writing this book, I am finally fulfilling Dad's desire that his story be known. My in-depth research into the events and personalities that shaped his life has given me a greater understanding of that desire—and of my father.

His is truly a story that needs to be told.

1

The Admission

"WORK ETHIC" COULD HAVE BEEN DAD'S MIDDLE NAME. Growing up on a farm in rural Iowa during the Great Depression, he remembered the anxiety of the Depression years, and he was well acquainted with the notion of keeping busy. Spending idle time was not a possibility in my family. If we weren't doing homework, practicing musical instruments, or playing hard, we were mowing the lawn.

So when my father, Wallace William Clauson, retired on August 31, 1984, he began looking for projects to fill his time. The fact that he'd just come off a bout with colon cancer didn't seem to matter. After he'd made every possible improvement to the home he shared with my mother in Bellevue, Washington, he started in on the homes of his four children. Because he was one of those guys who knew how to do just about anything thoroughly, it was a great deal. He was insistent upon making whatever repairs or upgrades he saw fit to both increase the home's value and make our lives easier, and we knew we'd be getting high-quality work entirely for free by an undemanding houseguest.

I'll always remember the day in 1987 that I moved my family into our Southern California home in Rancho Niguel, near Laguna Beach. My longtime employer, Johnson & Johnson, had transferred me from the Seattle area to take a management position in the new extended care division. Dad had flown down from Seattle with his tools at the ready.

While the movers were still unloading boxes, Dad thoroughly inspected the house. Nearly the first thing he had said was, "Johnny, we have to rearrange your electrical panel," as he grabbed his needle-nose pliers.

I said, "Dad, it's a brand-new house!"

He said, "Johnny, trust me: we are going to rearrange your panel." Everything was too loaded on the two circuits, and Dad spotted it right away. Mind you, the electrical panel should have been correct on a brand-new house. But it wasn't.

When he was finished redistributing the circuits to his liking, he set up a table saw to begin framing out the windows. He spent three twelve-hour days on this new project, and that was only for the *first floor*. He also made us furniture, and I still have a set of beautiful hardwood side tables, with oak veneer and hardwood spun legs, that he made for that house.

Ironically, a month later, the builder of our development of fifteen hundred homes, knocked on our door and said they would like to get to our service panel to rearrange it.

I said, "Don't you get near my panel."

They were shocked and inquired, "Don't you want us to fix it?"

"It's already been fixed," I offered with a look of disdain. I also felt a bit of pride that my dad had spotted the error within minutes of stepping foot in the house.

Two months after his last visit, Dad had driven down in my sister Nedra's van to my house in Rancho Niguel, California, again to finish the wood casings for the upstairs windows. Although the walls were so uneven he decided not to finish, he still managed to complete a redo on our yard. That included a new sprinkler system, new drainage ditches, expert landscaping, and the pouring of ten yards of concrete for an expansive patio.

When the welder showed up to do some plumbing, the guy had only just started to weld when my dad put his goggles on said, "Let me show you how you should do welding on stuff like this."

The plumber looked at me in total disbelief—and was probably a little offended. But Dad had instantly seen that the man didn't know the best way to weld this particular section of pipe, and Dad was trying to teach him. He said, "This is how you weld when you've got to do it upside down and you don't want it to drip." Now intrigued, the plumber listened and watched closely, because it was obvious my dad knew what he was talking about.

As always, he fashioned some rather unorthodox tools to complete various tasks. His version of a leveler to get the lawn's dirt ready for a concrete pour was a chain link fence *attached to my waist* by a rope. Like a work mule, I was compelled to drag the fence across the dirt, throwing bricks on top of the fence to increase the weight. I told Dad repeatedly that I needed to get to the office, but the truth was, I just wanted to get away from all of his grueling work requirements.

2

Moving to Jersey

TWENTY-TWO MONTHS LATER, we were moving again. I was to assume a new J&J management job in New Jersey. Celeste wasn't thrilled about the move, and I didn't blame her. Although life was sometimes stressful with three small children, my three-day-a week travel schedule, and Celeste's full-time job as a trauma room nurse, we loved that the kids could play outside all year round. We also enjoyed relaxing in the backyard hot tub at night.

We were living in the five-bedroom home of our dreams in Laguna Niguel at the end of a cul-de-sac, three miles from the Pacific Ocean. We had gotten involved in the church, the neighborhood, and the kids' schools, and now I had to yank her away and move her to Jersey. To this day, I've never met anybody who would willingly move from Laguna Beach to New Jersey.

Our first house-hunting trip, in and around Princeton, New Jersey, with Celeste was disappointing. We spent most of the time arguing about the move itself, about leaving our family-friendly home with the great brick and stone patio in the back, and moving to New Jersey for my job. *Again.* It seemed we were always moving because of my job.

After one particularly big argument, Celeste wanted to immediately fly home, and I talked her out of leaving. Still, we didn't see any homes we really liked that weekend. A few days later, when it was time to plan the second exploratory trip, Celeste, frustrated with being uprooted again for my job's sake, backed out. "It's your move. You get it done," she said. "Why don't you take your dad instead?"

As it turned out, taking my dad was a great idea. He was brilliant when it came to identifying structural issues and shortcomings, and for knowing what a house would need to become a comfortable home. He knew what was right about a house, and was tops at gauging home values. Because he had always had an uncanny knack for all things construction, mechanics, and structural design—none of which were handed down to me in the Swedish family gene pool—Celeste and I decided it was easier to take him along than have him point out our errors later.

When I called to tell Dad we were moving east, I was afraid he would express his displeasure, given all the work he'd just completed on our Laguna house. He'd put in countless hours on projects that increased our home's usability and value, and I worried he'd be disappointed that we'd be leaving all his handwork behind so soon. I should have known better.

"Jersey! Well, that's a great place!" he said with enthusiasm, the possibility of new projects getting his blood going. He was five years into retirement now, and he loved keeping himself busy. Mom loved it too because any projects involving building and design made him happy. And seeing Dad happy was a relatively new treat for all of us.

One week later, we were together in central New Jersey. I was surprised that Dad knew as much about the area as he did, and for a moment or two I wondered why. I didn't remember him ever talking about spending much time in New Jersey, but I didn't bother to ask him about it.

For two days, we scoured the area around Princeton, finally driving to view a new model home on three acres in the town of Titusville, in Hopewell Township. When we saw it, my dad confidently said, "This is the one you want to buy."

Lucky for Dad, who lived for home renovation projects, there was no fence around the house, and he quickly pointed out its great necessity with our three small children and two dogs. The builder's foreman let us in, and Dad immediately began to take measurements for the twenty-by-thirty backyard enclosure, and said, "Johnny, I'll fly back and we will do the fence." When he was done with that, he continued his measuring in the kitchen, proclaiming we were in need of a shelf for the TV.

I hadn't even made the offer to the builder yet, but Dad was dreaming up projects, seeing the house as it could be. I had to admit it was a very nice home, and by the end of that trip, I'd called my wife to tell her that this house was the one.

Celeste had resigned herself to going along with whatever home we found, having one less thing to focus on. But as I described it, she agreed that it sounded like a beautiful home.

That weekend Dad and I stayed at the Nassau Inn in downtown Princeton. Because it had nearly two hundred rooms and ample space for meetings and conferences, Johnson & Johnson uses it a lot for meetings and for employee travel. When we walked through the front door, my dad had an almost odd, quirky smile on his face, but I didn't know why. I thought he must have liked the look of the place. As it turns out, the famous old hotel was a favorite among scientists back in the '40s and '50s for meetings. Dad had indeed been there before, perhaps many times. But he wasn't ready to share that with me just yet.

Soon after the house-hunting trip, we got the call that the house was ours. We packed everything up again, our children tearfully said their good-byes, and we moved into a rental house for sixty days until the home was finished and we could close on it. I didn't have a fence that spring or summer, but we kept an eye on the kids and the dogs, and they loved exploring their new home and neighborhood.

The following October, when we'd been living in the new house near Princeton for three months, Dad called from Seattle. "I'm flying back there to help you build that fence. Get the materials lined up," he said. "And I've got the kitchen shelf ready. We'll hang that too."

Two weeks later, on Monday, October 16, 1989, Dad stepped off the plane at Philadelphia International Airport, wearing his usual "Mister Rogers" sweater and clutching the eighty-pound TV shelf—sturdy enough to hold several hundred thousand pounds due to the corbels on the sides—via a convenient twine-and-wood handle he'd devised. I'd prepared for his trip ahead of time, taking time off work, and ordering the concrete and wood as he'd instructed. I was excited to finally have a fence, and even more excited to spend time with my dad.

Everything was ready and waiting in the backyard. Celeste was looking forward to seeing Dad; she really was enjoying the new house. And the kids were over the moon, knowing Grandpa was coming to visit.

We headed north on 95 from the airport past downtown Philadelphia. Dad made it clear he was very eager to begin constructing the fence. But when we passed through downtown Philadelphia, his voice trailed off as his gaze connected with the Broad Street exit sign, and an unprovoked admission came forth as he looked north toward the city's heart.

"Down that road is a YMCA with a basement where a lot of big decisions were made," he said out of the blue. "Ten men sitting around for two weeks disguised as a basketball team, talking about the future of nuclear weaponry . . . ten men who designed the weaponry system this country has used to this day. They designed it all: the warheads, the testing options, the delivery systems—trains, silos, buses, balloons, airplanes, you name it."

The words came so far out of nowhere that I barely paid attention. But then he started naming them—the men on the fake basketball team. Enrico Fermi was the first name on the list. I perked up at that name, recognizing it from news broadcasts in my adolescence. Dad reeled off seven others I didn't recognize, reached number nine, and groped for the name. "It was that guy from Georgia. Doggone. Can't remember. Just when I was one away." Dad was upset at himself, his once-uncanny memory apparently not quite what it used to be. He looked down at his lap, trying to recapture a ghost from the past. "Figures I'd be just one away from remembering all of them . . ."

Dad was in his midsixties then, and I saw aging memory as the culprit. "Dad, if you can't remember number nine, you're not going to remember number ten either," I said as gently as I could.

"No, Johnny. Ten's the easiest," he said, looking up again. "Number ten was your father."

Stunned, I felt my heart pounding in my head. The tires drifted to the right, drumming on the roadside rumble strips for a split second before I regained my composure and straightened the steering. I glanced at him suspiciously. "You and nuclear weaponry? What are you talking about?" I asked in disbelief. I kept my eyes on the road ahead, gripping the steering wheel a little tighter.

"I've got some things to tell you, son," he said, his voice taking on a taut, foreboding tone. Then he lapsed into silence without further elaboration. Confused, I followed his lead.

He perked up again roughly fifteen miles later when we passed the exit sign to Lakehurst off Interstate 95. "That's where I was," he said, nodding to the sign. "The Naval Air Engineering Station there. Then they sent us to the YMCA to review our findings." I glanced at the sign as we whizzed by, looking for any clue, words or otherwise, that might help me understand what he was saying.

Just as suddenly as he'd spoken, he grew silent again for a while, and eventually changed the subject entirely before we reached my home in Titusville near Princeton, forty minutes away.

As we pulled up to my house, I could see Dad's mind at work as he searched the front yard for possible future projects. "Might use a new flower bed over there," he said, which meant he'd probably get to work on it as soon as we finished the fence. I knew it would be as meticulously laid out as was his perfect garden in Seattle.

I took his bags; he took the shelf. After he'd given Celeste and my kids—Chris, Caitlyn, and Joey—a warm hello, he turned back to me. "Mind if I get started?" Barely waiting for my nod, he went to the garage, choosing tools to hang the sturdy handmade shelf for the television.

I couldn't help but think that he must be very disappointed in the basic options I owned, and hence, in me. Dad used to say that if you had the right tools, you could fix anything, and he always had the right tools for any occasion. In fact, he had three of everything—one for routine projects, a higher-grade version for challenging projects, and a tool of "exquisite quality," saved for the most special of times.

I helped Dad hold the shelf in place in the kitchen as he marked the appropriate spots for nails. "Johnny, if we get the studs right, this thing can take up to over three thousand pounds," he said. I didn't doubt that—it was a TV shelf on steroids.

Though I was curious to know more about the mysterious YMCA men, I didn't pry, and he didn't bring it up again that night, leaving me to wonder if he was telling the truth, or if this story was a sign the cancer was spreading.

After dinner he went outside and stood alone in the backyard to satisfy himself that the fence components were in place. They were all there—twelve sections of fence and a premade gate, four-by-four treated wood posts, concrete, and bags of nails. The fence-building project would involve digging twelve postholes around the perimeter of our backyard, and I would need to rent a large auger tomorrow morning to dig them.

Dad knew the house with a three-acre yard well, because that summer he had helped me find it in advance of my corporate transfer from Southern California. Before we'd even moved in, he had already measured and marked the spots for the fence and told me what materials to order.

A cool, crisp breeze gently brushed his short, gray hair as he inspected our workspace. I stood alone in the kitchen next to the new and indestructible TV shelf, hung high upon the wall. I watched him, wondering what was going on inside that head of his.

The earlier interstate confession was completely out of character for my father. And because of that, it rattled me deeper than I initially realized.

After watching him for several minutes and feeling as if I was intruding on his privacy, I went to my room with my mind still reeling, unsuccessfully trying to forget the few details he'd told me. Celeste had seen us talking, and as I was getting ready for bed, she mentioned that he appeared "chatty"—a tendency he had never had.

"Yeah, he is," I said, not offering any further details. I didn't know what to think of his stories. I sure wasn't about to offer an explanation to my wife.

Sleep didn't come easy that night. In fact, what I would soon learn would consume my waking thoughts and my nightly dreams for years to come.

3

Building the Fence

THE NEXT MORNING, I was at the local hardware store as soon as the shop opened to rent an automatic posthole auger. Before Celeste had even left the house, Dad and I had gone to work, digging the holes for the fence. That piece of equipment could have been already ten to fifteen years old by the time we rented it. But it would do the trick.

The auger was attached to a small motor about three feet above the blade, and it had a footplate at the base of an extension shaft to stand on, in case you needed to add extra weight. From head to toe, the machine was about four to five feet tall and weighed around twenty-five pounds. If your clothing got caught, you were going to spin around and around until someone stopped the motor or your clothes were ripped to shreds—and that's if you were lucky.

It was very dangerous, but safety concerns were a lot different back then. When I was a kid and would go to visit the family farm in Iowa, the gossip at church on Sundays would always be about who had gotten injured on the farm equipment. But my dad was vigilant when it came to safety, so the only thing I needed to worry about was keeping up with his incredible work ethic.

When we started to dig the holes, it was tough going. The Downer, the soil in New Jersey, is made of a mixture of sand, silt, shale, and clay, which meant it wasn't necessarily the easiest to dig through. We needed to dig down to a depth of around twenty to twenty-four inches to sink the posts with fancy sculpted ends. (Those fence posts are still there today.)

At the moment, we were drilling into heavy shale, and it was proving to be harder to break through than I'd anticipated. We needed more weight on the machine, and only when I stood on one side of the footplate and Dad on the other, his dirty work boots standing on top of mine, did the power auger get traction in the earth. The blade was now at least a foot in the ground and was stabilized.

We spun slowly around, facing each other at close range, his strong hands on my sweaty arms. The strangeness of it overwhelmed me as the auger's motor hummed along, digging through the sandy loam below. I can still see the look on his face, as if it was one of the best rides of his life.

Dad had never been a jostler or a hugger. In fact, in my entire life I could only recall a few times he hugged me or said he loved me. Our physical proximity alone told me something had come over him.

He had also never talked about his work. Even five years into retirement, as he was now, he didn't care to reminisce about his long career in sales. Yet there we were, on the posthole auger, spinning slowly on our ridiculous carousel, our skin covered in a mixture of sweat and dirt, as the metal teeth bit into the earth. Even while working up a sweat, Dad looked oddly happy, an expression I wasn't very familiar with, at least coming from him.

Dad was much more of a perfectionist than I could ever be. He refused to move on to the next hole until he was certain the hole we were drilling was deep enough. We continued to spin in silence on our private merry-go-round for the first three postholes. But after the third hole had been dug, he said, "John, I'm not going to be around eighteen months from now."

The statement lingered in the autumn air. I could hear my children playing inside. I said nothing.

"The cancer's back and it's spread," he continued, confirming my worst fear. Over the last few months, Dad had started to feel strange and had begun a whole battery of tests. After his original colon cancer diagnosis in late 1984, he'd undergone surgery and treatment. With a follow-up surgery in Seattle in 1986, he had been in remission ever since.

I started to object and he stopped me. "I know, I know," he said. "I look good. I feel good too. But I'm gonna go fast."

My stomach sank. I struggled to catch my breath as I tried to hold eye contact.

"And you know, it's time," he went on. "My life was the Cold War, and it's dead, too, thank God. Dead as a doornail. It was my whole life, and all these years I was sworn to secrecy. I haven't been able to tell anybody a word about it." He looked me in the eye, his gaze unwavering.

"But now I gotta tell someone. I'm telling you."

He turned and moved to the next hole. I heard him exhale a great sigh, almost a whoosh of relief, as if an ax had been pulled out of his back. I followed, carrying the auger, unable to form a complete thought.

We positioned the auger in place over the next mark on the grass for a hole to be dug and cranked the motor. I was too dumbfounded to make a sound. Instead I studied his face looking for any trace of uncertainty. There was none.

"And I'm gonna do that right now," he said, making eye contact again.

That was Dad. Never could just sit you down in a living room to have a talk. He had to be building something. Very Swedish.

He started talking as the auger spun again.

4

Second Chances and a Gift from God

DAD WAS BORN ON NOVEMBER 16, 1922, in Kiron, Iowa, a small farm town fresh in the middle of nowhere, between Sioux City and Des Moines. His father, John Eldon Clauson, was known as the town alcoholic. When the senior Clauson was a very young man, he'd take a break from work in the fields to stop by the communal still out by the communal windmill. A habit developed at a young age can be very difficult to break.

Eldon was usually drunk on corn moonshine by early afternoon, and that loosened his tongue and stoked his temper. He had always been a drinker, and so were some of his relatives. You could say he came by that trait honestly.

On days when my grandfather failed to show up for dinner, Dad would go out searching, usually finding his car in a ditch, Eldon slumped over the wheel. Dad would pull him out, drag him back home, and clean him up. Sometimes Dad's best friend, Dale Lindberg, went along for the ride, but otherwise, Dad told no one of his father's way-wardness. Turns out everyone knew anyhow. In a town of fewer than three hundred people, Eldon's shortcomings were visible to all.

Eldon often became hostile and abusive when he was drunk. Although Dad's sister, Dolores, was never physically harmed, Dad was the recipient of way more whippings than he ever deserved. The few gruesome stories I heard of the beatings my dad took as a kid were enough to turn my stomach. I can't help but wonder if it was somehow a way to get back at Eldon's own father, Charles William Clauson, after whom my dad was named.

Some weeks Dad didn't get to go to school much. If he got lucky, he was forced to work in the fields, and Eldon would take his portion of the money and drink it away. On bad days, when Eldon was feeling particularly evil, he would tie Dad to a stake and whip him to a bloody pulp. His mother, Dorothy, was never physically harmed, though she was emotionally tortured during Eldon's drunken furors, especially at the sight of her husband beating their son.

Wally Clauson, though, had gifts, even from a young age. One was a fearless curiosity that drove him to take things apart to see how they worked, and he commanded the mechanical skills to do that flawlessly. From the earliest days of radio, says our family lore, he knocked on neighbors' doors to inquire if their sets needed fixing, which he would happily do for free. More than the thrill of getting out of the house and away from his father's abuse, he enjoyed the challenge of taking something apart, seeing how it worked, and putting it back together, leaving the item better than when he found it.

His other skill, which shaped his professional life and led him into the world of Cold War secrecy, lay in mathematics. Beginning in his early twenties, he wielded a logarithmic slide rule as if it were a fighting sword, making quick, sure thrusts among the numbers until the final blow, the coup de grâce, produced the answer. And that in itself was a bit of a miracle—a blessing in disguise from a horrific car accident when he was eleven years old that he hadn't been expected to survive.

One Sunday morning, on the way home from church, Wallace Clauson sat patiently in the front passenger seat, staring out the window, as his mother, Dorothy, drove home through the cornfields of Kiron. His sister Dolores had stayed home that day.

With stalks seven to eight feet tall, the corn was almost ready to be picked, and the rows created tall greenish-yellow walls on either side of the two-lane unpaved gravel road. Dorothy had just begun to drive through the blind intersection when a drunk teenager in a pickup truck ran the stop sign. He T-boned the car at a high speed, totaling the car, injuring Dorothy, and with no seat belt to hold him back, launching Wallace from his front passenger-side seat through the windshield, cutting his face wide open. He landed facedown in the cornfields a great distance away.

As Wallace lay unconscious and bloodied, his body twisted between the stalks, Dorothy tried to find help, but it would be hours before anyone would find them. The teenager, now very sober, offered his shirt to cover the wide-open wound on Dad's face, and then left the scene in his battered but still drivable car. Wallace's chances of survival decreased with every minute he remained in the cornfield.

Help did arrive later that afternoon as a local resident came upon the intersection and the wreckage. But without money for medical care or a simple doctor's visit, the only option was to wrap Wallace in a blanket and bring him home to be buried.

Death from car crashes or farm accidents wasn't uncommon back then. There were no skilled surgeons or physicians back in that era, like we have now, and no anesthesia capable of dealing well with head injuries. The Clausons would have had to drive to a major city to find the nearest hospital, and without money for medical attention, and a drivable car, the only option was to go home and pray for a miracle. Wallace's fate was solely in God's hands.

Back at home that night, his grieving family placed Wallace on the couch, and discovered only then that he was still alive—barely. Thankfully, Dorothy was a nurse and knew the medical basics. Since her injuries from the crash were not crippling, she was able to tend to Wallace's wounds while he remained in a coma for several days, but she was limited in her physical resources.

A prayer warrior descended from a long line of pastors—eight or nine in a row in the family history before her—she may have lacked in medical aid, but she more than made up for it in faith. In a closet in her house sat a chair, nothing more. That was her prayer closet, taken very literally from Matthew 6:6: "But thou, when thou prayest, enter into thy closet, and when thou hast shut thy door, pray to thy Father which is in secret; and thy Father which seeth in secret shall reward thee openly." And that's where she did her best work.

Dorothy Clauson was a Greene by birth, related to General Nathanael Greene, who was second in command to George Washington in the Revolutionary War. As the story goes, when George became sick now and then, Nathanael would take over the Continental Army. While Nathanael wasn't a pastor, he was an excellent leader, and he sired a long lineage of pastors. Dorothy certainly knew the proud heritage—both of faith and of freedom—that had been passed down over the centuries, and taught it to her two kids. They'd need both to survive.

Day in and day out, between tending to Wally's wounds, taking care of her family, and trying to maintain peace in the midst of uncertainty, the chair in her prayer closet practically stayed warm from frequent use. If there was a healing prayer to be lifted high, Dorothy did it with fervor. She knew praying was even more powerful than nursing care. Still, there was only so much that could be done.

The family covered Wallace's gaping facial wound with a rag, changed it every so often, and waited for him to die. But he didn't. Surprising everyone, his breathing never slowed, he eventually awakened from his coma after several days, and soon he was coherent enough to drink liquids. His wound slowly closed, and in time his face would heal entirely on its own, with a large scar to show for his near-death experience.

Upon awakening, Wallace appeared to be a changed boy in many ways. If he had an out-of-body experience, he never spoke about it, but the difference in his behavior would suggest a spiritual encounter not unlike the stories often heard from those who have escaped the grasp of death and come face-to-face with heaven, only to be told they have more work to do on earth.

Indeed, after Wallace regained his strength, his faith multiplied, and he became zealous for the Lord. Dorothy, overjoyed at her son's miraculous recovery, was more than happy to guide Wallace into a deeper relationship with God and His Word, no doubt giving thanks for yet another generation of strong believers. For the rest of his life, Dad would find great solace in church and the Bible, counting down the days each week until Sunday, when he could relax and recharge, both physically and spiritually.

It also soon became apparent that he'd experienced a bit of God's favor in more ways than one. Surviving the wreck would be proof enough to most. But there was more—he emerged from the wreck as a mathematical savant, a certified genius.

Sudden savant syndrome, also known as acquired savant syndrome, is little understood by the medical and psychiatric community to this day. Many savants are born with extraordinary abilities, but the acquired savant's gifts manifest after a disease or injury affecting the central nervous system, such as my dad's massive childhood head trauma.[1] The condition is extremely rare and is estimated to occur in less than 10 percent of an already small savant community. Wisconsin psychiatrist Darold Treffert has been studying savants for more than fifty years and keeps a list of savants. Of the 330 he had interviewed as of 2012, only 30 acquired their abilities *after birth*.[2]

One case in particular mimics that of Wallace Clauson. In 2002, during a bar brawl, a forty-three-year-old community college dropout and furniture store worker, Jason Padgett, was knocked unconscious by a blow to the head. Waking the next morning in the hospital, Padgett could suddenly see repeating geometric patterns, or fractals, in everyday objects, and could draw these patterns from memory. The mathematics behind fractal sets is insanely difficult to comprehend, and Padgett's gift allows him to also delve into the mathematical components of his visual acuity.[3] He literally sees numbers floating in the air.

As crazy as that sounds, Dad's gift was very similar. In later years, he would explain to my brother, Bill, that when he was presented with a mathematical equation—no matter how difficult—he could just *see* the solution. He didn't have to compute it. The answers would just materialize before him.

In a small community like Kiron, no one suspected he'd been gifted with a miraculous ability upon recovering from the crash. The town was understandably overjoyed that he'd survived at all; some whispered behind closed doors that perhaps Eldon would take it as a sign to reform his wily ways.

Even though Dad had escaped death, he still maintained a rambunctious streak. Dad *was* mischievous in those days, perhaps acting out against his father's unabated abuse at home. He refused to apply himself in school, preferring to give the teachers trouble. Nevertheless, everyone could see that he was brilliant in math.

One day, the school's superintendent, frustrated with my dad's blatant lack of effort, sat him down and told him that he'd never seen anyone waste *so much raw talent*. He called it a tragedy. That comment penetrated Dad somehow. It was the first time someone had openly recognized his intelligence. And it was also likely that it was the first praise he'd ever received, even more powerful coming from a man his own father's age.

Dad began to turn things around. He shot right up to the top of the class. His best subject was still math, his test scores always 100 percent, until one day his teacher handed back an exam with two problems marked incorrect.

Having graded perfect test scores all semester from his student, the teacher told Wally he was a little disappointed to see that he'd gotten two answers wrong.

Dad, all of twelve at the time, took the paper back and studied the questions and his answers. Minutes later, he raised his hand, and when the teacher called on him, he said, "These aren't wrong. I didn't get these wrong."

Answered the teacher, "According to the textbook, they're wrong."

"Then it's the textbook that's wrong," Dad responded.

The teacher was taken aback by his definitive tone, but he thumbed through the class math text to the question-and-answer section at the back and called out the page number. Dad and the rest of the class— eight in all—found the page. Dad looked at what the textbook had to say and shook his head. "No," he said, "the answers *here* are wrong."

After hearing Dad's explanation, the teacher was impressed, even more so after he did the math himself and duplicated Dad's results. Curiosity piqued, he asked Dad to review the entire textbook. Eager to please, Dad went over the entire book that night and discovered several more wrong answers and instances of badly formulated questions.

"Sometimes they just don't set it up right," he told his teacher the next morning as he handed over his revisions.

The saga continued when the teacher sent the text with Dad's edits to the publisher. When Dad told me that, I wondered how many teachers today would take that extra step. Maybe the teacher saw a ticket out of a remote town for a bright student who might not be cut out for farming. It was also likely that his teacher knew about Eldon's heavy drinking and was pained by the bruises my dad no doubt tried to cover up.

The story might have ended there, except that the publisher also was impressed.

Soon after, Dad received a letter addressed to "Mr. Wallace Clauson." It came from New York in a creamy white envelope with the return address in raised letters. "Mr. Clauson," it began. The publisher was in the process of correcting the math text and wondered if my dad would be willing to look at some of its other high school–level math texts.

Dad went to work, pleased to finally have a way to aid his family's beginning-of-the-month struggle to pay the bills. He was embarrassed in front of his peers, however, asking his teacher to keep it all a secret because he was worried how it would reflect on his father, and he'd do anything to keep from fanning those flames. The teacher kept his secret, and his classmates thought he was doing free secretarial work, typing for the school administration.

"I must have made a hundred dollars doing that that year," Dad said. "I gave the money to my mom. It helped our family quite a bit." What money his mother didn't immediately use on groceries, other items, and paying off her husband's debts, his father drank away. And the fact that twelve-year-old Wallace Clauson was now earning more income than his father likely didn't help the family dynamics.

Not surprisingly, Eldon's drinking worsened, as did the physical abuse to my dad. It became increasingly difficult for Dorothy to withstand her husband's alcoholic rages. She eventually fled with the two children to a cousin's home in Denver, Colorado, where they lived for nearly a year. Eldon called and wrote her repeatedly, finally convincing her to return to Kiron with his promise to stop drinking. (Dad also wrote a letter, to his classmate and crush, Marilyn, during his time in Colorado, saying, "I sure miss you, Marilyn," but he forgot to put a return address on the envelope, so she couldn't reply.) After a year away, Dorothy returned home with her children, hoping Eldon had sobered up but he did not keep his promise.

Dad must have continued to review the publisher's textbooks, though, because when he and his mother returned to Kiron a year later, Dad found more books awaiting his review. He looked at them all, returned them with notes and corrections, and continued to supplement the family income.

This continued through high school, with the math becoming ever more advanced. Now a teenager and confident in his mathematical abilities, he wore his slide rule the way other boys wore baseball gloves.

Eldon never sustained enough effort or accumulated enough cash to buy a farm, a piece of land, or even a house of his own. He made some money in concrete projects, which Dad usually had to finish for him.

The extra income Dad provided helped stave off crises for a while, but it was not enough to pay all the bills for the family. With unreliable income, eventually the Clauson family found it necessary to leave their rented farm for a rented house in town.

Dad began his senior year of high school in September 1939 wondering what his future held. That year, the most he was paid was the princely sum of *twenty dollars* for each astrophysics textbook he could review and correct. During the 1930s, when the Great Depression gripped America, a public school teacher made just over $1,200 per year, so this was a very unexpected, but greatly appreciated, blessing. Still, it wasn't enough to fund his escape.

Dad dreamed of going to college, but had no idea how to pay for it.

5

The Problem Solver

FAR AWAY, IN WASHINGTON, D.C., the economic crisis of the Great Depression was giving way to a greater threat. Germany invaded Poland in September 1939, plunging Europe into World War II. The United States, with a strong isolationist wing in Congress, stayed neutral, but President Franklin D. Roosevelt's administration realized the war to come would be decided by superior technology and, with the help of the National Academy of Sciences, began scouting the country for mathematical and scientific brainpower. Among the sources they probed were publishers of mathematics textbooks.

Dad started his senior year in high school the same month Poland was invaded. Two months later, in November, he turned seventeen. Looking forward to graduating the following spring, he wondered how he could afford to go to college. His family didn't have any money to spare, and although the income from correcting textbooks helped, it wasn't enough for college tuition. Unbeknownst to him, an answer was on its way.

By 1940, news of the war in Europe was coming in a steady stream. Dad would stop by the Malmquist farmhouse most days to flirt with Mom and sit with her by the floor-to-ceiling wood radio in the parlor. The war wasn't going too well for the Allied forces, and although the United States was not officially involved in the conflict, the country was suffering great losses, with German U-boats sinking American vessels all across the Atlantic.

Dad understood that what the United States needed at the time was advanced radar technology. Not only was it difficult to know when the Germans were approaching underwater; American forces weren't too swift in detecting the Nazi air approaches either. What Dad didn't know was that a great effort was already under way to solve the radar crises.

The newly formed National Defense Research Committee (NDRC), led by the Carnegie Institute's Vannevar Bush—a Tufts- and MIT-educated electrical engineer—and reporting directly to President Franklin Roosevelt, was in the midst of forming four top-secret committees (divisions) composed of the nation's most brilliant scientists and mathematicians. These experts were tasked with designing "mechanisms for warfare," as outlined in FDR's official authorization. One division was formed to study armor; another to study bombs, fuels, gases, and chemistry; a third to research communications and transportations; and a fourth, under the leadership of Karl T. Compton, president of the Massachusetts Institute of Technology, was concerned with radar, fire control, heat radiation, and instruments. There was also a special project called the "Uranium Committee," which would later transfer to the Army and become the Manhattan Project.[1]

As more American vessels went down, this fourth committee took center stage, advanced radar development becoming the national number-one priority. In addition to having vastly increased accuracy, the new radar equipment needed to fit on an airplane, and hence, must be compact. Each of these goals was lofty. To reach both was a major stretch.

The NDRC asked the National Academy of Sciences for a list of America's fifty most brilliant mathematicians. The NAS scoured the country for men who, in an age of no digital computers, could use a slide rule to conduct quick, accurate calculations outside of an academic setting, or even in remote, foreign, or alien territory. No stone was left unturned in the search. The NAS contacted publishers of mathematics textbooks and came up with a few names in the expected age range of twenty-five to thirty.

They also focused on Yale, MIT, Harvard, and the supposed "math schools," seeking young professors. So it was by sheer chance that one of the editors at a publishing house of math textbooks, as a side note, recommended a young man in a small town in Kiron, Iowa, who was only seventeen but was editing their astrophysics textbooks with impeccable accuracy.

The NAS wasn't sure. Seventeen seemed too young. But when the powers that be reviewed Dad's corrected textbooks, they opted to put age aside. That winter, Dad said, another letter in a creamy white envelope arrived for Mr. Wallace Clauson. It invited him to a meeting the following week at Kiron's only diner, Cronk's Café. From the Academy of Sciences letterhead, he assumed he was being invited to a college recruitment interview.

The interview happened to be scheduled during basketball practice. Unfortunately, Kiron was to play against the high school in neighboring Odeboldt the following weekend, and the coach was drilling the team hard—the hometown boys needed all the practice they could get. Dad asked the coach for just a half an hour off. "There might be a chance I can go to college," he pleaded.

With his coach's approval, Dad ran to the diner straight from basketball practice, wearing a jacket and jeans over his uniform to buffer the winter's cold, his ever-present slide rule on his belt. Having practically sprinted the whole way, he was out of breath as he opened the door. At the back of the diner, three men in suits and overcoats waited for him in a booth, warming their hands around steaming mugs of black coffee.

"Are you Wallace Clauson?" asked Suit #1.

When Dad nodded, Suit #2 introduced himself as Archly Holt

from the National Academy of Sciences and told him that he and the other men had driven *eight hours* from Chicago to be there. "We'd like you to come up with a solution to this math problem," he said, sliding a piece of paper toward Dad. "If it takes you longer than two hours, we're not interested."

Suit #3 never said a word, but his expression said it all. *No way will this farm boy in a basketball uniform ever solve this problem correctly.*

Dad didn't stop to wonder why college recruiters had come all the way from Chicago. He just assumed that what Holt was "interested" in related to a scholarship they were offering. *This is my one shot at going to college,* he thought. *I just hope I'm done in time to make the end of basketball practice!*

He took the math problem he was given, seated himself at a neighboring table, and went to work, moving his slide rule's center strip left and then right, and fast-scratching the results on the paper.

Two of the men excused themselves to the restroom, probably assuming they'd be at the diner for a while. But soon Dad got up too, already finished with the work. Approaching Holt, he spoke tentatively as he handed the paper back and pointed to the test question: "You know, this equation is way longer than it needs to be. I rewrote it for you."

Holt was stunned. What was supposed to take *no more than* two hours had taken *under two minutes.* Holt watched in disbelief as Dad ran out the door and back to basketball practice.

When the remaining two suits returned to the table a few minutes later, Dad was long gone. There's no way of knowing what the three interviewers thought or said, but it probably looked something like this:

"Did we scare him off already?"

Holt glances over Dad's answer—clearly the marks of genius on paper. "I don't know who should be more scared—us or him."

The NAS sent their list of fifty brilliant mathematicians to the NDRC committee in Washington, which then matched the skill sets of each individual to the agency's needs. They found a perfect fit for Dad. Within a month of his interview, he received a telegram from the

National Academy of Sciences, asking him to report to the windmill out in the cornfield at noon a few days later.

Dad associated the windmill with the still that used to be there, and hence, with his father's alcoholism, so it wasn't a meeting place he fancied. But he did as he was told, walking out into the field at the appointed hour. Off to the side of the access road, hidden by the cornstalks, sat a lone black sedan. He spotted the car just before he entered the windmill.

Once inside, he found Archly Holt waiting to give him his orders. Dad had been recruited for the National Defense Research Committee, and was to go undercover at Iowa State College of Agricultural and Mechanic Arts in Ames as a freshman student.

Actual class attendance would be entirely optional, Holt said, and it was doubtful Dad would even have the time. He'd be working on an intensive program involving military project secrets with Professor John Atanasoff, a brilliant mathematician with great expertise in calculations by slide rule.

Now, in 1940, Atanasoff was building what would become the world's first digital computer. But Dad didn't know any of those details just yet. A young man excited to see the world, he likely viewed this opportunity as his only way out of an abusive home and a small town.

Dad was the perfect candidate for the NDRC job not only because of his impressive ability to solve complex equations so quickly, but also because of Kiron's proximity to an Iowa state school and how easy it would be to justify his attendance there. Although Holt and his associates probably didn't know it at the time, Dad was also a perfect candidate for another reason. Very reserved, he was not an easy person to get to know: he would not likely divulge secrets.

"Are you ready for this kind of assignment?" Holt questioned, gazing at the soon- to-be eighteen-year-old. When Dad said yes, he was ready, Holt swore him to the utmost secrecy about his work, a promise Dad would keep religiously for the next fifty years.

In a matter of a few days, Dad received his formal acceptance letter saying he would be attending Iowa State College (now Iowa State University), one hundred miles away, in Ames. He was *going* to college after all—just not as he'd envisioned it to be.

6

An Invitation from the NDRC

IN APRIL 1939, Germany began its nuclear energy program. By October, FDR realized that radar technology was feasible, as was the possibility of an atomic bomb, and knew there was an urgent need to evaluate them. The government recognized that with all the scientific work that was progressing, they would need to find the smart people—the nerds—to do the high-powered calculations.

FDR needed to authorize a formal government project to evaluate radar technology, so in June 1940 he formed the NDRC (National Defense Research Committee), which was composed of brilliant mathematicians and scientists who could make devices of warfare. You can think of the NDRC as being the *beginning* of what President Dwight Eisenhower deemed the "military industrial complex" in his farewell speech twenty years later, in 1961.[1] A document entitled the "Report of the National Defense Research Committee for the First Year of Operation June 27, 1940–June 28, 1941" lists which universities and schools would be utilized for the projects. Iowa State and the University of Minnesota, which Dad would later attend, are both listed.

The NDRC was officially in operation from June 27, 1940, to June 28, 1941. Their job was to "correlate and support scientific research on the mechanisms and devices of warfare, except those relating to problems of flight included in the field of activities of National Advisory Committee for Aeronautics."[2] Its goal was to bridge the gap between private industry and the United States military, and was the purview of Vannevar Bush.

Born March 11, 1890, Bush was a Tufts- and MIT-educated electrical engineer who founded Raytheon in 1922 before heading the NDRC during the Second World War. (Raytheon is a major defense contractor and is best known for the Patriot antimissile system used extensively in the 1991 Persian Gulf War.) The word *visionary* would aptly describe his talents in the field of electrical engineering. Aside from forming Raytheon, Bush performed work on early analog computer systems and foresaw the hypertext link in the form of what he called the *memex*. In a 1945 essay written for the *Atlantic Monthly*, titled "As We May Think," Bush postulated the development of a microfilm system that contained a person's library, correspondence, and personal records on a *single device* where each item could be easily accessed through "bookmarks" on a microfilm page. It should sound eerily familiar. His article was highly influential and arguably influenced the development of the Internet.[3]

Bush's inroads into Washington came in 1938, when he was appointed to the National Advisory Committee for Aeronautics (NACA), the precursor to NASA. From his post at the NACA, and through experiences during the First World War, Bush became acutely aware that any cooperation between private-sector scientists and the government was virtually nonexistent. This was especially true when speaking of development of technologies with military applications. The old guard of Washington politics had no real mechanism to understand verging technologies, nor any advisors to give counsel on military contracts past the good-ol'-boy networks.[4]

To bridge the gap between politics and science, in early 1940 Bush worked up a proposal to Congress that would form the National Defense Research Committee (NDRC). The Germans invading France in May 1940 punctuated the need for a liaison between government and corporations on military matters, and Bush set up a fifteen-minute meeting with FDR on June 12, 1940. Roosevelt was sold on the idea and gave clearance for the formation of the NDRC, with Bush as the chairman.[5]

The NDRC was originally managed by eight members: Vannevar Bush, president of the Carnegie Institution; Rear Admiral Harold G. Bowen Sr.; Conway P. Coe, commissioner of patents; Karl Compton, president of MIT; James B. Conant, president of Harvard University; Frank B. Jewett, president of the National Academy of Sciences and president of Bell Telephone Laboratories; Brigadier General George V. Strong; and Richard C. Tolman, professor of physical chemistry and mathematical physics at California Institute of Technology. They formed four separate committees, one of them being the "Radar Committee" and another special project called the "Uranium Committee." Instead of the government forming their own facilities, they wanted to use universities as their "research labs." That way, the researchers could work under the cover of being students or faculty, for the sake of secrecy, which is also why they sought out younger men, who could pass as either students or first-year professors.

When I finally began my research, years later, after Dad's confession, I reviewed the documentation for the four initial NDRC projects (divisions), and that is where I first found the mention of radar knobs. My dad had mentioned that one of his specialties was in tuning knobs, and as time went on, I'd see why this seemingly simple-sounding skill was a major component of radar accuracy. (But for now, just know that fine-tuning microwave radar is not that easy.) Other NDRC projects included proximity fuses and underwater explosives, both of which reminded me of old James Bond movies.

At the exact time the NDRC was forming, Winston Churchill formed the MAUD Committee in June 1940, to investigate whether applying nuclear technology to make a bomb was, in reality, feasible.[6] England, with all their nuclear secrets and radar—an acronym for *radio detection and ranging*—technology, was in a very similar position as we were as far as knowledge, but England knew they could not continue to develop the technology because the possibility of being bombed by Germany was great. The United States had greater development and production, and England was eager to share their technology with their U.S. allies.

So on September 6, 1940, the Canadian liner *Duchess of Richmond* docked at Halifax Harbor in Nova Scotia, carrying a revolutionary microwave radar transmitter called the *cavity magnetron*.[7] The United States rushed to establish a secret lab, dubbed the Radiation Laboratory, at the Massachusetts Institute of Technology (MIT), to exploit the magnetron. The facility opened just two months later, in November 1940, staffed by the country's top scientific minds.[8]

When the NDRC was initially forming, they initially sought out fifty scientists; they added more as time went on. They figured that if you were a top mathematician, you likely knew another one or two you could recommend. In high school, Dad didn't know any other math geniuses. (He didn't even know he was a genius himself!) But he would soon be surrounded by likeminded thinkers in an environment that both stimulated his gift and encouraged his inclination to secrecy.

Once the NDRC had the manpower in place, research began across all four divisions. I have a sheet that itemizes the NDRC funding, specifically, how many dollars were spent in each department. In one year's time, during 1941, a total $6 million was spent. That's the equivalent of $98.5 million now! Radar was actually the biggest spender. The radar group was designing and making the microwave radar sets.

The next step was to calculate how much money it would likely cost to create *one pound* of uranium to make the atomic bomb. In the spring of 1941, researchers estimated that it would cost a *minimum* of $100 million ($1.6 billion today), which was unheard-of back then.

Meanwhile, Vannevar Bush's role within the government changed again in June 1941 as he chaired the newly formed Office of Scientific Research and Development (OSRD). The scope and funding of the OSRD was greater than that of the NDRC in that the OSRD was directly financed by Congress, had the authority to develop weapons and technologies without direct involvement of the military, and was not limited to only developing weapon systems. For example, the OSRD was instrumental in facilitating the mass production of antibiotics for battlefield use.[9] Removing this layer of bureaucracy was expedient during the Second World War, but arguably was the footing for Dwight Eisenhower's military industrial complex.

Bush's management style and decision-making process was fairly simple for a detailed-oriented engineer. His singular inquiry was, "Will it help to win a war; this war?" and he set strategic goals without bogging himself down in the minutiae of individual projects.[10] And we needed a fairly simple decision-making process because we were still trying to determine how to even make the fuel; there are five different ways to do it. Now the NDRC was in full gear, and good thing: shortly after that funding development, FDR approved the bomb to be built on October 9, 1941.

The NDRC laid the groundwork for advances in both radar and nuclear weapons, as well as other, more "mad scientist-y" operations. This was the group into which my father, a fresh-faced teenager, was inducted right out of high school, in March or April 1940.

The NDRC was officially launched on June 27, 1940.

* * *

As fascinating as all this was to hear, and as much as I was enjoying this gift of one-on-one time with Father—made even more rare by his unprovoked monologue—it was equally confusing.

In my mind, yesterday my father was a retired IBM lifer whose job in computer sales had supposedly taken him around the country and to foreign assignments in Switzerland and England. He didn't smoke or drink alcohol, and he and Mom had attended a conservative Protestant church every Sunday for as long as I remembered. His life seemed to be that old cliché, an open (and not particularly interesting) book. Now, in the middle of a backyard project, that book was closing and reopening to reveal someone steeped in secrecy, the reticence and evasions with which I was all too familiar sheared from his innate personality and now given the weight of national interest.

A few minutes later, his treetop box of apple juice empty, we went back to work. As we stood facing each other on the posthole digger again, his feet on mine, spinning slowly as the auger dug into the shale-flecked earth, he continued his story. I had no other choice but to listen. Strange though it was, the bright-eyed boy inside leapt at the opportunity to spend this much time with my father, even under the unique circumstances. Though our relationship had never been strained, it had also never been very close.

With all the traveling he did throughout his long career—whether it was really for computer sales or something else—he was gone a lot, often months at a time, with no explanation, and sometimes without any contact, even with my mother. How she managed to raise four children and manage a home never knowing when her husband would call or come home is a mystery to me, but she did, and she never let on that she was worried or frustrated.

I, on the other hand, was far less patient with my father's absences. Even worse, when he was home, I often felt that although he was physically there, he was mentally consumed by work. He also did his best to be invisible in public situations, embarrassing me more than a few times when I thought I would finally get to introduce him—my elusive father—to friends or classmates, only to turn around and find him gone.

Just as I began to get frustrated at the memories of all the times he'd left, I remembered what he'd told me the day before and it shook me out of my pity party and into an intense awareness. According to his doctors, he'd be *gone for good* in less than two years. *You'd better pay attention now while you have the chance*, I reminded myself.

7

A Real Education

IN MAY 1940, Dad's graduating high school class numbered a meager six students instead of the usual eight. A pair of twins, Lloyd and Lynnel Baker, were kept from the ceremony because they were needed on their family's farm for chores.

Marilyn Malmquist, a bespectacled brown-haired beauty standing five foot nine, was another member of the Kiron class of 1940. My mother and father were born just months apart, Dad in November 1922, and Mom in January 1923, so they entered kindergarten together at the lone Kiron school. My mom, Marilyn, was a fabulous seamstress, an excellent pianist, a talented cook, and was always at the top of the class. She was even the class valedictorian, though later, after they were married, they were both coy about the family rumor that he'd botched a question on a history test to let her win the honor.

Both Dad and Mom were of Scandinavian heritage and they both came from farm families, but they would have been living on opposite sides of the tracks, if there were any tracks. Dad's father, Eldon, was never sober enough to go to church in the morning, but Mom, a devout Christian, was there every Sunday. Dad primarily went to church to get out of the house and away from his father, although since his near-death experience, he was showing much more interest in developing a personal relationship with God. Being able to look at the woman who would one day be my mother—with her curly brown hair—from across the pews didn't hurt either.

In a class of eight, you don't have a big pool to pick from, but the interest each felt for the other was genuine. My mom had eyes for my dad early on. "I had a crush on him in eighth grade, and I knew I'd marry him by the twelfth grade," she confessed with a smile years later.

Dad didn't like Mom talking to other boys. When working out at the farm owned by his aunt Lila, who shared a party line with the Malmquist family, Dad would pick up the phone to listen in when the Malmquists' three-ring signal would sound. Once he'd made sure it wasn't a boy calling for my mom, he'd hang up. If it was a boy, he'd stay on the line. My mom, hip to what Dad was doing, would always say, "Wallace, are you on? Get off the phone!" My dad was a little possessive, but he won my mom over. I never heard of them *dating* in high school, per se. But then again, there wasn't much to do back then apart from walking together to and from school.

As a kid, to get out of the house early and to keep his sanity, forever embarrassed by his father's reputation as a moonshiner, Dad would walk the few miles to the Malmquist farm, and accompany my mom and her sister Marjorie the rest of the way to school. He'd retrace his steps back down the dirt roads once the final bell rang each day. He continued this routine throughout high school.

I think everyone assumed that those two were soon going to be an item. And sure enough, they were.

Immediately after graduation, Dad informed Mom and his family he'd received a scholarship from Iowa State. He would soon be "enrolled" in an electronic engineering program. Too young to enter nursing school just yet, Mom moved to Storm Lake, Iowa, to attend pre-nursing classes. She and Dad exchanged letters and phone calls, Dad promising to visit her.

By summer 1940, as Dad was preparing to move to Ames for college, only England held out against Hitler's Nazi war machine in Europe. Prowling German U-boats ravaged not only England's military fleet, but American and other merchant shipping bringing supplies to the beleaguered islands, while the German Luftwaffe rained bombs down on English cities. Radar detection was the key to anticipating both sea and air attacks and targeting the attackers, especially the German submarines.

In June, Roosevelt created the NDRC and intensified the search for scientific brains for top-secret work in several fields, including bombs and radar. The bulk of the research went into creating accurate microwave radar, compact enough to be mounted in airplanes. It was soon centered at the Massachusetts Institute of Technology's Radiation Laboratory, known as the Rad Lab. And Atanasoff at Iowa State was among the scientists charged with the advancement of radar technology.

Atanasoff was no doubt informed that a young math savant would be joining him soon in the lab, but he didn't know what my father looked like.

They'd meet soon enough.

* * *

John Atanasoff, known as the inventor of the first computer, was born in Hamilton, New York, on October 4, 1903. His father, a Bulgarian immigrant, was an electrical engineer, and his mother, a mathematics teacher. By age nine, John had taught himself how to repair faulty electric wiring in the family's home.

He received his master's degree in mathematics from Iowa State College, and a doctorate from the University of Wisconsin in 1930. To write his doctoral thesis, "The Dielectric Constant of Helium," Atanasoff was required to perform many complicated and time-consuming computations. Although he utilized the Monroe mechanical calculator, first produced in 1912 and one of the most advanced machines of the time, its shortcomings motivated the young man to dream of developing a more sophisticated machine. The story goes that Atanasoff got tired of using the hand crank on his mechanical calculator and wanted to devise a better way of running calculations.[1]

When Atanasoff subsequently returned to Ames, joining the mathematics department at Iowa State as an assistant professor, he set up a lab, and between 1939 and 1942 worked toward his goal step-by-step in the basement of Iowa State's physics building. With the help of graduate student Clifford Berry, he produced the Atanasoff-Berry, the world's first electronic digital computer, a machine that would allow the user to calculate linear algebraic equations up to twenty-nine equations at one time.[2]

But this was only one of Atanasoff's projects. Atanasoff had become chief of the acoustics division at the Naval Ordnance Laboratory, a position that was paying him a salary well above the $10,000 cap on government salaries at the time.[3] In addition to being in charge of developing a computer for the United States Navy, he worked on a variety of acoustics tests, monitoring different types of explosions, including the first atomic test in the Pacific. He was also deeply involved in work for the NDRC as one of the chief scientists charged with advancement of radar technology. Later in life, interestingly enough, Atanasoff would be the head of Atlantic Aerojet, and in the inherited workbench my dad left me were numerous cards from employees at Aerojet General.

When Dad went to Iowa State in the fall of 1940, he took a Greyhound bus the hundred miles from Kiron to Ames. Still carrying his suitcase, he found the Iowa State campus and went straight to Atanasoff's office in Beardshear Hall. The professor was just about to conclude his visiting hours, nearing the end of his workday.

"How can I help you? What seems to be the problem?" Dad remembered him saying as he looked up from his desk. Atanasoff must have assumed Dad was just another student in need of help or encouragement.

"I don't have a problem. I'm here to help you solve yours," Dad replied. When Dad took out his slide rule and began to show Atanasoff what he could do with it, the professor was stunned.

*　*　*

By the time we had sunk several postholes for the fence, we were sweating profusely though the day was still young. It was October, but still warm. I was wearing jeans and a T-shirt, and Dad wore cotton work pants and the kind of sleeveless, "wife beater" undershirt that Marlon Brando had immortalized in *A Streetcar Named Desire*.

He had told me yesterday that he was dying, but at sixty-six he was still strong and capable of hours of nonstop work. I headed inside to splash some water on my face, and he called after me to bring him a small carton of apple juice, his favorite beverage. When I returned, he pulled the straw off the side of the juice carton and poked it through the tinfoil hole in the top, the cool sweet liquid within a well-deserved reward after several hours of hard work.

I was reeling with the stories he was throwing at me.

Why have I never heard any of this before? I wondered. *Why didn't he tell my mother and my siblings? Is it true?*

Did I even want it to be true?

8

Hidden Genius

DAD WAS AT IOWA STATE ostensibly to study electronic engineering. However, Iowa State official records from the 1940–41 academic year indicate that Wallace Clauson's GPA was 1.11, partly based on his failing algebra. Of course, there was no way my father could *fail algebra*. The bad grades were trumped-up by a government agency intent on making absolutely certain Dad wouldn't be identified by enemy spies as a math genius. "The truth was," Dad told me, "I never went to class. My job was to work on math problems for Atanasoff."

The NDRC didn't want the Russians to have any idea that they had a savant on their hands, so in addition to his failing grades, they put my dad in the trumpet and drum corps at Iowa State as a decoy, to make him look like a flunky, because that is the last place you would think a savant would be hanging out. And they succeeded. I've seen the group picture of the Iowa State College trumpet and drum corps in the photo section of the 1941 edition of *The Bomb*, the annual publication of the student body of Iowa State College at Ames. The irony of the publication's title wasn't lost on me. What's even funnier is that he didn't play any instrument at all. He was not very musical—it was all a cover.

"Johnny, they wanted me to look like the village idiot," he said. But even I knew better than that. My dad could fix anything. He also raised us to be honest—just like he was—except, apparently, concerning his career. When it came to that, as it turned out, he was a fantastic liar.

Increasingly more Americans were dying from attack by German U-boat, the 260 killed in 1939 increasing to 3,300 in 1940 and 5,600 in 1941. With more and more American vessels sinking every month, the pressure was intense to come up with a microwave radar set that was not only small enough to fit onto a plane, but accurate enough to identify an underwater target from the air. Fortunately, Atanasoff had discovered that using a small knob, instead of handwheels, could allow the finger muscles to achieve finer control in aligning radar frequencies and tracking than could a larger dial with coarser hand and back movements, which had previously been the norm.[1] This greatly increased the move toward miniaturization, and my dad would be fascinated and propelled by the drive for miniaturization the rest of his career.

Atanasoff and others constantly presented Dad with mathematical problems that needed to be fixed and challenges that had to be met. Despite the fact that he was the youngest participant in this NDRC program, he quickly became known for his ability to pinpoint the exact location of a target by measuring the strength and intensity of the radar waves pinging off an object and then bouncing back to their origination point. In a sense, he was using mathematical equations to reverse engineer the process. The studies he did would later become a key factor in the development of the Polaris missiles, the first to be accurately fired under water at varying depths, at the Rad Lab in Livermore, California.

As the first missile with underwater launch capability from a moving submarine, fireable at various depths, it was seen as a great technological advance. The calculations used on this weapons system, many formulated by Dad, were so complex that the Soviets couldn't unravel the work until a decade later. It wasn't just the missile's trajectory that was formulated, but also how the missile would be moved onto the submarine, how it would stay in place, and how the missiles could be hidden underwater and launched from varying depths at sea.

It was in Ames that Dad began to develop a longtime quasi-obsession with vacuum tubes, used to control and magnify current during the radar frequency experiments. There he started his tube collection, which steadily grew well into the thousands. Years later, at least fifty buckets of varying tube sizes lined our San Jose garage when I was in my early teens. He used them to conduct experiments, as well as to fix TVs, speakers, amplifiers—anything that would take them.

Dad's fascination with computers also began to develop at that time, and he later told me how honored he was to have witnessed the birth of the world's first version. Although his main responsibility lay with the NDRC projects, as well as with projects relating to the Ordnance Lab, Atanasoff often came to him with difficult-to-solve equations related to the computer project.

In addition to computer projects, Dad also worked on fine-tuning radar. The archives noted that the NDRC Project at Iowa State was fine-tuning radar by the use of small knobs that could be easily manipulated by the tiniest finger movements. Atanasoff would have introduced Dad to that project and set him loose. This would have been at the same time he was with the other nine men in the YMCA basement that he'd mentioned to me earlier. I pieced together that he must have traveled to Lakehurst to study the importance of balloons. And it would also be the beginning of his numerous trips to Princeton with John von Neumann.

Perhaps partly because of the many fascinating extracurricular projects he was involved in, it was in Ames that Dad developed the workaholic tendencies he exhibited the rest of his career. He would work late into the evening, then stop by an all-night diner for dinner, finishing off the meal with his favorite: tapioca pudding. He'd then make his way back to the downtown rooming house to catch a few hours of sleep before returning to the lab early in the morning.

Dad said he interspersed his work for Atanasoff with occasional bus trips to Iowa City to see my mom, Marilyn, who was by now working on her nursing license, having met the educational qualifications for nursing school. Now and then Dad went home to Kiron, where he gave his mother some of the money he was making. Those visits were always short, he said, because his father's drinking and abuse continued unabated. He'd find himself wanting to leave Kiron almost as soon as he arrived, very glad to no longer be forced to withstand his father's tirades. He would often urge his mother to leave his dad, but scared of a new life, she refused to budge.

As difficult as it was to face his father, I think Dad was angrier at his mother, who never took him or his sister out of the situation permanently when she should have. Apart from the year they spent in Colorado with a relative to get away from his father, his mom seemed resigned to accept the abuse for herself and her kids. Once both kids were out of the house, she was the lone recipient of whatever foul mood Eldon Clauson found himself in. "The Lord put me with him, for better or for worse," she always told my dad. He could likely have accepted that she was weak and couldn't be strong, but I don't think he appreciated her using faith as her reason to stay. And faith or not, he'd never understand how his mother could stand by and watch her husband beat him savagely without trying to intervene.

* * *

Through the summer of 1941 and into the fall, Dad spent most of his time in Ames, in Atanasoff's lab. There's no record that he enrolled in any classes for his sophomore year. It was certainly not the college experience that most students have.

Toward the end of 1941, American boat casualties were up in the thousands. The German U-Boats were having a field day with Allied cargo and transportation ships. Dad's primary mission, working on the development phase of the advanced radar, was near completion, the shorter-length microwave dishes now ready for mass production.

Then, on December 7, 1941, the Japanese attack on Pearl Harbor brought the United States into the war, and the need for advanced radar systems was all the more crucial. My mom was already a working RN in the maternity and delivery ward when Pearl Harbor occurred, and soon transferred to Mounds Midway Nursing School and Hospital in St. Paul, Minnesota.

A week after the attack, Dad had another visit from the NDRC's Archly Holt, although the name of the organization had now been changed to the OSRD—the Office of Science and Research Development. By this time the committee membership and structure had been reorganized, and the committee consisted of Harvard president James B. Conant (chairman), professor Richard C. Tolman (vice-chairman), organic chemist Roger C. Adams, MIT president Karl T. Compton, and Frank B. Jewett, president of the National Academy of Sciences, along with the commissioner of patents (Conway P. Coe until September 1945, and then Casper W. Ooms) and the periodically changing representatives of the Army and Navy.[2] Dad's new mission would involve enlisting in the Navy as an officer, and he was excited about joining the military.

* * *

Dad stood up straight to stretch his back. I gladly took his lead and did the same. We were making great progress but still had hours and hours of manual labor to go. I knew I'd be incredibly sore into the coming week, but for now, I was instituting mind over body, totally focused on Dad's story. I didn't want to forget a single detail.

Dad wiped his sweaty hands on his pants, dirt mixed with pure determination, before making his next earth-shaking statement: "Johnny, you must always remember that World War II for the U.S. was all about building the bomb. Everything! It's why we got into the war, and it's how we got out of the war."

The bomb? Did he mean the atomic bomb?

This was about to get even more interesting.

9

The Setup

BORN IN 1887, ALFRED LOOMIS, a brilliant mathematics guru and inventor, was worth nearly $300 million by the mid-1930s, and had a research lab on the top floor of his house. He was privately funding a lot of the foremost scientists' work projects and invited every key physicist to his personal lab to conduct research. These scientists included Niels Bohr, the Danish physicist who made foundational contributions to understanding atomic structure and quantum theory; Einstein, "the Man"; and Werner Heisenberg, the head of Germany's nuclear program. Alfred especially liked hanging out with Ernest Lawrence (founder of the Lawrence Livermore National Laboratory) and bought $30,000 in copper so Lawrence could make his cyclotron, a circular particle accelerator, in 1929.[1] Fascinated by human behavior, Alfred also gave each of his sons $1 million when they became teenagers just to see how they would spend it.

Alfred's uncle was Henry Stimson, then the United States secretary of war, and the man ultimately responsible for building the atomic bomb. In 1940 Alfred's son Henry (no doubt in part named after his uncle, who had a considerable influence on Alfred during his upbringing after his own father, Henry Patterson Loomis, died while Alfred was in college), dropped out of Harvard his senior year to enlist in the Navy.

Most articles say Henry did this because he felt it was his civic duty, having been so fortunate to grow up in a wealthy family. While that may have held *some* truth—how often do you hear about the children of millionaires dropping out of Ivy League schools to join the military?—it's more likely that he enlisted because both his father and his uncle had already planned his next career move for him.

At the young age of twenty-one, Henry, straight out of Harvard, was appointed commander in chief of the Pacific Fleet Radar Headquarters in Pearl Harbor, which meant he was in charge of training and installation. I'm sure people wondered how he'd gotten appointed to such a high-level position with so little military experience. Yet now he was over all of the radar training. *What a lucky break*, his acquaintances must have thought. In reality, his father, Alfred Loomis, had invented some of the radar equipment—including the Loomis chronograph, for measuring shell velocity[2]—and likely trained his son on all of it.

Remember that Alfred Loomis, unarguably the world's guru on radar, was the head of the NDRC's radar project. Six top nuclear guys were initially involved in the radar project, including Ernest Lawrence of the Lawrence Rad Lab. It was a tight-knit group, and Henry would have been familiar with all of the men, since his father was notorious for hosting parties, inventing and experimenting, and also allowing other scientists into his home laboratory.

By coincidence, I was reading the *Washington Post* on November 8, 2008, and read Henry Loomis's obituary.[3] And that's when I made a connection I'd never made before: When Henry Loomis was named head of Pearl Harbor Radar, it created quite a bloodline—Henry Stimson, Alfred Loomis, and Henry Loomis—all tied into the atomic bomb. All three of these individuals knew of the building of the bomb, and the costs associated with it.

There's even *another* scientist under Alfred Loomis in the NDRC, an F. W. Loomis, most widely known for his contributions in the field of physics. He attended Harvard as well, and was born two years after Alfred, making me wonder if they might be cousins. They could have quite the family reunion at the NDRC meetings, conversing about atomic science while passing around the appetizers.

To young Henry's credit, he was a brilliant whiz kid on radar, just like his dad, and he played an active role in many of his father's scientific experiments, even as early as his adolescent and teenage years. In one seemingly devious experiment, while Henry was sleeping in a sound-proof room, with electrodes attached to his head, his father, Alfred, to prove that emotional disturbance altered human brain waves, whispered, "*Land's End* is on fire!" through the microphone. *Land's End* was the family boat, and Henry, half-awake, tried to climb the wall of the room as if it were a ladder, fearing that he might be trapped in the fire.[4]

Unquestionably gifted in science, Henry had also studied Japanese history at Harvard before enlisting in the Navy. Later, during the war, in a discussion with United States Secretary of War Henry L. Stimson and Lt. Gen. Leslie Groves, who was head of the Manhattan Project, which developed the atomic bomb, about which cities to bomb in Japan, Loomis dissuaded them from targeting Kyoto, citing the city's art treasures.[5]

What bothers me to this day is the public's perception of Pearl Harbor and what really happened. Without fail, the rhetoric goes something like this: "Radar was so new, we really didn't understand it." But that's simply not true. Both Alfred and Henry were so skilled at the use of radar that they could have spotted a scourge of mosquitoes coming in. And as head of Pearl Harbor Radar, Henry was in charge of training the team, so we can assume that he was doing his job and that those under his command were, in fact, being trained on the equipment.

So how could Pearl Harbor have happened?

10

Bombs Away

ON DECEMBER 7, 1941, servicemen George Elliot and Joseph Lockard were on duty at Kahuka Point on the northern tip of the Hawaiian island of Oahu. Lockard was instructing Elliott—an apprentice—in the use of the new radar equipment that morning.[1] The SCR-270-B Radar Unit was the state-of-the-art device at that time, and Lockard, an experienced radar operator, manned the oscilloscope while Elliot did the plotting and kept a log.[2]

There were six radar stations around Oahu (with only five working), but there was no real chain of communication or reporting set up. "At one point the operators of one of the sets were instructed to phone in reports from a gas station some distance away. By explicit order by General Short [a lieutenant general in the United States Army and the U.S. military commander responsible for the defense of U.S. military installations in Hawaii], the radar stations were to only be operated for four hours per day and to shut down by 7 a.m. each day."[3] Like clockwork, the other three stations shut down at 7 a.m. But this morning, said Elliot, "at 06:54 I was advised over our tactical line to shut down the Radar unit."[4]

Elliot and Lockard were waiting to be picked up for breakfast, but the truck was late, so the pair decided to get in some extra training time, since, as Elliot put it, "we had received previous permission from our platoon sergeant to keep the system operating so that I could learn how to operate the oscilloscope. I had less than three months radar experience under my belt and Lockard agreed to keep the unit running."[5]

At 7:02 a.m., Elliot spotted a huge blip on the screen 137 miles out, and described it as a "large number of planes coming in from the north, three points east."[6]

It was completely out of the ordinary and Elliot called it in to Fort Shafter minutes later, only after convincing Lockhard that it was worth calling in. Lockhard's initial response when Elliot said they should call it in was "Don't be crazy! Our problem ended at seven o'clock."[7]

When a call back came minutes later from Lieutenant Tyler at Fort Shafter, Lockhard confirmed "an unusually large flight—in fact, the largest I have ever seen on the equipment."[8] That should have raised an eyebrow at least, but from there, the communication completely broke down.

Instead of taking the report seriously, Lieutenant Tyler told the men not to worry about it, but they continued to track the radar blip, which grew so large that Lockard assumed the radar set was broken. The men turned the radar off at 7:45 a.m., after the blip disappeared behind Oahu's mountains.[9] Three minutes later, the first bombs began falling on Pearl Harbor.

Of the one hundred ships in Pearl Harbor that morning, the primary targets were the eight battleships anchored there.[10] All eight U.S. Navy battleships were damaged, with four sunk. The attack sank or damaged three cruisers, three destroyers, an antiaircraft training ship,[11] and one minelayer. That day 188 U.S. aircraft were destroyed, 2,403 Americans were killed, and 1,178 others were wounded.[12] Terrible damage and loss of life for sure, but it's not a coincidence that not a single U.S. aircraft carrier was in the area. They were pulled away. In war, you can lose a lot of battleships, but you can't lose an aircraft carrier.

On December 7, the United States had three carriers out on various patrols. Carriers *Enterprise* and *Lexington* were taking part in operations in preparation for war with Japan. The *Saratoga* was in San Diego to pick up bombers and ferry another ship carrying Brewster fighters.[13]

What's interesting is that two months before Pearl Harbor, FDR authorized the building of the atomic bomb on my brother's birthday, October 9, 1941. If you've approved a bomb to be built, you obviously have a budget in mind because you can't go to Congress otherwise. They knew the bomb would be so frightfully expensive, and it had to be done top-secret. So what do you do? *You get attacked. You go to Congress. And you tell them that since you're now at war, you can't share a lot of the details about the bomb.* FDR shoves the whole program over to the Army Corps of Engineers, which is part of the military. You talk about doing an end-around on Congress.

"At the time of the attack on Pearl Harbor," according to Congress, "the United States had been investing significant sums in military spending for the preceding year and a half, particularly with regard to infrastructure needs."[14] In fact, in the year before Pearl Harbor, $45 billion had been added to the defense program, bringing the total available funds to $75 billion.[15]

Eleven days later, President Roosevelt signed the "First War Powers Act, 1941" into legislation, "empowering the President to, among other things, redistribute functions among executive agencies,"[16] which meant he could move funds around however he saw fit since this was now the budget of a nation at war.

In the actual war budget for World War II, Roosevelt wrote, "War plans are military secrets. . . . I cannot predict ultimate costs . . . I can only say that we are determined to pay whatever price we must to preserve our way of life."[17] Remember: the bomb had been approved three months earlier. FDR admitted that $2,000 dollars was allocated to the War College, and $39,000 for lepers on Guam. They soon allocated $2.9

billion for naval ordnance and stores, and $4 billion for construction and machinery costs for replacement of naval vessels.[18]

You can sneak in the building of the bomb with those kinds of dollars.

11

The Problem with Pearl Harbor

WAS PEARL HARBOR AN INSIDE JOB? Or did we provoke the Japanese? I think it was a little of both.

In 1940, a Gallup poll showed that 88 percent of the American population was against getting into World War II.[1] Something had to be done to change public opinion, because more than $100 million needed to be raised to get one pound of uranium. The majority of the population didn't want to get into a war, but that was the only way to fund the building of the bomb.

The book *Day of Deceit: The Truth About FDR and Pearl Harbor* (2001), by Robert Stinnett, alleges that FDR's administration had ample evidence warning us of an attack, and that the United States deliberately *provoked and allowed* the Japanese attack on Pearl Harbor, to bring the United States into World War II. We needed to become involved in the war to generate the massive funds necessary to create the atomic bomb before our enemies did. To create the bomb, we needed enriched uranium. And to produce that, K-25 at Oak Ridge had to be built quickly, which would prove to be the world's most expensive building.

On the other side of the coin, five months before the attack, FDR had cut off the sale of oil and scrap metal to Japan—a major point of provocation. He had long since favored the Chinese, since his ancestors had made money in the China trade.[2] Because Japan has few natural resources, many of their industries had to rely on imported raw materials, including coal and iron ore or steel scrap, among others, many of which came from the United States or from European colonies in Southeast Asia.[3] Without these resources, Japan's industrial economy would have ground to a halt, but thanks to international trade, the Japanese had built a fairly advanced industrial economy by 1941.

In June 1940, Henry Stimson, who had been secretary of war under Taft and secretary of state under Hoover, became secretary of war again, and favoring the Chinese over the Japanese, he pushed for the use of economic sanctions to obstruct Japan's advance in Asia.[4] On July 2, 1940, Roosevelt signed the Export Control Act, which prohibited the export of essential defense materials—namely, to Japan. On October 16, 1940, FDR placed an embargo "on all exports of scrap iron and steel to destinations other than Britain and the nations of the Western Hemisphere."[5]

On July 26, 1941, five months before Pearl Harbor, Roosevelt froze Japanese assets in the United States, bringing commercial relations between the nations to an end.[6] One week later Roosevelt embargoed the export of such grades of oil as were still in commercial flow to Japan; the British and the Dutch followed suit.

In his diary, after a meeting of the war cabinet on November 25, 1941, Henry Stimson wrote, "The question was how we should maneuver them [the Japanese] into firing the first shot without allowing too much danger to ourselves."[7] That seems like an ominous admission to me of one country trying to lure another into taking action.

After the attack on Pearl Harbor, instead of feeling a range of normal emotions, like anger, sadness, or absolute rage, Stimson confessed, "My first feeling was of relief . . . that a crisis had come in a way which would unite all our people."[8] As you can see, the economic sanctions were a huge supporting link to the allegation that FDR was trying to poke the Japanese bear. And poke it we did.

The United States was unprepared for the attack, *but it was intentional.* I've spoken with Robert Stinnett, author of *Day of Deceit,* and he has outlined an incredible number of incidences that happened on December 7, the day of the attack. The thing is, even statistically you can't have that many coincidences all happening at once. There are more than two thousand documents that are still classified regarding Pearl Harbor.

Still not convinced? Let me give you an example: The radar stations were all supposed to be connected to each other—at least in theory. The operators took the stance *If we are attacked, then we'll link all the stations together,* when we should have taken a proactive approach. Why would you take a reactive stance with national security and decide that you'll only link up all the radar stations *if* you're attacked? That's like a prizefighter who's been hit in the face and knocked down on the mat, and *then* he decides to put his mouth guard in.

It simply makes no sense. What good would the radar stations be then anyway? If one station were attacked and they were not already hooked up, how could they notify other stations? That's not only a waste of money, training, and talent; it's a gaping wound of oversight, ignorance—or worse.

Another point to make is that while radar wouldn't have necessarily prevented Pearl Harbor from happening—the Japanese were already on their way—if the warning had been taken seriously, the United States might have had time to react if they had gone into war mode when they first saw the giant blip, instead of taking time to figure out if it was low clouds, radar malfunctions, or a flock of seagulls. That could have potentially saved lives, saved ships, and created a different outcome.

Fewer than five minutes after the Pearl Harbor radar station picked up something mysterious on their radar, they called in to central command to see if other radar stations had also seen it. But the main station was shut down not even five minutes before the sighting, and the men were initially told there was nobody on duty to take the information, although they did get a call back a few minutes later from Lieutenant Tyler, telling them not to worry about what they were seeing. We were bombed at 7:48 a.m. Hawaiian Time. And as noted, they were supposed to stay open until 7:00 a.m. every day. But on this day, they shut the station down at 6:54 a.m.[9]

This tragedy is now a comedy of errors. Rear Admiral Husband E. Kimmel was the commander at Pearl Harbor, and both he and General Short were dishonorably discharged after the attack. Their families, to this day, are still trying to have that reversed.

So when Dad told me that everything was about the atomic bomb—although I was initially skeptical, it makes sense! If you need a secret source of unlimited money to build K-25, becoming involved in war was the only way to raise the funds. Of course, that leads to all kinds of ethical and moral considerations, including the idea of sacrificing the lives of some to potentially protect the lives of many, none of which I am qualified to entertain. I am, however, extremely thankful that I will never be faced with such a decision. I can only speculate as to what my dad's stance would have been, had he been posed that exact situation in one of the meetings in von Neumann's living room.

After Pearl Harbor happened, The K-25 building of the Oak Ridge Gaseous Diffusion Plant, which was used solely to create enriched uranium, had to be built. It was a mile-long, U-shaped plant that covered forty-four acres, was four stories high, and measured up to four hundred feet wide.[10] It cost $512 million to build in 1944 (nearly $7 billion today), which makes K-25 the most expensive single building in world history—and one of the largest, covering thirty-five football fields. It took two years before the plant was able to produce uranium.

I haven't been able to find any building project in the history of this country that cost that much. The idea of a single structure costing more than the equivalent of $7 billion can't be found. Perhaps the city of St. Petersburg, Russia, cost more to build—but that is an entire city in 2016 dollars. Another point of comparison might be the Pentagon, which cost $83 million to build.

Years before, when the science was fairly new, Leo Szilard, a Hungarian physicist who conceived the nuclear chain reaction in 1933 and patented the idea of a nuclear reactor with Enrico Fermi,[11] initially approached FDR in August 1939 with a letter signed by Einstein, alerting the president to the potential of nuclear power and a nuclear bomb, but FDR was busy and couldn't arrange a meeting. Alexander Sachs, an unofficial adviser to President Franklin Roosevelt, helped the cause by roping Einstein into the letter-writing process months before, in July 1939, so that FDR would take note. Eventually all three men wrote letters (see the appendix) to FDR regarding the potential of an atomic bomb, and Sachs delivered them to the president on October 11, 1939, reading his own letter out loud and handing the others to the president. At the end of that meeting, FDR called his aide into the room, "Pa" Watson, and said, "This requires action."[12]

FDR agreed then that the United States didn't want Germany dropping an atomic bomb on New York City; thousands upon thousands of people would be killed. Prompted by these letters, by late 1939 FDR was already thinking that the United States needed to get the jump on creating the bomb first. And these three documents "set in motion the machinery which produced the Bomb."[13] My dad was recruited into the NDRC in February 1940 while still in high school, so we know that once FDR saw the writing on the wall, action was quickly taken.

TIMELINE LEADING UP TO THE BOMB

- **October 21, 1939:** Budget of $6,000 allocated to Lymann Briggs, the head of the National Bureau of Standards, to explore the topic of an atomic bomb.

- **February 1940:** Wallace Clauson is recruited by the NDRC during his senior year of high school.

- **March 1940:** Frisch-Peierls memorandum notes the possibility of having a bomb with .45 kg of enriched uranium.

- **April 10, 1940:** MAUD committee meets in England to discuss the feasibility of an atomic bomb.

- **June 12, 1940:** Roosevelt officially creates the NDRC (National Defense Research Committee).

- **September 1940:** Lymann Briggs receives $40,000 for a uranium study.

- **Fall 1940:** Wallace Clauson enrolls at Iowa State under false pretenses.

In the early days of NDRC, they spent more from the budget on radar than on the uranium committee. They also discovered that an atomic bomb was theoretically feasible. The NDRC's first year report reads, "There has appeared recently, however, new knowledge which makes it probable that the production of a super-explosive may not be as remote a matter as previously appeared."[14]

TIMELINE OF BOMB DEVELOPMENT

- **June 28, 1941:** Office of Scientific Research and Development (OSRD) under Vannevar Bush absorbs the NDRC's Uranium Committee.

- **July 15, 1941:** MAUD Committee issues final detailed technical report on design and cost to develop an atomic bomb.

- **October 9, 1941:** Head of NDRC (Vannevar Bush) takes MAUD report to FDR; FDR subsequently approves project to confirm MAUD's findings.

- **December 6, 1941:** The United States authorizes the development of "gaseous fusion" and "electro-magnetic separation" to accelerate the development of nuclear fuel.

- **December 7, 1941:** Attack on Pearl Harbor.

- **December 19, 1941:** First meeting of OSRD-sponsored S-1 Uranium Committee meets to discuss the building of nuclear weapons; Ernest Lawrence receives $400,000 to develop a large cyclotron.

- **January 19, 1942:** FDR formally authorizes the atomic bomb project (later to be known as the Manhattan Project).

- **March 1942:** FDR places the atomic project under military command, headed by Henry Stimson (secretary of war).

Of the nearly $2 billion overall cost of building the atomic bomb, the bomb itself represented only 15 percent of the spending. The real expense—85 percent of the cost of the atomic program—was the uranium and plutonium fuel. Although my dad never spoke about K-25, I'm quite sure he was well aware of it and may have even visited a few times. After all, Cuthbert Hurd, head of IBM's Applied Sciences Department, and the man who hired my dad, formerly worked at Oak Ridge, where K-25 was located. Dad was thrown immediately into the Applied Science group under Hurd, where IBM admits their best engineers were sent.

COST OF THE BOMB

- Costs projected to development were between $100 million and $500 million.

- Ninety percent of the cost of building the bomb related to all facilities and land purchases needed to support its development, including the fuel.

- Cost, development, manufacturing, and dropping of the atomic bomb was roughly 18 percent of the entire war effort.

- Between K-25 and the Hanford Nuclear Reservation in south-central Washington, more than 160,000 people were hired to work on the bomb and lived in secrecy from 1941 to 1945.

- The cost of building K-25 was $512 million.[15]

- The cost of building Hanford in 1945 was $390 million; the site itself covered 586 square miles.[16]

- Two pounds of fissionable uranium cost more than $150 million to produce.

- The Los Alamos project, also known as Project Y, was a bargain at only $74 million.[17]

So, regarding Pearl Harbor, when we look at where the funds for the atomic bomb were coming from—it was the war budget: 18 percent of the entire cost of World War II went to building the bomb. That's remarkable, and no one knows about it.

On June 28, 1941, the NDRC was absorbed into the Office of Scientific Research and Development (OSDR). The NDRC still technically existed, but in a limited capacity in that it lost the ability to fund projects (that falling to the OSDR) and took on an advisory role to the OSDR.

From this point, it's easy to view the NDRC and the OSRD as being the same organization with a name change. No matter the name, we're looking at the marriage of government and private industry in the development of military-related technologies. The Manhattan Project, proximity fuses, radar, and antibiotics were all under the watchful eye of the NDRC/OSRD.

Regardless of department names, Dad still spent most of his time in Ames in the lab with Atanasoff until he "quit" school and joined the Navy. He was in uniform less than a year after Pearl Harbor, entering naval service on September 29, 1942. He said that putting on the Navy uniform for the first time was one of the more memorable moments of his life. He wore it home with pride that Christmas, surprising everyone, including Mom, who was also home for the holidays, and posing for pictures with enthusiasm.

He told both his mom and my future mom a white lie: that he'd decided to drop out of school at Iowa and join the Navy since, at nineteen, he was likely to be drafted anyway. He really joined the Navy to lead the installation of the radar sets at the Naval Air Station in Jacksonville, Florida.

The people directing his mathematical contributions to national defense work told him that, as a navy officer, he'd be assigned to help monitor quality control and component compatibility, making sure production was meeting the appropriate standards, in the manufacturing and installation of SCR-535 radar sets by Philco,[18] which had entered into a partnership to manufacture the SCR-535 radar equipment for the Naval Air Corp in the summer of 1941.

Of course, he'd be under the supervision of the National Defense Research Committee, spending a great deal of time at Atanasoff's lab. As Dad told it, he didn't know what was ahead of him, or how serious things were about to get on the world stage.

12

In the Navy

FOUNDED IN 1892 IN PHILADELPHIA, the Philco Corporation was a pioneer in battery, radio, and television production. They ranked fifty-seventh among United States corporations in the value of World War II military production contracts,[1] and had committed to producing two prototypes for Jacksonville, Florida's Naval Air Station by January 1942. Although this required an extremely intense pace of development, the company exceeded expectations, delivering twenty-four radar sets to the Jacksonville base rather than the promised two.

Dad, upon joining the Navy, would be spending time in both Pennsylvania, where the SCR-535 radar sets were manufactured, and in Florida, where they would be installed at the Naval Air Station in Jacksonville. After the prototypes were so well received, the Philco Corporation had an initial order for eighteen thousand of the radar units and expected orders to only increase, requiring additional quality control officers like my dad. The radar units all used the same, or at least similar, technology, but tuning was different depending on whether a set was underwater, on a ship, or in an airplane, since there were different wavelengths to be manipulated.

The Naval Air Corp went to work immediately, installing the equipment on airplanes, submarines, and ships. Meanwhile, Philco continued to improve the equipment, Dad on the assist in Pennsylvania, as they constantly shrank the size of the vacuum tube, thereby increasing sensitivity and accuracy.

The Army and the Navy both used IFF (identification friend or foe) units because they wanted some unified systems for all U.S. forces and allies (especially the Brits) for radar stations to be able to differentiate friendly and enemy air/sea units, and they all had their separate tuning issues. Dad was a master at adjustments. Once he determined the "size knob" for the enemy signal, operators could "tune in on the enemy," the knobs allowing for finer control by utilizing fine motor skills, as opposed to larger handwheels.

Tuning is a term for accurately finding a certain location or signal. Back then, you'd tune in to your hi-fi radio station. And now that America was in the war, demand was sky-high for these IFF radar sets, which allowed the planes that used them to be identified as friendly by the antiaircraft batteries guarding England's shores.

When Dad wasn't installing radar units, he was working in Atanasoff's lab. Atanasoff was good friends with John von Neumann at Princeton. In fact, a lot of top nuclear scientists were in the NDRC's radar group and were intermingling with the nuclear group—the nuclear guys and the radar guys were all interconnected. In fact, von Neumann was so entrenched in the development of the bomb that he was on the committee that decided which cities they would target if the bomb was dropped. The close-knit community allowed for my dad to shuttle back and forth easily and often, designing the radar sets.

Atanasoff would leave Iowa State later in 1942, moving to the U.S. Naval Ordnance Lab in Maryland, where he became chief of the Acoustics Division, monitoring different types of explosions. He and

Dad would work together again, but for the time being, it seemed that for the majority of his Navy career, most of Dad's duties apparently lay in Jacksonville, not Pennsylvania.

It is important to mention that the Jacksonville Naval Academy was like the think tank and design center for the military—equal in importance and brilliance to Silicon Valley, if you will—during the war. Dad was asked for input on fixing top secret "rocket engine issues." This is the first time he had mentioned to me that he liked to examine the schematics of machines. He also mentioned that he worked on "vibration issues" and only needed to see the schematics to find the problem.

In Jacksonville, he lived in a Quonset hut with five other radar engineers, each directing a group of installers. In many ways, this was as close to a real college experience as my dad would get. Palling around with these guys, he found a camaraderie he'd never experienced before, forged from the close proximity of his living quarters, the shared mathematical genius, and the common purpose of the war effort.

When they weren't working, they frequented ice cream parlors, and he later admitted to me that during this time his six-foot frame filled out from indulging his addiction to tapioca pudding, by then eating a quart of it a night. It was on one such evening excursion around town that one of Dad's engineering buddies told him of his idea to package and sell frozen orange juice, suggesting that Dad should go into business with him when the war was over. This fellow had figured out how to concentrate orange juice, package it, and then add water to reconstitute it later. Dad declined, and often regretted the decision when his friend's idea took off into the stratosphere.

His attraction to Marilyn Malmquist—who would one day be Mom to me—also blossomed during the war into a full-blown romance. She remained in nursing school at Mounds Midway, and he wrote her frequently. During one of her school's spring breaks, she took a bus to Jacksonville to visit him, staying in a motel near the base. They spent most of their time on the beach during the five-day rendezvous, Mom's fair Scandinavian skin turning red as a lobster, making the two-day bus ride home more difficult.

Although they continued to write, it was six months before they saw each other again, this time in Kiron, when Dad was on leave from Jacksonville. He proposed to her then, but didn't have a ring at the time. He sent it to her later via the U.S. Mail, along with a poem he had written:

> *I wished I were there in person*
> *To slip on this token of love.*
> *Circumstances hamper such a mission*
> *But my sub-conscious self is there, my Love.*
>
> *So to the ends of the earth may we cherish*
> *This love that we do so much adorn.*
> *That never shall there be any blemish*
> *To this love that is now officially born.*

* * *

Dad and I were halfway finished digging postholes by now. After more water on my face, and more apple juice for Dad, he surveyed the forty-four bags of concrete mix he'd told me to buy, and nodded in approval. I'll never forget that detail as long as I live; 44 was first baseman Willie McCovey's uniform number on the San Francisco Giants. Stacked alongside the bags stood the prefabricated fence sections I'd bought and had delivered with the concrete days before. We'd be mixing and pouring the concrete as soon as all of the holes were dug.

"The war ended," he told me, returning to his story, "but the government wasn't finished with me yet."

Still unsure of what would come out of his mouth next, I hung on every word.

13

The Rise of Radar

THE RADAR DEVELOPMENTS in which Dad played a small part were a major factor in turning the tide against the Nazis and carrying the Allies to victory in Europe.

The SCR-535 radar sets did exactly what they were supposed to do, significantly reducing the number of Allied casualties by U-boat. The 1942 loss of 8,400 American lives decreased to 3,800 in 1943 and 1,100 by 1944. The new equipment was credited with saving scores of Allied lives during the fight for England.

Dad left the radar project in the autumn of 1945, the OSRD and the Navy determined to bring his mathematical skills, now more extraordinary than ever, to the nuclear weaponry world, which in terms of NCRC resources, had replaced radar as the number one priority. The NDRC's top-secret nuclear weaponry committee was now under the leadership of Harvard University president James B. Conant.

As Dad related it to me, "getting into the war was all about the bomb," with FDR and his generals manipulating events at Pearl Harbor in order to motivate the country not only to war, but more important, into spending the billions of dollars it would take to keep up with the Germans in terms of nuclear weaponry development.

Since Pearl Harbor, $5 billion had been poured into nuclear research. Although Germany's nuclear development was over, Soviet activity in this area was burgeoning. Dad was certainly not the only one who moved in between radar technology development and nuclear development. Ernest Lawrence, considered one of the greatest nuclear minds of the twentieth century, and a Nobel Prize winner in 1939 for his work with the cyclotron, had moved over to the radar project for a time, but was now moving back.

But it was the atom bomb that ended the war, with Japan's surrender on August 14, 1945, after the strikes on Hiroshima and Nagasaki. At that point, radar was old news; the military technology that held the attention of the scientific world was exclusively nuclear weapons. America had beaten Germany in the race to build the bomb.

Now, in the wake of Germany's defeat, the Soviet Union emerged as the military counterbalance to the United States. And General George S. Patton was in favor of taking out the Soviets after the war. The weight that would tip the scales was more destructive—nuclear warheads. No sooner had the hot war ended than the Cold War had begun.

This was the war, Dad said, as he mopped his brow with a red handkerchief pulled from the pocket of his stained work pants that had defined his life. I paused briefly to wipe the sweat out of my eyes, no longer trying to hide my expression, which shifted from suspicion to complete surprise with each new revelation.

At this point I had no idea how to judge my father's story. I was in my midthirties at the time and had a job I'd always thought was similar to his, except that I traveled, selling medical devices for Johnson & Johnson, rather than computers. His overseas assignments were the one exotic note of separation, or so I thought.

I was a high school junior when we moved to Thalwil, Switzerland, a suburb of Zurich, and he worked on what I understood to be a water project in Iran. In reality, my dad was busy making Iran a nuclear power back in the '60s and '70s; Iran had nineteen nuclear reactors slated to be built in 1970.

In 1966, America stood out as one of the few arms dealers to Iran. In 1972, "President Richard Nixon and his then-national security adviser, Henry Kissinger, agreed for the first time to 'sell Iran virtually any conventional weapons it wanted.'"[1] The trend continued. "According to a Senate Committee on Foreign Relations staff report in 1976, Iran was the largest single purchaser of US military equipment then. Military sales had increased more than sevenfold from $524 million in 1972 to $3.91 billion in 1974."[2]

It never occurred to me to question the link between being a computer salesman who'd just moved his family to Switzerland and working on a water project in Iran. Apparently the rest of my family was just as oblivious as I was regarding Dad's career.

Later, when the company sent him to England in the years preceding his retirement in 1984, I was out of college, and only my mother joined him there. As far as I knew, these had been interesting but not earth-shattering assignments, but as we worked together on my new fence and he talked, they would take on a darker hue. I remember him telling Mom that he thought IBM wanted him to retire, and this technology project in England was his last hurrah. All that came later in his story, though, and being methodical—one posthole after another, in a row—he was following chronology, for the most part.

Leaving Jacksonville behind, Dad spent six months in the Philadelphia area, evaluating the feasibility of placing nuclear warheads on giant LTA (lighter than air) dirigibles. The testing was done at the Naval Air Engineering Station in Lakehurst, New Jersey. Dad lived on the base in Lakehurst, riding up in a balloon virtually every day, no matter what the weather—rain, sun, or snow—to conduct trajectory calculations at various altitudes. An entire Quonset hut–like structure was cleared out to make room for his experiments. Dad skated over the details of those experiments, and at the time I didn't know enough to ask for additional information, so I was never clear on what all of the experiments were.

The Naval Air Engineering Station Lakehurst achieved fame as the site where the German dirigible the *Hindenburg*, a huge passenger airship, caught fire and burned during a docking attempt in 1937. Filled with hydrogen, the transcontinental blimp burned in less than a minute. Thirty-six people—both passengers and air and ground crew—died. The *Hindenburg* disaster ended lighter-than-air passenger flights, but according to Dad, dirigibles still remained in play as potential nuclear warhead delivery vehicles.

Although it was finally decided that LTA craft were not acceptable as part of nuclear weaponry deployment systems because they crashed too easily and presented too large a target for possible attack, it was discovered that the blimps were a useful tool for *testing* nuclear weapons.

I chuckled when Dad said that the military brain trust decided that big, slow aircraft filled with hydrogen weren't suitable for delivering nuclear warheads. I told him I thought that would have been clear from the beginning.

"No, no," he said. "That's what that basement meeting at the YMCA in Philadelphia was all about, where we were supposed to be a basketball team. There was a tournament actually going on. We just stayed there in the basement in a kind of barracks. We suited up, but we didn't ever play. Instead, we talked about delivering bombs by train, by missiles, by plane, of course. And in my case, balloons."

It was while living in Lakehurst that Dad was invited to attend this clandestine meeting at the YMCA facility on Broad Street in Philadelphia to discuss nuclear weapons systems delivery. The Navy gave him leave for two weeks. Each of the ten participating mathematicians and scientists—all of them virtual geniuses—reported on a particular nuclear weaponry delivery system, from trains to silos to, just as Dad had said, balloons.

At the time, I didn't know much about Enrico Fermi, who was

one of the "players" my dad had named. But now when I think of the Nobel Prize–winning physicist—in his midforties then and in shorts and a basketball jersey, instead of the tweeds, bow tie, and lab coat of a genius—the mind boggles.

My later research led me to discover a group called the Teapot Committee—a code name for the Strategic Missiles Evaluation Group—formed in 1953 to research nuclear warhead delivery systems, including a variety of air force missiles. Fermi wasn't part of it; he died in 1954 at age fifty-three. But it did include eleven leading scientists and engineers who fit Dad's description of the high-ranking brain trust into which he'd been recruited. Dad's involvement in the YMCA group was to give initial input so that when the Teapot Committee formed several years later, they would have reliable information. Dad supplied many of the statistics used to make the future decisions.

As it turned out, hydrogen balloons weren't the answer, although Dad's balloon testing technology was perfected and used extensively at the Lawrence Livermore National Laboratory. "The balloons were good for testing the bombs," Dad said. "Just think, Johnny. The whole thing incinerates. No radioactive contamination left behind."

When I didn't respond, he looked around to survey our progress. "Let's see . . . How many holes have we got left?"

Just a few, as it turned out. The fence stretched from the deck to my asphalt driveway, where a gate would eventually go.

After a brief break to stretch our backs, we started in again.

14

Love and Marriage

MY DAD, EVER THE STOIC SWEDE, wasn't known for expressing much emotion, good or bad, which makes me even more curious about the few artifacts I found from his time in the Navy, September 9, 1942, to March 6, 1946. Those three and a half years saw a lot of change for the military and for the advancement of radar technology. And while I'm sure Dad was immersed night and day in research and development, I can't help but wonder if he didn't enjoy it a great deal.

He was a hard worker, and his OCD was undoubtedly an asset in the arms race. I can also imagine that being inducted into a brotherhood of sorts, being in the Navy, and being surrounded by those of likeminded purpose and abilities, likely felt like the family he never had.

In my collection of family photographs, I have two pictures of Dad smiling overtly, hands on his hips in his Navy outfit, with another gentleman from the Jacksonville naval station. He looks immensely happy—comfortable, even. A third picture shows him in his Navy uniform, smiling in front of the Philco building, where he made radar sets. Mom said he was so proud to be in uniform, and he wore it everywhere when he would come back from Jacksonville, Florida, on leave.

Dad was honorably discharged from the Navy on March 6, 1946, as an aviation electronics technician's mate, petty officer, first class, after nearly three and a half years of service. During his time in the Navy, he was at the ground floor of numerous developments, including what became the Patriot missile, which would be used to shoot down incoming missiles. When he was discharged, he continued to work on the same projects with the same groups of people. In many ways the only thing that changed was his home address.

His family and the love of his life were in St. Paul by now, and so was his new project, so that's where he was headed too. "That's when I moved to Minneapolis," he said. By this time, Atanasoff's early tabulating computer had morphed into more advanced versions of machines able to do high-speed calculations. Dad relied on the machines, but resorted to his slide rule too.

Dad's parents and his sister, Dolores, had moved to St. Paul a year or so after he joined the Navy, nearly three hundred miles away from familiar Kiron, Iowa. Dolores attended Bethel College in St. Paul, and then Minnesota University, in preparation for teaching home economics. And by now, my mom was an RN, working on the maternity floor of a local hospital.

Much to everyone's surprise, Dad's father had apparently cut down on his drinking and gotten a job during the war, building gliders, thoughtfully nicknamed the flying coffins of World War II. These combat gliders were commonly towed by C-47s, the military version of the iconic twin-engine DC-3, to carry additional troops and equipment in the European theatre. After the war, Eldon worked as a handyman for homeowners on upscale Summit Avenue.

Dad lived with his parents temporarily after his time in the Navy, but spent most of his time working or actively courting Marilyn Malmquist, who lived and worked nearby.

Less than a month after he left the Navy, he began college at the University of Minnesota, on April 1, 1946 (the University of Minnesota is also mentioned as an NDRC university that received government contracts[1]), to be involved in the Allegany ballistic tests.

It was during this time that he would have met John von Neumann at Princeton and traveled to Lakehurst. His ultimate mentor, von Neumann, who was also in the NDRC and the Radar Committee, was the head chairman of this strategic missile-planning group, which was the Teapot Committee. It was a close-knit, fraternal group, so all of the members would have been well aware of my dad, and quite familiar with one another.

For the second time, Dad was supposedly undercover as a university student while doing top-secret work on ballistics missile control for the government. To maintain his cover, the University of Minnesota requested and received a copy of his "transcripts" from Iowa State in the spring of 1946, and despite his supposed failing grades in classes to which he had never shown up—and a terrible, 1.11 GPA—U of M awarded him full credit and accepted him into their electrical engineering program, which is asking a lot for someone who—at least on paper—isn't even able to add two plus two. His developing expertise in the Minnesota unit, he said, lay in ballistics control, one of the toughest areas facing American scientists as they tried to build an effective missile arsenal—how to launch a missile accurately from either a fixed or moving vehicle.

Ever since the Germans' V-1 rockets began hitting England (the V-2 was used for the same purpose), war technology had taken a major turn toward missiles that did not come from airplanes overhead, and once the war was over, the United States was determined to focus on developing an effective missile arsenal. Studies began on the efficacy and accuracy of liquid versus solid powder fuels, as well as on how the missile would control itself in space. What proved especially challenging was the ability to shoot a missile accurately from a moving vehicle. But over time, Dad became something of an expert in this area.

While in Lakehurst, Dad, still in the Navy, reconnected with

Atanasoff, who was now the chief of naval acoustics at the Naval Ordnance Lab in Washington, D.C. Once Dad was out of the Navy, Atanasoff asked him to come on board a ballistics project that was tied into the Navy-owned Allegheny Ballistics Laboratory, a tactical propulsion, warhead, and ammunition production and research facility in West Virginia. Although the project was headquartered at Allegheny's headquarters in Pinto (later, in Rocket Center), West Virginia, satellite groups of scientists and mathematicians were clustered at the University of Minnesota, the University of Wisconsin, and Duke University, as well as at commercial research facilities such as the Budd Whell Company of Detroit and the Bell Telephone Laboratories in New York City.

Things were looking up for my dad, on both professional and personal fronts. Finally after years of remote courtship, he and my mother, Marilyn, were married on Monday, December 30, 1946, at the First Baptist Church in Kiron, Iowa, where both of their families could attend.

Even though he had shown himself to be different from his alcoholic relatives, Mom's family—and especially her father, Albin Malmquist—was initially against the marriage. Grandpa Albin's aunt had married a Clauson, and he'd turned out to be a drunk just like my dad's father.

Love won in the end, and my grandfather Albin attended his daughter's wedding ceremony anyway, though disgruntled and aloof both in person and in pictures. If there was only one human being who was more stoic than my dad, it was my grandpa Albin. They could sit side by side for two hours and the only words exchanged would be "You want a cup of tea?" Needless to say, it probably wasn't a very lively wedding ceremony. It was also relatively small; Dad's best friend, Dale, wasn't able to participate as initially planned, as he was married on the same day.

We have a lot of pictures from the wedding, and most are of my dad kneeling down, almost being subservient to my mom. There's one picture of my dad on his knees and my mom sitting, and it's as if she is perched on a pedestal. I think that picture describes somewhat how much my dad respected my mom. He would never be able to tell her the truth of what he was doing, but he must have had a great deal of respect for her to trust her to manage the household and the children, without asking questions, acting as a single parent most of the time.

I found it curious that a lot of the old family pictures are of my dad trying to be affectionate, when in real life he wasn't. In fact, I only recall my dad being affectionate with my mom once. He only hugged me once or twice my entire life.

Hours after the ceremony, the newlyweds were soon back on the road for the four-and-a-half-hour drive back to Minneapolis. With money tight, Dad and Mom moved into the upstairs section of a home in Minnesota that they rented with another young couple, and promised themselves a proper honeymoon sometime in the future. The two couples split the seventy-dollar monthly rent and shared the kitchen and the single bathroom. While Mom and Dad were thankful to have their own bedroom, the close quarters required some creativity. To get Dad off to work, Mom had to fetch water from the bathroom sink and make the morning coffee on a hot plate.

Dad was known to be a workaholic, but he apparently had *some* free time, since he told me they sometimes went on weekend picnics with his parents.

But sadly, Mom and Dad's dreams of a honeymoon were postponed, first by the Soviet Union's announcement of its nuclear program in 1947. The Soviets had their first working nuclear reactor, with uranium confiscated from the Germany's now-defunct atomic bomb program in December 1946. A honeymoon was further delayed by the birth of their first child, my brother, Bill, in late 1947.

When Bill was born, Grandpa Eldon was so proud to show off his first grandchild. He had mellowed considerably by his later years, so despite his abusive parenting, Grandpa was able to enjoy at least a cordial relationship with my dad, likely made easier by proximity. I'd like to think Dad eventually mended his relationship with Grandpa—at least he appeared civil in front of us children.

Meanwhile, though, it was still 1947. I had not yet been born, the Cold War was just beginning, and Dad's life would be consumed by it for the next thirty-five years.

15

The Farmer with an Engineering Degree

DAD GULPED ANOTHER CARTON OF APPLE JUICE between the final post-holes for my fence, then told me he'd worked practically around the clock at Allegany Ballistic testing, while he was at the University of Minnesota, calculating accurate trajectory parameters for various missiles. He added, with a tone of regret—maybe even heartache—that he had hardly taken any time off when my older brother, Bill, was born, to bond with him.

As his second son, I felt the ache from my end too. It had followed me throughout life—the ever-present yet unfulfilled dream of spending more time with my dad. I wondered if my older brother had a clue about any of this. I also wondered why my dad was telling me and not Bill, though I did feel a sense of pride that I was being entrusted with such information.

I wasn't around during those early years of Mom and Dad's marriage, of course, but from conversations with my parents and what

I observed in later life, I can imagine how their personalities and the stresses of Dad's work defined their roles at that early stage. He described a level of secretiveness I sometimes found bizarre, but he took it seriously. He wouldn't talk about his work, even with Mom. That divided their worlds from the start: she changed diapers and kept house; Dad maintained a strict divide between traditional husband and wife roles, something that served his commitment to confidentiality in a way that might not be possible today. He went off in the morning and returned at night, with the hours in between a blank.

Dad was very much the head of the household, somewhat authoritarian in his attitude. The perfectionism required by his work—calculating accurate missile trajectories and keeping quiet about it to all but his coworkers—followed him home, where it found a target in Mom's casual housekeeping skills. Frustrated with what he perceived to be her lack of attention to detail, he'd stalk about the house, muttering, "Oh, Mary. Oh, Mary," (a nickname he had for her). Then, feeling guilty but unable to bring himself to say, "I'm sorry" for hurting her feelings, he would volunteer to scrub the floors to make up for his ranting. He seemed to enjoy that particular chore, and of course the floors always looked perfect when he was finished. Sometimes I wonder if he didn't pick a fight just to spend some down time doing mindless work, like cleaning the house.

It was at this point in his career that Dad's anxiety about his top-secret work began to overtake him at times. His obsession with security verged on paranoia. One afternoon Mom went out with Bill to do some shopping. When two hours passed and they hadn't returned, Dad got so worried that something had happened to them that he called the police. Mom showed up not long afterward from her shopping expedition, carrying a large grocery bag and pushing Bill's stroller with one hand.

That embarrassed him, Dad said, but it didn't make him worry less. He was always a worrier—he worried about providing for the family, he worried about having the resources to send us to college—but his more intense worrying at this time was influenced by the paranoia the U.S. government was exhibiting.

Dad told me that in those postwar days of the late 1940s, with the Soviet Union nuclear-capable and worries about Communist expansion at a fever pitch, his program took every precaution. The Soviets had already infiltrated the Los Alamos program, and it was of great concern that they could do it again.

In the spring of 1948, as he arrived at the lab one morning, Dad was met by his Navy superiors, who immediately took him for a drive in a sedan because they couldn't be sure the building was safe. They told him they had reason to believe that a mole was on the inside at the OSRD program at the University of Minnesota. The OSRD had expanded the role of the National Defense Research Committee even before Pearl Harbor. Now, as Dad's employer, it had a stake in protecting its most valuable minds.

Given his great facility with computers, and hence his bright future, the last thing the Navy and OSRD wanted was for Dad to be compromised. Several American corporations were on the verge of installing large computers for massive defense projects. IBM, for one, was in the fledgling stages of the establishment of what was eventually called the Military Products Group, and Dad's abilities and knowledge made him invaluable to the cause. As such, the damage to national security if he were exposed would be incalculable.

The same fear, he said, led his handlers to declare him "graduated" from Minnesota in 1949. The government made certain that the University of Minnesota awarded Dad a degree to justify his cover, and U of M records show he graduated on June 11, 1949, with a degree in electrical engineering. His degree was questionable. I'm sure he knew that, but he didn't need it anyway.

He was immediately sent back to Kiron, Iowa, with a new cover, this time as a farmer, while he waited for a new assignment. His handlers told him, "Wallace, you tell Mary you are going to be a farmer. Say you can't find an engineering job." So he did.

If someone were going to try to "turn" him, any unrecognized vehicles in and around a small farming community would be noticed immediately, and both he and his security team could easily spot a stranger approaching. He was to lie low while they sniffed out the potential rat in the project.

Dad told Mom to prepare to move back to the Malmquist farm, where they would be living with Marilyn's father, Albin, in his farmhouse. He was graduating the engineering program early at the University of Minnesota when engineering jobs were scarce, he told her. Of course, with the computer in its infancy and the Cold War in full swing, engineering jobs weren't scarce at all—it was just another one of Dad's cover stories. So was his claim that he had come around to thinking that his true calling may lie in farming. In fact, farming was the *last thing* Dad wanted to do with his life, although he would come to be quite good at it, as with most things he attempted.

Mom was unable to comprehend why Dad refused to stay in Minnesota at least an extra couple of days to attend his graduation. He told Mom he wasn't interested in attending the ceremony because it was a waste of time. But he told *me* it was because he'd never been to class, spending his time working on special projects. He knew if he did attend, other graduates would have been wondering, *Who is* that *guy?*

It turned out to be a good move, health-wise.

Dad insisted that the black-and-white newspaper clip from St. Paul's *Pioneer Press* be kept in our family photo album, showing the crowd gathered in the school's football stadium for the spring 1949 graduation. The photograph's caption reads:

Twilight Graduation March: Thousands of spectators watch the long lines of academic robed University of Minnesota students file from the track of Memorial stadium Saturday night as the candidates for degrees are ushered to their seats in front of the commencement platform. The stadium was sprayed in the early evening with DDT to keep the bugs away from the bright lights thrown around the setting of the ceremony. —Pioneer Press Photo.

DDT is the insecticide that was later used in the Vietnam War. It made bald eagle's eggshells thin and almost rendered one of our nation's most powerful symbols extinct. While not as toxic as Agent Orange, also used in Vietnam, it probably isn't the greatest chemical to be sprayed with.

I don't think Dad knew about the DDT ahead of time, and even if he had, DDT use wasn't scrutinized until 1962, when Rachel Carson highlighted its dangers in her groundbreaking book *Silent Spring*. Even then, it wasn't banned for agricultural use worldwide until 2001.[1] Still I wonder just how many of those students and spectators experienced ill effects from that night's ceremony.

Looking back, it did seem odd for such a drastic career switch—from engineering student to instant farmer—but the family went right along with it. Grandfather Albin was happy to have help on the family farm; Mom and Dad would inherit the farm one day anyway. Mom was thrilled about the move back home, admitting in a 2010 interview, "I was really looking forward to moving back to the farm." Farming was part of her blood, her heritage, and her childhood memories. And maybe after a few years of being moved around and kept relatively in the dark as to why, the farm life offered a welcome peace and familiarity to her.

And with Dad's previous farming experience, he never missed a step—the transition was so seamless. In fact, I have very fond memories of working that farm as a young boy every summer, cutting the weeds out of the soybean fields with a machete, baling hay, shucking corn, slopping the pigs, and spending time with my father.

While his God-given talents lay elsewhere, I think farming was his solace. He was completely isolated on the 160 acres when he was there, which gave him a feeling of security. He loved to do physical work—for him it was his R & R. You have to remember, he didn't really have R & R during the year. But when he would go to Iowa, he would spend some time farming. Then he would vanish for three or four days, undoubtedly working on one of his top-secret projects, and then he would show up again. When he was able to work on the farm, he was more relaxed. He would actually have a crooked little smile on his face while he worked his tail off. There is definitely a connection between the body and the earth, and when my dad was on the farm, he became one with the soil. And every August, no matter where we were living in the world, he'd send me to the farm to work for baling season.

Where Dad got his endurance from, I'll never know. I sure didn't inherit it. I was a hard worker; don't get me wrong. But even in my youth and teenage years, when I was on the bale rack, stacking bales of hay, I'd get so dusty and tired after a few hours. Someone wrote on my back once, "Wash me." I didn't care what it said. Dad, on the other hand, could work for twelve solid hours without a complaint, as long as he had plenty of water and apple juice.

You need an incredible amount of balance so you don't get knocked off the bale rack because it isn't a smooth ride as the tractor hauling the baling machine rolls down the dirt rows, forming the hay into bales, tying it with string, and stacking it on the rack. One time I got bounced off while holding a hook in my right hand to grab the bales with. I somehow poked myself in the ribs with the hook, which bled a bit, but of course, the family didn't stop working. They said it would quit bleeding eventually, which it did.

After dinner we'd all go to the porch and talk about what the weather was going to do the next day, and maybe watch a little 6:00 news. We'd all be in bed by 8:00 p.m. Dad never wanted me or any of the kids to forget what hardworking, deliberate people do on a farm.

If you milked the cows, you got up early. I'm not an early-morning person, so I only went *once* as a kid with my grandpa Albin. Unable to focus my eyes in the dark, I fell in the barn and landed in one of the cow pies. Then, when I was situated on the milking stool, I wasn't assertive enough in getting the milk. Those cows know when you're not comfortable, and having never milked a cow before, I was *very* uncomfortable. They can smell fear, and in no time at all, a dirty cow tail came around and whacked me in the head. My grandfather, milking his cow nearby, just laughed!

After that adventure, I was happy to stick with slopping pigs and baling hay.

* * *

We had dug the last posthole by now, and rested in the shade of the eaves at the corner of the house, watching the colors undulate on the orange-leafed trees that marked the property line. Looking back and analyzing what Dad was telling me, so much of it seemed fantastic.

Maybe I was listening to the story of a man whose life wasn't as much as he wanted it to be, so he was spending his remaining days enhancing it through vivid and creative storytelling, bolstered by cartons of apple juice. After all, it was difficult to see my dad as one of the most sought-after men, maybe in the world, at that time. And it seemed even more ludicrous that someone supposedly so brilliant would trade in his lab coat for beat-up blue jeans at his employer's request.

But then again, maybe he was telling the truth.

After a lengthy break, Dad drew a long tape measure along the postholes, to be sure they were spaced right. Of course, they were. Then, with the sun starting to get low, it was time to mix and pour the concrete into the holes, and then place the wooden posts. We'd hang the fence sections on the posts tomorrow, after the concrete had time to cure overnight.

Finished with the auger, we didn't have a rusty old machine to keep us in close proximity. We had something even better—concrete.

If my dad was going to tell me his life story, it wasn't going to include a cup of tea and a warm seat by the fireplace. He was at his peak when he was immersed in hard labor, working up a sweat. One of his favorite mediums to produce that sought-after level of nirvana was concrete.

I never quite understood his passion for concrete work. Maybe it was part psychological and part sentimental. His own dad was an incredible concrete guy. It was easy to forget that *he* had any talents at all besides consuming record amounts of alcohol and wielding his fists like hammers. But Grandpa Eldon had such a knack for it that any concrete project he poured could nearly be considered art.

Sadly, in the early years, if my grandfather began a concrete project in the morning, by noon he would be drunk and couldn't continue. Still, I think my dad always wanted to be a great concrete guy like his dad. Maybe he thought that if they had something in common, he could gain his father's elusive favor.

My dad's stories began again as soon as we emptied the first bag of concrete into the wheelbarrow, including the one about his use of a windmill to transfer secret calculations, and a onetime run-in with his father-in-law.

16

The Windmill

ONCE HE GRADUATED FROM MINNESOTA and was back in Iowa, Dad told me, he stuck with his story that he was considering a farming career. Many in town were surprised, never expecting that from him. He was different from other people around there, after all. He had chances others didn't have. Yet, Dad could work the bale rack with the best of them, and he was very adept at sitting on the porch, chatting about the weather, as Swedish farmers are wont to do. He managed to convince everyone of his farming credentials—except for his father-in-law, Albin, who found Dad's frequent traveling suspicious.

Even though Dad had already told my mom that there were no engineering jobs available, hence the sudden switch from an engineering degree to farming, he said that he had meetings about *possible* jobs on the East Coast. He'd disappear at times, sometimes leaving for three or four days, and then he'd return, ready for farming. In reality, that year on the farm, Dad made numerous trips between von Neumann's lab, Lakehurst, and meetings with Enrico Fermi, where they conducted assessments and discussed the different warhead delivery systems.

While in the Navy, under the NDRC, he had been responsible for doing research on whether balloons could be used to transport missiles. (He was still involved in that research as a makeshift farmer.) In fact, it was at one of these meetings at John von Neumann's home where he first met Albert Einstein.

The head of the Institute for Advanced Study in Princeton, von Neumann immigrated to the United States from Germany in 1933, and had originally been hired to work with Einstein on institute projects. Von Neumann had invented the "game theory," a branch of mathematics that brought new insights to fields as diverse as economics and evolutionary theory. He called the meeting of esteemed scientists and mathematicians in late 1951 to introduce the new code—the C-code—he'd developed, and to discuss how it pertained to nuclear ballistic calculations.

Dad soon found himself in a roomful of the most brilliant minds in the country. When Einstein, then already in retirement, arrived, a hush fell, Dad feeling his skin tingle in the presence of "The Man." The discussion soon grew into a heated debate about whether or not nuclear weaponry was indeed viable from defensive as well as offensive positions. Another topic to be discussed was whether it was morally and ethically sound to even use such knowledge for weapons, understanding that if it fell into the wrong hands, the destruction to the earth—and to humanity—could be cataclysmic.

Before Einstein left, von Neumann inducted the inside nuclear guys, presenting each mathematician at the meeting—four or five of them—with a slide rule, complete with a leather-tooled carrying case bearing his initials, to thank him for his contribution, and to form a united brotherhood. Today that slide rule, given to my father, is one of my most cherished possessions.

These meetings with Einstein would continue for three to four years, and over that period Dad had a very close friendship and working relationship with Einstein. Dad was recognized as a younger protégé, and he would love to get into mathematical discussions about compression of time and space and black holes. Einstein was still very popular, but he was trying to develop another theory of relativity that didn't quite pan out. With his brilliance and popularity being surpassed by John von Neumann, Einstein looked at Dad basically as *his mathematician.*

At Princeton at that time, the two greatest mathematical minds were obviously Einstein and von Neumann—my dad's closest mentor, who eventually surpassed Einstein. Their offices were across the hallway from each other at the Institute for Advanced Study.

* * *

Once back at the farm, Dad was contacted regularly by the same group of men from the diner who'd first tested my dad's abilities. A new routine soon began: He'd receive instructions hidden in an abandoned windmill outside of town, just on the edge of his father-in-law's property. They were, he said, OSRD packets that were left for him in burlap bags containing mathematical problems to be solved.

Dad kept a locked case in the attic, and I can only imagine it contained the contents of the packages he brought home. He would slip away to the attic every few days for a couple of hours, suitcase in hand, lowering the set of folding stairs from the hallway ceiling and climbing up into the attic of the farmhouse. There he'd work silently, sometimes early in the morning or late into the night.

I remember holding the thin wooden handrail, walking up the narrow stairs as a kid, and then playing with my sisters in the large, unfinished room. Grandpa Albin could have framed in another entire floor up there—it was much bigger than a typical attic. There were a few pieces of furniture and some kid toys for us to play with. In fact, it was the perfect space for a playroom. It was also the perfect space for my father's makeshift office.

If anyone asked about his frequent trips upstairs, Dad would say he was looking for peace and quiet to read up on the latest farming techniques, but in fact he was conducting calculations for the government on his slide rule. And after working out the answers, he would drive to the windmill and leave the packet in the same hiding place—in burlap bags at the base of the windmill. They'd disappear in the middle of the night.

He didn't say how he knew *when* they'd arrive or how frequently, but if a light was left on in the farmhouse attic, it meant he was going to deliver his corrected papers into the windmill floor. That was the signal to inform his employers to pick up his work, and to deliver any new instructions. He'd drive the short distance, fetch the burlap packages, turn off the light to signal he had received the package, and go to work with his slide rule in the farmhouse attic, working on calculations that needed to be finalized, critiqued, redone, or revamped.

Why would government men take the risk of moving top-secret calculations off-site and leaving them in a windmill? Theoretically the men could be followed or a package could be compromised in the transfer, perhaps stolen or damaged by overzealous rats. Why not bring my dad to a secure location, like Los Alamos or Berkeley, to do the math problems instead of leaving documents for him on a farm?

As it turns out, the farm was perfect for such an intelligence transfer since no one in the wider intelligence community—outside of the OSRD and NDRC—knew about my dad or his incredible gift yet; at least that's what his handlers were banking on. The windmill was very isolated, and could be watched 24/7 to see if other people approached it. If anyone had approached the site, they certainly would have been apprehended. Grandfather Eldon had long since given up his drinking post at the windmill, and it wasn't used as a fun hide-and-seek spot by the local farm children either. So, when Dad hid the packets inside of the base of the mill, they would be undisturbed until pickup, when his calculations would be transferred to a remote site where they were needed.

While there were initially fifty scientists recruited for the NDRC, not all received the same cloak-and-dagger treatment as my dad. Some of his peers—like von Neumann and Loomis—led fairly public lives. But between his introverted personality and the oath he took as a teenager, he'd spend the rest of his days blending in to his surroundings, never wanting to stand out.

With Dad becoming more and more comfortable with his farming assignment every day, his superiors also wanted to use this time to see if anyone was going to try to "turn" him. His mind was beyond unique. As a mechanical and theoretical savant, he was very rare, somewhat of a national treasure. Not only did he know how to do nuclear calculations, but he could devise how to build the delivery system and the guidance control of a missile, no matter the size or range. He literally was a one-man shop for nuclear power!

The government didn't have any reason to suspect that Wallace's gift was known to any other agencies, but they couldn't be 100 percent sure, especially since a mole had been discovered at Minnesota and Dad was deemed as having graduated early to get him out of that facility. Remember: there was a four-year, thorough investigation going on as to how deep the Russians had penetrated our nuclear program. If there were other agencies or countries that were going to make a move on Wallace, they'd no doubt have done it on the silent acres of a family farm. If he *was* turned, a foreign country could become a nuclear power literally overnight.

While Dad's newfound passion for quiet time in the attic no doubt puzzled my mother, she never really questioned his actions after he'd explained that he was reading up on farming techniques. By this point, she had known my father long enough to realize that he exhibited strange behavior at times. Maybe she accepted that as one of his lovable quirks.

However, Grandpa Albin's suspicions were on high alert. After all, he was the only one who was up early enough on a regular basis to see the lights being turned off and on in the farmhouse attic. His military intuition reignited after years of farming, he suspected that he was observing signals to an unknown entity. And that meant an unknown entity was watching his farm closely.

17

Albin Smells a Rat

ALBIN MALMQUIST WOKE EVERY MORNING at 4:30 to milk his cows, and on a number of occasions he noticed his son-in-law driving away from the farm, heading toward the windmill. Fewer than fifteen minutes later, my dad would return home with a burlap sack, unaware that his father-in-law was watching him.

Born in October 1889 in Stockholm Township, in Crawford County, Iowa, Grandpa Albin was a well-educated man, especially for those times. After his normal school education, in 1911 and 1912, he continued his education at the Denison Normal and Business College, later returning to help his father at the farm until he entered the military in February 1918.

Grandpa Albin served for two years during World War I as a private in a machine gun company, a grunt in General Pershing's army, spending much of that time in France. Out of a large troop that he led, he was one of only two men to survive being gassed in the trenches.

We never knew many other details about his service, other than a brief glimpse into life in the trenches, in the form of a letter he wrote to his father, John Lars Malmquist, which was included in the town newspaper. Grandpa Albin wrote, "Dad, we shot the machine guns at the Germans today. I've learned now how to put on my gas mask now in seven seconds and I've learned to sleep with the cooties [rats] on my face." In the same article, there's a note that his dad sold a pig that weighed 315 pounds. On the back page, there's a picture of General Pershing. They were in the thick of it in World War I, and while he likely had a great many stories to tell, Grandpa Albin refused to talk about the war. He *especially* refused to talk about the Germans. Unfortunately for his children and grandchildren, he also failed to pass down his gift for multiple languages that made him quite the commodity.

Grandpa Albin was highly educated and spoke three languages, although it's a mystery how he learned them. He did attend school in France while he was there, but there's no record of him learning any language besides French. Perhaps he had an ear for those other languages and enough interest to become fluent.

At that time, England's Windsor Castle had twenty thousand to thirty thousand acres around it, so American troops coming out of France would typically station themselves in tents around the big fence surrounding the Castle, waiting to get the ships back to the United States. But somehow, during the war, word of Grandpa Albin's impressive education made its way to the castle. Not long after that, he became the private tutor to King George V of England for nearly a year. Every day the king would come and get him, and surrounded by guards on daily morning walks, he would teach the king science and agriculture.

After he was discharged in June 1919, his stint as a royal tutor finished, he came back to Iowa to farm, just like his parents. The family farm was 160 acres, a quarter of a section. Back when all the immigrants were coming into the country, the government chopped up what they called "quarter sections" for all these immigrants to buy, and Grandpa Albin was eager to get to work on the farm his parents had purchased under the Homestead Act around 1890. In February 1920, he married Sadie Johnson, who was a servant in a home in Kiron. Together they had four children—my mother, Marilyn; her sister Marjorie; and two other babies—a boy and a girl—who died in infancy.

A very stoic-looking Swede, Grandpa Albin was hardworking, very frugal, and in some ways, ahead of his time. In Iowa's often-harsh farming conditions, wooden fence posts always seemed to be breaking down or rotting out, and once that happened, it was only a matter of time before the cattle would get out. To put an end to that, Grandpa Albin waited until farming season was over each year and hand-poured concrete posts for the *entire farm's perimeter*—eventually covering all 160 acres. In the winter the frozen soil can't be farmed, so a lot of Iowa farmers would go to Arizona or some other warm place in the winter. But not my grandfather. Forever clad in overalls, he would spend hours outside, pouring concrete fence posts. Then, when the land would thaw or he just had some spare time, he'd anchor them deep in the ground

Grandpa Albin chose to spend the majority of any down time on work projects. Needless to say, he was very fit—both mentally and physically, and had not an ounce of fat on him. He was also a very strong Christian with a big heart. A man of few words, if he spoke, you listened. I sure wish I'd known him longer because he no doubt had some amazing stories to tell.

In the 1930s and '40s, the Germans and the Swedes in Iowa both shared a love of collective farming, but they really didn't interact with each other. While I don't believe there was any deep-seated disdain on either side, the cultures and languages were different enough that the communities mostly kept to themselves. Memories of World War I didn't help relations either.

I went back home each summer to help on the farm from the time I was born until I was eighteen, like clockwork, and we only interacted with the Swedish folks in the farming community. The town itself consisted of only a couple of hundred people. In collective farming, all of the families would gather each morning in a central location, and

then a manager of sorts—usually Aunt Mae, who also directed wed-
dings—would create work groups with the men, and divvy up the jobs
that needed to be done that day between ten different farms, depending
on the season, weather, and harvest times.

Aunt Mae would call out, "You four are doing Augustus's lower
forty today, and you three are going over to the Larsons'." Workers
would come help on someone's north forty on Tuesday, and then the
next day they'd go over on another farm and help them, until all the
work was done on each farm.

The women would come together every day and make a mid-
morning snack and lunch for the men. My Aunt Nelda and Aunt Nancy
would drive the pickup truck to bring food and punch around all day
while we were baling hay.

The younger kids wouldn't go far, usually staying home to do
chores or going to help the neighboring farm next door. It was a true
communal deal, and it was unbelievable to see how everybody helped
everybody, with no questions asked.

There was always a window of time to get the job done each season,
but with rotating help from multiple families, the work was done in a
timelier manner, and it was certainly never mundane. I was very familiar
with all of the Swedish family farms in Kiron, but we never worked on
German farms. As we found out much later, Grandpa Albin was very
familiar with his German neighbors.

On his farm he had five hundred pigs, cattle and chickens, and
eight big horses—Clydesdales and Belgians. He had a reputation as a
prosperous farmer in a town where prosperity was hard to attain during
the Depression. He made tremendous money, off the chicks and pigs
mainly. But a big issue on a farm like that is feeding all of the animals.
They can eat you into the poorhouse. Yet Grandpa Albin always had
the best crops on his farm. God blessed him, and he, in turn, did his
part to quietly bless others.

My grandfather was ultraconservative and saved every penny he
made. During the Depression, he gave out loans that he didn't expect

to have repaid—and he did it in secret.

When Bethel Seminary in St. Paul, Minnesota, was going bankrupt in the mid-1930s, Grandpa Albin literally bailed them out with his own money and kept them from going under. And when he got wind that some of the area residents—including three German families in Schleswig, the German community next to Kiron—were in financial trouble and were about to lose their farms to the bank, he tried to help them save their farms. He couldn't stand seeing banks taking over farms and displacing hardworking families—no matter what accent the owners had.

When he died in 1983, the regular Swedish congregation crowd came to his service. The surprise came when three older, German farmers showed up at the funeral to pay their respects. My mom was shocked and asked me, "Why are they here at the funeral?" It wasn't until then that we learned how Grandpa Albin had personally saved several German families from losing their farms and their livelihoods.

When asked why he was at the service, one man said, "He lent me money so I could save my farm." Another man told my mom that if it weren't for her dad, the government and the banks would have taken over all *three* German farms.

All of the debts had long since been paid back to Grandpa Albin. But the men were doing their duty, paying respects to a good man who had helped each of them survive the Depression when he really had no reason to.

We were all shocked, of course—and pleasantly surprised in a time of great mourning. My mom considered it such a beautiful blessing to learn about her father's compassion in action, and to hear firsthand the testaments to the Christian love he felt for his brothers in need—*whether they were Christians or not.*

I personally found this revelation fascinating because he refused to talk about what the Germans did in World War I, yet he had such a disdain for what the bankers were doing to the German farmers. Somehow—even with the atrocities he'd witnessed in war—he was able to show genuine compassion to his neighbors in need, regardless of politics. As I mentioned, I never once, in all the eighteen years I visited the farm, saw any of the Swedish folks intermingling with the Germans. But somehow, Grandpa Albin found a way to cross the cultural borders.

While he was away during World War I, his mother's wedding ring fell off while she was ploughing the field behind a horse. By the grace of God, after twelve years in the soil, being tilled upside down every year, a sparkle grabbed my grandfather's eye after his return to the farm, and he located the ring. He wore it as his wedding ring, tucking it away in his wallet after Grandma Sadie died. At Grandpa's funeral, my mom pried the ring out of his wallet, and I have worn it ever since.

Now gracious as he was, Grandpa Albin was by no means naïve, and my dad's strange sneaking around the farm during the early morning hours triggered his curiosity. Because of Eldon's long history of drinking and being a nuisance, Grandpa Albin had serious questions about his daughter's marriage to a Clauson from the start, even though my dad never touched a drop of alcohol his whole life. In Grandpa's mind, the hard-drinking Clausons were on the wrong side of the track.

Yet, living in a small town, he saw that my dad was different from the other Clausons at a young age. As a young man, Dad would come by to fix Grandpa Albin's tractors when they broke down. He would fix his engines and anything else that needed repair. He would openly walk from his house to pick up my mom and her sister Marjorie, and he'd walk with them the entire five miles and carry their books to school.

Grandpa Albin no doubt appreciated Dad's kindness toward his daughters, but when it came to marriage, he wasn't too excited about being related to the Clausons. In fact, I've got a picture from Mom and Dad's wedding where you can see Grandpa Albin, and his expression is priceless. It's as if he's thinking, *Oh my God. I'm now part of the Clauson household. We're DOOMED!*

Now, years later, while out to milk his cows as the day was just starting to get light, Grandpa Albin had more than once seen Dad heading to the windmill. One morning, unable to stand the mystery any longer, he finished his milking early and approached Dad in the kitchen, just as he walked back inside after the latest secret deposit.

"Wallace," he said gruffly, "in the first war I fell asleep in the trenches with rats crawling on my face. I think I am starting to smell a rat in my family with you in that windmill."

Not missing a beat, Dad said, "Albin, you defended this country once. I'm defending it, too, just in a different way."

That was all that was exchanged between them. Dad's guarded confession must have satisfied Grandpa Albin's curiosity, because he left Dad alone after that—never once bringing it up again.

18

The Greatest Living
Room Debates

HAVING FINALLY FINISHED POURING THE CONCRETE, Dad and I loaded the rented auger into my car to return it. As much as I hated the day's conversation to end, I wanted to get to the hardware store before it closed, to avoid paying an extra day's rent.

We drove in silence to return the rented automatic posthole auger, Dad beside me on the front seat. As we approached a light, Dad said, "Turn left at the next light."

"But Dad," I protested, "the equipment rental place is that way, and if we don't get it back by six, they'll charge us an extra—"

Dad interrupted. "Just turn here."

The turn took us down a residential street in the old section of Princeton. At a substantial turn-of-the-century Victorian home, he asked me to stop. Then he told me something else I hadn't known. The previous summer, when I'd flown east from San Jose, looking for a house in advance of my transfer to the Princeton area, Dad had joined me rather than my wife, Celeste, and we'd stayed at the Nassau Inn. What I didn't know was what he'd done while we were there.

"When we were here on the house-hunting trip," Dad said, "I snuck out from the hotel one night and walked around town. It was that night it rained, and I borrowed an umbrella from the hotel. And when I got here to this street, I saw this house and I just stared into that living room." He pointed to the stately old home with a big glass front window, perched on a knoll.

I did remember that it rained that night. That's the reason I went to bed as early as I did. We'd already had dinner, and although he wasn't ready to call it a night, there was nothing else to do.

In addition to the excitement Dad felt from visiting his old stomping grounds, he was also on West Coast time, and as you know, when you fly east, your clock goes forward, so my dad really wasn't tired yet. Instead he went downstairs and asked to borrow an umbrella so he could take a walk, first to von Neumann's house, where he just stared into the black windows, then to Einstein's house to do the same, no doubt reliving each conversation he'd heard in those homes as if it were only hours ago.

The hotel is about a two- to three-block walk away from John von Neumann's house. Dad could have absolutely walked there and back and had plenty of time to reminisce in less than an hour and a half. Apparently, I had slept through this nighttime excursion, because I was in my own hotel room, doors down from Dad's room, either asleep early or watching TV, and had no idea he went walking that night in the rain.

Now I looked up the rise of the lawn to the living room window, but with the waning daylight casting a golden glow on the windows, there was no clue as to what was inside. Still, I knew I was looking at one of my dad's treasured memories. I'd never seen him exhibit such reverence about anything before that wasn't church-related. And that was huge! When I was growing up, our family went to church Sunday mornings, Sunday evenings, Wednesday midweek service, and that was just part of our natural protocol. Then again, maybe this was just a different kind of church for Dad.

"Somehow it felt like home," he continued. "Because I'd been there. I had the most fascinating conversations and most incredible debates of my life in that room. All scientists connected to the government, but split into two camps, one for and one against." His time inside the home would have been after the bomb had been dropped in Japan, likely when he was at Lakehurst and driving into Princeton.

"For and against what?" I asked, my dirty hands gripping the steering wheel, straining my neck to get a better look at the house.

"Nuclear weapons," he said matter-of-factly.

The house, he said, belonged to John von Neumann. Later I learned what a towering figure von Neumann was, a mathematical genius who advanced quantum mechanics, conceived game theory, helped pioneer computing, and for the discussions Dad referred to, made calculations vital to the success of the Manhattan Project and the atomic bomb. He developed the first computer codes that were eventually used on the IBM 701 Defense Calculator at the nuclear weapons facility in Livermore, California.

Born in Hungary in 1903, von Neumann was a child savant. He became an academic star in Germany, and was invited to lecture at Princeton in 1929. As mentioned earlier, he emigrated permanently in 1933 when Hitler came to power, and headed Princeton's Institute for Advanced Study from its founding that year until 1942. He lived in Princeton until his death in 1957. An extrovert socialite who loved to entertain, he often had parties and gatherings at his house. This no doubt helped him attract a number of the fairer sex—he was known as a bit of a womanizer.

Along with celebrities and other socialites, von Neumann also entertained the top scientists at that time, including, I soon learned, my dad, who would often meet with von Neumann to discuss the latest findings and projects.

"That's where *The Man* gave me the slide rule," Dad continued, still looking into the window of the house. He had always treasured a particular slide rule that he kept in a beautifully tooled leather case with his initials in a line down the front. He let me play with it when I was a child but always retrieved it afterward and put it away. As kids, we never quite understood why it seemed so special to him.

"We each got one," he said of the small group of mathematicians. "Except *The Man*. He was there just listening."

"What man?" I asked him, waiting for a name.

"*The* Man," he said, the exaggerated inflection in his voice showing great reverence. I knew Dad well enough to know that was his signal that he wouldn't say the name. But by now, from the revelations he'd made throughout the day, I had an inkling.

"Einstein?" I said. I knew Einstein had lived in Princeton.

"Yeah," he answered, again without voicing the name. He never took his eyes off the house.

* * *

The tension in the room was extremely high on the night the mathematicians were awarded with their slide rules—the equivalent of a police officer receiving his badge. These men would save the world with the power of their minds. This would have been around 1950, during Dad's farming year. He told Mom he was going out on interviews, and he would be gone for weeks.

On that night, nearly twenty men gathered in von Neumann's living room. The high-profile nuclear scientists, including Einstein, made their case—they wanted to push the genie back in the bottle, but the knowledge was already public. Lise Meitner, an Austrian-Swedish physicist living in Germany under Hitler, had discovered the science behind nuclear fission, mathematically proved the chain reaction, and released the calculations in the late 1930s.

Lise should have been awarded a Nobel Prize; her associates were— all men, of course. They named an element after her called "Meitnerium" to appease her family, but she was never given proper credit. She had to flee Germany because she was Jewish, and she ended up in Stockholm, revered as a great scientist.

Her calculations were now being used in several countries to build weapons, and they knew a fusion bomb was capable of ending the world as we know it. In fact, a *fusion bomb*, if released, would be a thousand times more powerful than the *fission bomb* dropped on Nagasaki in 1945—the only thing left of the entire city and surrounding areas would be granules of glass. One side of the camp wanted to halt all nuclear development because they feared the power and the knowledge falling into the wrong hands.

On the other side of the camp was my dad, whose specialty was fusion. And with him were the mathematicians who favored moving forward with experiments and trying to control the power, rather than run from it—it was already out there. In fact, beginning in January 1939, *Naturwissenschaften* (science of nature), a science magazine similar to *Scientific American*, printed articles for six months on how to create a chain reaction. The scientists realized this needed to stop, but it would be impossible to erase Lise's discovery from existence.

The two sides debated for days in von Neumann's living room, heated arguments and moral convictions pleading for each side's cause. The high-profile scientists finally conceded to the mathematicians that since the science already existed, it should at least be managed by those whose priority was national security rather than mass destruction.

"But we all agreed on one thing," Dad said. "If we're going to get into this and we're going to stay in it, we're going to have to know how to control it, monitor it, and direct it. Nobody disagreed on that."

After staring at von Neumann's house for a few more moments, he directed me to drive into an adjacent neighborhood and to pull up in front of a whitewashed wooden home with black shutters. "That's where *he* lived," he said, eyes fixed on the structure, memories of his friendship with Einstein buzzing through his mind like electricity.

Another moment and he motioned that I should carry on. As I turned the corner, he abruptly changed the subject.

"We'd better get that auger back to the shop before it closes," he said. "You don't want them to charge you for an extra day."

19

The Math Tutor

AS I DROVE THE REMAINING MILES to the hardware store, I thought back on the day's revelations, and I must confess, along with a stirring of excitement, I also found myself growing a little resentful. Although my brother, Bill, had excelled in math, my math skills were average at best, and I'd always struggled with the subject as a student. Now I was hearing that I'd grown up under the same roof as a bona fide math genius who had the unique ability to think in a kind of mathematical extra dimension. He had a mind so valuable the government had gone to great, even improbable, lengths to keep it a secret. *And he'd kept it a secret from me too.* Not once, when I was growing up, had he asked how I was doing with my schoolwork or whether I needed help with anything, or given any hint at all that he could guide me through the tough spots. In fact, anytime I needed help with math, he told me to ask my mother!

Hmm, I thought. *Maybe he's bluffing.*

We reached the hardware store a few minutes before it closed. Dad waited in the car, and I lugged the heavy auger from the trunk into the store. Other renters were returning tools, and as I waited in line, a pair of high school girls came in and spoke to one of the store clerks—apparently the mother of one of the girls.

The girls were study partners, and they were upset because, as one of them explained to their mom, their math tutor hadn't shown up and they were worried about a test they were taking the next day.

What are the chances? I thought.

"Excuse me," I said. "I couldn't help but overhear. I know somebody who can help you out."

With a burst of energy, I leaned the auger against the counter and went out to the car. "Dad, a couple of girls in there need some math help. Why don't you come in?" This was the perfect opportunity to see if he really knew what he was talking about. I was about to call his bluff.

"Johnny, I'm worn out. I'd really rather not," he said, avoiding eye contact. Dad didn't want to budge. He said he was too tired.

My memories flashed to several times throughout my adolescent years when I'd wanted my father's approval or his presence, and he'd let me down. Much to my dismay, he had always shied away from being introduced to my friends or classmates. In fact, the only time he did any socializing was at church, and even that was low-key.

In my mind's eye, one specific instance stood out from the rest. I saw myself walking up to the podium in my senior year of high school to receive the outstanding athlete award during graduation. My father was seated at the back of the room, always next to the exit door.

Thinking I would finally be able to introduce him to my classmates, I said into the microphone, "I'm pleased that my father is with me," and I looked to the back of the room where he had sat moments before. A roomful of heads turned to finally see this mysterious man, but he was gone. I was so proud to have him with me, but he must have ducked through the door as I was excitedly walking up to the front of the room to accept the award. His reaction left me feeling as though I had failed him yet again. Even worse, my entire class had been present for my moment of disappointment.

Crestfallen, I received the award and quickly left the room.

When I found him later, I accused him of being ashamed to have a jock for a son and said he probably couldn't stand to see me receive an *athletic* award. He only responded with, "No, Johnny. It's got nothing to do with you."

As we walked to the car, he said, "We are going to Roland's for graduation luncheon."

I replied, "Dad, he didn't graduate." My friend Roland Gerig hadn't bought the biology book and so he hadn't passed the class, rendering him ineligible for graduation.

But Dad was adamant. "They are still having a get-together at his parents' apartment, and no matter what, he is still your best friend," he said. "All of his gears in his brain are moving in the right direction."

My other best friend tagged along with me, and still in a sour mood from my dad walking out on me, I noted to my friend, "I bet you we are the only graduating seniors going to a senior's graduating party who didn't even graduate."

He did finally graduate, attending a private school to finish up, high up in the Alps in a town called Gstaad, where I visited him. It was a town composed of a lot of movie stars, and both David Niven and Liz Taylor had homes there.

But for now, I was still fuming about my dad's unexplained rejection.

Maybe he was embarrassed that we had a beat-up, cheap car. After all, as we sat in the parking lot earlier that day, before going inside for the ceremony, my classmate's father parked his brand-new Bentley right next to us, and I pointed it out. Instead of complimenting the car, he quickly pulled out of the Baptist seminary parking lot and parked across the street in a remote field where his was the only car. I could sense my dad's anxiety.

Looking back, I'm sure he positioned the car to drive directly out of the field onto the road without having to reverse, perhaps for a quick getaway, if necessary, in case there was a diplomatic emergency.

(One never knew.) Maybe he wanted to avoid the risk of being pinned in by a carload of Russians who wanted to kidnap him. But at the time, Russians would have been the farthest thing from my mind. I interpreted his strange parking as a not-so-subtle escape route from the graduation ceremony and the shame of having a jock son.

Dad's late-life confession had shed new light on a lot of his behaviors when I was growing up. I'd have to process each scene over time through new lenses. But even now, as an adult, I still felt hurt. And I knew I wasn't the only one.

Dad's relationship with Dawn and Bill, my two oldest siblings, seemed strained at times too. Dad was always kind of frustrated with Dawn, and she always seemed intimidated by him, spending most of her time at home with Mom. I don't know if it was her lack of math genius or just their different personalities, but they were never very close.

Bill had his own struggle with Dad. He was—and is—naturally gifted in math and science, but he isn't a savant, like Dad. When my brother was in fifth or sixth grade, he couldn't answer sophisticated algebra or physics questions yet, and my dad would start yelling at him. My mom would have to step in and say, "Wallace, stop!"

See, my dad had no idea why Bill couldn't work the problems, because he *was* able to do it at that early age. So, I guess he expected that his abilities were normal and that my brother should be able to just *get it* like Dad did. Maybe if you are naturally that smart, you just assume everybody can be like that too.

In later years, Bill got very emotional when I asked him about doing math when he was a young kid and why Dad had to quit doing homework with my brother. That is probably why my dad never helped me once. I only asked him one time, and he refused, saying, "No. Can you go ask Mom? She can help you." He was probably thinking, *I can't deal with my kids in mathematics.*

Snapping back to the present, I looked at my dad sitting in the front passenger seat and I thought to myself, *He refused to help me with my homework. But I won't let him refuse these girls.* I felt a sudden urge to somehow force him into making up for all the tutoring he *hadn't* done for me.

So I persisted, mostly out of frustration. "Come on," I said with a snip of sarcasm. "Let's see how good a math tutor you *would have been.*"

When I did get him out of the car, I told him he had to change out of his wifebeater. He quickly snapped back at me and said in an intense voice, "I have never beat your mom!"

I had to explain to him that a "wifebeater" is what a sleeveless white tank top is called in the ghetto.

Since I wouldn't let him out of helping the girls with their math, after a change of shirts, he finally opened the door and trudged into the store.

It was closed for business now, and while I wrapped up the transaction for the auger, the main clerk found three chairs for Dad and the two girls. Dad arranged them in a semicircle with him in the middle and the girls on either side. Showing no outward signs of exhaustion, he addressed them with a kind and inquisitive voice. "Now, what's the problem?"

The girls posed math questions more advanced than anything I'd ever mastered. Dad borrowed a nubby pencil and a memo pad from the hardware counter and dove right in, scratching figures and equations on the pad. The store manager brought a couple of Foster's beers from a cooler in the back and offered one to me, which I gladly accepted. For the next few minutes, we were forgotten spectators.

Dad solved everything quickly, pointed to what he'd written on the pad, and then explained it clearly. The girls watched his eyes, then looked at the pad and nodded. "Ah!" one of them exclaimed. "See?" she told her friend. "That's it. I see it now."

Dad smiled—to himself or them, it wasn't clear. Then the church-goer and abstainer glared at me and the cold beer I was enjoying, as if I were doing something terribly evil. I'd been drinking beer since high school, but that didn't mean he'd accepted it. I ignored his displeasure, still reveling in the slightest victory of a payback.

Several minutes later, he wrapped up the tutoring session and we said good-bye to the girls. "Let me know how the test goes," he told the girls, with genuine care, and gave them my home number, instructing them to call him the next day.

I was still feeling a bit of the cold shoulder a few blocks from home; I surmised it was because I had drunk the beer in front of him while he was tutoring the girls. It was worth it, though—a passive-aggressive jab for not helping me with my own homework.

"Well, Dad," I said, "I guess I couldn't have been on your team. Is that right?"

"Yeah, you're right, because you were drinking since high school," he said in that displeased dad voice I was quite familiar with.

My momentary mental tantrum finished, I was proud of him. But I had stopped myself earlier from bragging to the girls about his associations. It was still too new to me to talk about with confidence. I still had too many questions; there were still too many unfilled gaps. These I would ask, and try to fill in, as time went on.

* * *

We walked back into the house after the first hard day of work, just as the kids were taking their evening baths. Celeste had left some dinner for us out on the counter. Dad wasn't halfway through dinner when he noticed that one of our small wooden children's chairs was falling apart. He pushed his food aside, more interested in fixing that chair. The man could not sit still.

"Dad, why don't you just relax?" I said. But he just kept going, pausing just long enough to play with the kids for a few minutes when they came into say good night. He was never all that great at playing with young children; they made him uncomfortable somehow. He wasn't allowed to be a kid when he was younger, and he wasn't really around when we were growing up, so I guess he never experienced the freedom of childhood playfulness or knew what to do with it when he saw it. When my son, Chris, sat down in the chair he was in the middle of fixing, curious to see what his grandpa was doing, instead of interacting with him in a playful manner, Dad quickly admonished him to get up.

The kids were now in bed, with Celeste getting ready for bed upstairs. It was Tuesday, October 17, 1989, and Dad and I sat down around 7:45 p.m. to watch game three of the World Series—the Oakland A's up against the Giants in San Francisco. It all seemed surreal in a way. Here we were, watching baseball like we'd done in the past, and here we were, in the middle of a project, like we'd been in the past, yet everything was so different now. Everything had changed. My father was a different guy now. With all the thoughts swirling around my head, I spaced out for a few moments.

"What the heck?" Dad asked, very surprised.

My attention was directed back to the TV, where the screen was now blank. My dad suddenly became very concerned. If it had been a nuclear blast, I am sure someone would have reached out and gotten ahold of him quickly. But that wasn't my default thought, even with the day's conversation.

I said, "Dad, something's happened. The TV doesn't get blacked out during the World Series game unless something horrible has happened in San Francisco." Growing up in California, you get kind of used to earthquakes, so after a few seconds, I said, "I wonder if there has been an earthquake."

We sat in silence until the picture returned about thirty seconds later with an announcement that the World Series game had been canceled due to a serious earthquake that had just struck the Bay Area. Dad, relieved that there wasn't a nuclear detonation, now immediately began to worry about my brother, Bill, and his family, who lived in a neighborhood called Atherton, a very affluent area in Palo Alto. We called Bill several times, but to no avail. Later, we did reach my brother and found out that everything was fine.

Exhausted, I decided to call it a night, and dragged myself up the stairs and into bed. I knew two things: One, tomorrow morning I would be incredibly sore. And two, I was determined to keep Dad engaged in telling me more of his story.

With the postholes dug and concrete poured, when tomorrow dawned, we still had a fence to finish.

20

An Unlikely Cover

DAY TWO OF THE FENCE-BUILDING PROJECT saw us both up early again. My dad was out in the yard at, like, six thirty in the morning, working away, and Celeste had to come wake me up. "John, you need to get up. Your dad has already started." She shook me awake.

I woke with a start, but that quickly faded, as my entire body ached. Needless to say, I had kind of a rough sleep the night before. I slumped back down onto the pillow, trying to convince myself to get out of bed. *Here we are. Round two.*

Finally on my feet and somewhat coherent, I glanced out the window and saw that Dad was indeed already up and dressed. In fact, he had already walked the perimeter of the postholes, checked that the posts were still level—of course they were—and the concrete had set, and was calculating the effort and efficiencies of the job that day. The man simply had no off switch.

Downstairs, I saw the remnants of the breakfast he'd made for himself. That was Dad's whole life. Eat and work . . . eat and work . . . in a never-ending cycle, sometimes remembering to sleep. Meanwhile I tried to drown myself with coffee and Tylenol.

By the time I finally headed outside, he was beginning to nail the fence sections together. Dad gave me that "Johnny Boy, we have work to do" look, which was always accompanied by a slight smile. He already had all the fence sections lying on the ground in place, awaiting installation.

As we nailed the fir fence sections to the four-by-fours, the masterpiece beginning to take shape, he launched into another installment of his story. His words pulsed evenly through the air like a metronome, his actions in complete cadence with his speech.

* * *

After the move back to Iowa, Dad took to farming like white on rice, and could talk farming as if he'd done it his whole life. Grandpa Albin, having finally accepted that his son-in-law wasn't a traitor, and perhaps having assumed he was doing government work, was all too happy to have his family around him again. His beloved wife, my grandma Sadie, had died four years earlier, on November 27, 1945, at the young age of fifty-two, and he was very lonely, even if she was known to have a bit of a jealous streak in her blood.

The year before, Grandpa Albin's farm had been in the path of a horrible tornado, and he and his family had all gone into the cellar for safety. Hours later, when they came up, the only structure still standing was the house. Everything else looked like a war zone, including the crops, the barn, and what was left of the livestock. On a farm, the barn is more important than the house, since it's where the animals, the feed, and the farming equipment are all kept—and it was all gone.

Grandma Sadie, distraught over their loss, had a massive stroke within weeks that left her bedridden for nearly a year before she passed away. Grandpa Albin rebuilt everything that had been lost in the destruction, but Sadie was sad just the same. My mom was at school in Storm Lake, Iowa, then, so she came home every weekend to relieve the in-home caregiver, taking turns with her younger sister Marjorie, who had recently experienced a life-altering accident.

The story goes that Marjorie played trombone quite well and was in high school band practice one day when somebody ran into her, hitting her in the abdomen with his own trombone and rupturing her spleen. She never was quite the same after that. Always sick, she lived the remainder of her life on disability. But this unfortunate twist of fate didn't keep her from living as much life as she could.

In 1949, with Mom and Dad moving onto the farm, Marjorie moved to Mesa, Arizona, where she became a registered histologist in 1954. She worked for a number of years at Good Samaritan Medical Center, and St. Luke's Hospital in Phoenix. Although she was crippled the rest of her life, she was able to get around fairly well, only confined to a wheelchair in her later years. She eventually married a man who had polio, and they raised dachshunds. I remember my mom saying that Marjorie was the bright one in the family, and that her disability was very unfortunate, because she was always ill—and her husband was a bit of a "sourpuss," one of the few unflattering things ever to escape Mom's lips.

Traveling back and forth to school, taking care of her mother, and seeing her little sister in constant pain made that year very difficult and stressful for my mom. But she also felt very guilty for leaving her widowed father alone on the farm with Marjorie, who hadn't been able to do much farm work. Moving back to the farm ensured that Mom could keep an eye on her father.

Although Dad's cover was to be a farmer—and he was actually a very good farmer, as I noted earlier—he periodically went back to the East Coast, leaving the farm for several days at a time. He explained his absences to Mom by saying he was exploring job prospects. Instead, he was meeting with Enrico Fermi to discuss warhead delivery systems, programming computers with John von Neumann, and perhaps doing ballistic air balloon testing at Lakehurst Naval Station.

But whether on a farm in rural Iowa or at the heart of the American missile program, the sense of urgency undoubtedly increased on the evening of August 29, 1949. Only two months into their new lives as farmers, Mom and Dad were eating supper—little Bill was probably asleep—when the regularly scheduled radio program they were listening to was interrupted by a news bulletin. It told of the Soviet Union's first successful nuclear A-bomb test, which the propagandists dubbed "First Lightning." Dad said he and his colleagues in the nuclear arena had assumed the Soviets were five years from the bomb. They had gravely underestimated the Soviets.

Very much on edge for weeks after, Dad wondered how much longer he'd be stuck on this farm. Every time he went out to the windmill, he'd be anxious to find what was waiting for him.

One month later, on September 28, 1949, President Harry S. Truman announced the Soviet detonation to the world. Now the Cold War arms race would begin in earnest, and vital to it all was the expertise Dad had been honing for so long—finding and programming the trajectories the delivery missiles would use to find their targets if, God forbid, they were ever fired.

And though Dad didn't know it just yet, his brief farming career would soon end. The Cold War had other plans.

On April 14, 1950, the United States National Security Council released a fifty-eight-page top-secret policy paper outlining the United States' global strategy against Communism, and presented it to President Truman. According to scholar Ernest R. May, American historian of international relations, NSC-68 "provided the blueprint for the militarization of the Cold War from 1950 to the collapse of the Soviet Union at the beginning of the 1990s."[1]

In the midst of the Cold War backdrop and my father's frequent trips, my sister Dawn was born in Kiron, Iowa, in June 1950. My mom was thrilled to now have a girl.

Later that year, Cuthbert Hurd, an American computer scientist and entrepreneur with a PhD in mathematics, was instrumental in helping the International Business Machines Corporation (IBM) develop its first general-purpose computers. A year earlier, in 1949, Hurd had organized and headed the centralized computing facility at IBM and the department called Applied Sciences. The Applied Science organization, according to Paul Lasewicz, a former official IBM corporate archivist, was "focused on bringing advanced science to bear on current and future client scientific computing needs."[2] These men "were trained in sales and automatic computing, and then assigned to branch offices to assist with sales and installation of IBM equipment for solving scientific and engineering problems. They also provided feedback to IBM product development groups on new requirements."[3] And they needed people with genius mathematical abilities, like my father, to help them win the war.

When the higher-ups saw that no one had tried to "turn" my dad during his eighteen months as a farmer—that is, no outsider had tried to approach him on the farm—he was deemed safe to hire.

21

Hired by IBM

IN DECEMBER 1950, Dad was officially hired by IBM's Military Products Group in St. Paul, Minnesota, as part of the Applied Science Department under Cuthbert Hurd. Whether my dad was ever actually involved with the sales process, I'll never know. But at least on paper, part of his training was as a salesman. And that's what my mom—and the rest of the family—believed for his entire career.

Dad was to go to work in the St. Louis office, and he would travel to Poughkeepsie, New York, for training sessions. As a top engineer, he was tasked with making weapons, initially for radar, because now the missile race was on, and my dad's ability for quick, accurate calculations were desperately needed. The following year Dad became a CE (customer engineer) and was part of an elite group called the Applied Science Organization.

Mom wasn't happy to hear about the upcoming move. Her father had been widowed since 1945, and she hated to leave him alone again.

She liked life on the farm, and felt it was a good place to raise the children, the family numbering four since the birth of my sister Dawn over the summer.

After arriving in St. Louis, my parents became first-time home-owners with the purchase of a small brick house in a rural community just outside the city. And Dad became an IBM man. He went to Joe's Haberdashery, downtown, and stocked up on black, IBM-regulation suits, and he wore a version of these suits seven days a week for his entire IBM career, even while gardening or fixing his car.

In addition to the look, he also adopted the manner of an IBM man, especially one with a confidential objective. He was coached on how to deflect conversation away from himself and toward other people, and he became extremely adept at it, even avoiding innocent childhood questions about his job in general or what he'd done that day. If you asked him what he was doing, he would immediately turn the question around to, "What did you learn today?" You were not going to get him to say a word. He also never said, "I" when he was talking about work. He was professionally trained not to mention himself directly, instead always saying, "we" or "our group" or "our team." It was never, "I." He never wanted any attention given to him.

Every morning, Dad would go off to work at the McDonnell Aircraft Corporation's huge facility. The Military Products Group was working in conjunction with a McDonnell space missile development program. Just as he had done in Minneapolis, he calculated trajectories and accuracies. At one point he sent a black-and-white picture to my mom of him there, sitting at a desk, looking down into an open book. The caption on the back reads: "Here is a picture of me supposedly studying." He was also involved in the development of computers for the military, which were now engaged in the Korean War. It was understood that these computers would later be scaled to commercial application.

Concurrently, Dad underwent training on the new IBM 701 NDRC defense supercomputer at IBM headquarters in Poughkeepsie. He was working with von Neumann as part of his input source in the calculations. Having met years earlier, they had a great working relationship by now, and von Neumann likely put in a good word for my dad, who was recruited by the military products group a few years later. Cuthbert Hurd—the head of Applied Sciences Department at IBM—had hired von Neumann to develop the 701 and then the 704. IBM admits that my dad was later promoted to operations assistant, District 17 (usually a district means a geographic area, so perhaps Dad was the head of the Western region out of Minnesota), and became a western region special systems representative for the Applied Science Organization, part of the "Applied Science men" under Cuthbert Hurd.

The 701 was designed as a response to the outbreak of the Korean War in June 1950, after IBM chairman Thomas J. Watson Sr. asked the U.S. government what the company could do to help. He was told to build a large scientific computer that could be used for aircraft design, nuclear development, and munitions manufacture. It could perform more than sixteen thousand addition or subtraction operations a second.[1]

The design process started on February 1, 1951, and was completed a year later. Assembly operations would begin in Poughkeepsie, New York, as early as March 1951. On April 29, 1952, IBM president Thomas J. Watson Jr. announced that IBM was building "the most advanced, most flexible high-speed computer in the world."[2] The assembly of the first production machine began on June 1, 1952. Known as the Defense Calculator while in development, the new machine emerged from the IBM Poughkeepsie Laboratory later that year, and was formally unveiled to the public on April 7, 1953, as the IBM 701 Electronic Data Processing Machine.[3]

By this time, someone at IBM had determined that Cold War companies could make a pile of money if the Applied Sciences Department accepted projects for Cold War manufacturers, allowing the government to fund the R & D for computers and other projects. Once the technology was used for its intended purpose, all the scientists had to do—scientists including my dad—was tweak the technology and make it commercially available.

Consumed with innovative pursuits, Dad traveled east often, leaving Mom with a growing family that now included my sister Nedra, born in April 1953. Dad became something of a celebrity in the neighborhood, given that he was constantly boarding airplanes when none of the neighbors had ever been off the ground.

In late 1953, Dad was given orders to train full-time on the 701 at IBM headquarters in Poughkeepsie, where the top scientists and computer designers—"the best electronics thinking"[4]—were housed. I have a picture of my dad standing next to the 701 Defense Calculator, the top-secret thermonuclear computer that was being built. He wrote on the back: "You need a special badge to enter into this classroom."

With this move, my parents were forced to sell a home that had lost value since its purchase and move to Wappinger Falls, just outside of Poughkeepsie, settling into a small home that had once been part of a summer colony of lakeside cabins. What Mom didn't know at the time was that it was quasi-IBM housing used for long-term visitors to work on projects of a highly sensitive nature. The cabins were closely guarded, and the entire family was under tight security, unbeknownst to anyone but my father. Unfortunately, the Clauson unit was without a proper bathroom—just a sink and toilet, with no tub or shower—and Mom was forced to bathe my siblings in the kitchen sink, a routine that quickly got old, especially by the time Bill was seven.

Dad's training on the massive 701, referred to in its early days as the "Defense Calculator," was not simply operational in nature. The government was determined to limit access to top-secret 701 projects to only a handful of individuals, and the more those particular individuals knew about the machine, the better. In order to be adept at maintenance and repair, Dad was required to know how to take the machine apart and put it back together again, and that meant familiarity with *hundreds of thousands* of wires and their end points. He was also trained on C-code, the new software developed by John von Neumann that he'd heard about at one of the scientific-minded meetings at von Neumann's home. C-code software was very rare, very odd, and very difficult to calculate. Fission calculations were difficult enough; fusion calculations were a thousand times more complex and nearly that many times more expensive to produce. The 701 enabled the calculation of mathematical equations at extremely fast rates, and would also lead to eventual miniaturization.

In the midst of training on the 701, Dad was designing the Type 704 Electronic Data Processing Machine, a large-scale electronic digital computer—that was his baby. The difference in the 704 was its high-speed magnetic core storage or memory—a word or number stored in the magnetic core memory was available for calculation in *twelve millionths of a second.*[5]

With the 704 computer, the calculations that had previously been done on Dad's slide rule could now be done on a machine that he programmed. And that's part of what made my dad's talents so unique: not only did he make and program the machine, but he could do the calculations too. It, too, would be built in Poughkeepsie and trucked across the country to Lawrence Livermore Lab in California. A massive machine, it required the engineers to build a special room just for the air conditioning to cool the processors down. It was so large that it took three eighteen-wheelers to move it to its new location. I have a picture of Dad actually assembling the 704 at the lab.

At last, after four years with IBM, Dad got the assignment he'd been waiting for. In 1954, he was transferred to Oakland, keeping the same official job title of customer engineer. He would be one of IBM's men on long-term contract at the Lawrence National Radiation Laboratory in Berkeley, barely a forty-five-minute drive from Oakland, founded two years earlier to spur innovation and provide competition to the nuclear weapon design laboratory at Los Alamos, New Mexico. The labs were jointly competitive—and necessary.

* * *

At 8:15 a.m. on August 6, 1945, the United States dropped the bomb code-named "Little Boy" on Hiroshima, and it exploded with the energy of approximately fifteen kilotons of TNT, causing significant destruction to the city of Hiroshima. Little Boy killed sixty-six thousand people, mostly civilians, and injured at least sixty-nine thousand more, according to U.S. Army estimates made in 1946.[6] Designed by the Los Alamos Laboratory, it derived its explosive power from the nuclear fission of uranium-235. Three days later, the United States dropped another bomb, "Fat Man," on Nagasaki, which killed thirty-nine thousand and injured twenty-five thousand more, according to the same Army report.

While those were fission bombs, as explained earlier, *fusion* is a thousand times more complicated, a thousand times more powerful, if you can even imagine such a thing. When Russia first tested a nuclear bomb, Edward Teller, the theoretical physicist known as the father of the hydrogen bomb, and one of my dad's mentors, pleaded with the government that they needed to form another lab that focused on the thermonuclear experiments, because "if Russia has a bomb, and we have the same bomb, we want to make sure we've got a bigger stick than they've got—and first." So in 1952, the Livermore Radiation Lab was created and run by a group of young scientists who would design radically different weapons from those being designed at the Los Alamos lab.[7]

The labs did work together, like friendly competitors with the same end goal. According to the *New York Times*, the "rivalry between the labs played an essential role in the emergence of intercontinental ballistic missiles, which required lighter, more powerful weapons."[8] The scientists at the Lawrence National Radiation Laboratory were a different breed from those at Los Alamos. You really had to be a nerd to work in Livermore. The guys walked around wearing bow ties, assembling a computer the size of three eighteen-wheelers. Old photographs found at the lab reveal the "casual approach to designing weapons that prevailed at Livermore, in a significant contrast to the more formal, bureaucratic national security culture that was characteristic of Los Alamos."[9]

My dad would have traveled back and forth between the two labs, calculating equations for fission devices and programming defense computers. Fusion devices are thermonuclear weapons, and the hydrogen bomb (H-bomb) is an example of a thermonuclear device. A lot of people who can think in fission cannot think in fusion, because the calculations are so incredibly complex.

But my dad could.

I have often wondered what my dad's brain could have developed had he really been allowed to. He might have beaten Bill Gates in software development by twenty years. But once you are in the infrastructure of the top-secret world, you don't just walk away.

Then again, heck, maybe the world would have blown itself up if he had not been there.

22

Fear and a False Alarm

I WAS CONCEIVED ON THE EAST COAST but born on the West. Mom was four months pregnant when Dad came home one day from work to say the family was moving again—this time across the country, to Livermore, California. He would now be one of IBM's men on long-term contract at the Lawrence National Radiation Laboratory. Of course, we were made to believe it was just another sales territory switch for him.

The family had spent less than two years in Poughkeepsie, and while I'm sure Mom was happy at the thought of having a real bathtub in which to bathe her children, I can't help but wonder if she didn't roll her eyes at Dad's announcement. It was at this point that Mom, who would now be managing the family's third move in four years, began referring to IBM as "I've Been Moved."

Perhaps as an unspoken apology to Mom for all the uprooting and to make the best of the long drive—ten days and thirty-four hundred miles—Dad tried to make the cross-country trip into something of the honeymoon he and mom never had, driving through Idaho and Montana and visiting Yellowstone, three eighteen-wheelers following behind them a portion of the way, hauling the massive IBM 704 computer west to Livermore, California.

It wasn't much of a honeymoon for Mom, though, uncomfortable with the pregnancy and managing three young kids in the backseat. The only detail of note on the pseudo-honeymoon trip where the family was trying to be like regular tourists, to see the park, and perhaps some bears, was that Dad wanted to stop in Wallace, Idaho.

Though the town shared his name, it certainly didn't share his morals. Wallace, Idaho, was known as the brothel town of the miners. Even today they advertise their historic background as the "Home of the Brothel," complete with the Oasis Bordello Museum, which operated as a cathouse until 1988.[1]

The honeymoon over, Dad drove to the new home in Livermore, which was just a small town back then, nestled against the rolling hills thirty miles east and south of Oakland. The family moved into a small two-bedroom home, which became even smaller with my birth in October 1954, all four of us kids sharing a room, including me in a bassinet.

We'd stay in that home for the next four years.

Mom drove us around in our Chevrolet, continually frustrated by Livermore's fifteen-mile-per-hour speed limit. Every Sunday, the family piled into that same Chevy to drive the twenty-five miles to Tracy, in the Central Valley, where we belonged to a Baptist church. It wasn't long before Dad became a driving force in erecting a new building. He did much of the work himself. A picture of Dad on a tractor hung in the church lobby for years afterwards.

My earliest memories of Dad are on that tractor, clearing the ground for construction in the hot Central Valley summer sun. He used to talk again and again about how it made him want to return to farming. Of course, he didn't *really* want to return to farming. He was just making sure everyone knew it was a possibility in case some kind of security breach occurred. If he had to get out quickly, his cover was fully engaged.

While at that church, he and Mom became great friends with the Sassers. One of the few families we would ever spend time with. When the church service was over, we would stay at their house all afternoon and then go back for evening church.

Dad found a rare friendship with Martin Sasser. He worked on trains and had all sorts of machine parts in his garage. Martin and my dad would weld things together for hours—welding masks completing their look while wearing their Sunday best. Who knows what they were doing or why. But these were some of the only times I can actually ever remember my dad looking normal, or at least *acting* normal.

At the lab, Dad was part scientist, part programmer, and part technician—a jack of all trades around the 704 computer. One of my favorite black-and-white pictures of him shows him sitting on the ground with another engineer, assembling the massive computer. As a systems control engineer, and still very mobile with his slide rule, he was the primary interface for all calculations when it came to Project Whitney, the lab's weapons design program. He helped make sure that everything—including the combustion of fuels, telemetry, trajectory, computing, and more—worked well together and would also be compatible with the human body in terms of transport, installation, and launching. He was constantly in motion, moving among far-flung installations over the lab's huge testing ground. He often had to hustle from one part of the facility to another, frequently finding himself somewhere amid the thousands of acres of rolling hills that served as the lab's primary testing ground.

He must have also kept up with his tapioca pudding consumption. I have his ID badges for the lab. In looking at the pictures, I noticed something that made me chuckle. Between the first ID card, issued on March 25, 1954, and the second, issued March 13, 1956, Dad managed to gain five pounds—must have been all that tapioca pudding he loved so much.

Another of my early childhood memories comes from the night of October 4, 1957, when an emergency phone call came for Dad.

NORAD had detected a rocket or missile launch in the Soviet Union at 7:28 p.m. that appeared to be headed toward North America. They were using two 704s, the machine my dad had built and programmed, to track satellites. One was the Livermore 704 and one at MIT on the east coast, and they were used to track satellites—namely, Sputnik. NORAD Command immediately contacted the lab in Livermore; the lab immediately called Dad. He told them to send a car right away and to bring his slide rule from his office.

An active, sometimes mischievous three-year-old then, I would sleep all over the house, because we had four kids in one bedroom, and sometimes I just needed some space. I didn't care. As long as I had my blanket, I would sleep on anything.

On that night, I remember hiding behind the sofa near the front door when four men came to the door. I knew Dad was about to leave, and I didn't want him to go, so I sprang out from behind the sofa and grabbed for his legs in an effort to stop him. In seconds, I had wrapped my body around Dad's calf as if I were holding on to a pole, begging him to stay.

I didn't remember any other details, being so young at the time. But my brother, Bill, who was ten years old then, recalled a tense atmosphere in the home that night. He didn't care about what I was doing; he just wanted to see who these men were who were standing at our front door late at night and asking for our dad.

While I was wrapped around my dad's leg, looking up into his face as he was trying to step through the front door, Bill's eyes were locked onto the four large men at our front door. He recalls that they were clearly military members and were heavily armed.

My mom knew Dad needed to leave, so she was busy trying to unwrap me from Dad's leg, so her attention would have been elsewhere. Dad gently extricated himself, and upon seeing the look of terror on Bill's face, Dad mouthed the words, "I'll be okay," and hurried out the door and into a vehicle that was just pulling up.

My mother was likely too consumed with unraveling me from my father's leg to pay much attention to the men at the door. If she did notice the guns, she never spoke about it and certainly didn't act in any way surprised or frightened. But that was my brother's first hint that something was off. In fact, during the next fifteen years, he'd experienced enough strange occurrences, and noticed subtle details along the way, that he wasn't very shocked when I finally told him about Dad's confession years later. I guess that makes me oblivious, naïve, or a bit of both.

Being hurried away by armed men as Dad was that night doesn't at all sound like something that would happen to someone involved with just a sales job. But we knew he was working at the top-secret Rad Lab, and it was common knowledge that it was limited-access military. My mom was aware of all that, but she also thought Dad was involved with computer sales at the nuclear weapons plant.

IBM was very adept at doing heavy research with government officials. And after they'd paid for the R & D, engineers would tweak the product and make it commercially available for the general public. The 704 my dad designed eventually morphed into one of IBM's more successful computers, called the 360.

So even if Mom had seen the men's weapons, she would have likely thought something happened at the lab that needed his attention. And if that were the case, it wouldn't be uncommon to be chaperoned by armed military police, especially after work hours.

As the car rushed him to the lab, Dad told me later, he was handed the calculations and went to work with his slide rule. Military thought it was an attack and should be pushed. But Dad could look at the reports in a few seconds and tell what had really happened.

By the time he arrived at the office—a usually ten-minute drive cut in half, thanks to the military escort—he was certain that what the Soviets had launched was *not* an offensive missile attack. As he walked inside and faced a contingent of very nervous people, he cautioned, "Calm down, everybody. It's not what you're thinking. It's not an attack." That's the staggering amount of pressure my dad lived under, right up to the very end of his career.

With further calculations, Dad determined that the Russians had sent a satellite into space—what they later announced was the launch of Sputnik 1. With their deep space launch, the Cold War race for technological superiority went into hyper-speed.

23

NASA

BY THE SPRING OF 1958, the development of the Polaris missile was complete, and the 701 computer, which had evolved into the even-faster 704, was no longer in need of expert guardianship. Meanwhile, Operation Hardtack was a series of thirty-five nuclear tests conducted by the United States from April 28 to August 18, 1958, at the Pacific Proving Grounds.[1] At the time of testing, the Operation Hardtack I test series included more nuclear detonations than all prior nuclear explosions in the Pacific Ocean put together, and one of the purposes was to test new types of nuclear weapons and devices, some of which were created at the Los Alamos lab. According to the Nuclear Weapon Archive, a total of 35.6 megatons were shot during this series.[2]

In the middle of these nuclear tests, Eisenhower started NASA in July 1958. Dad left Livermore the exact month that NASA is formed, and went to Long Beach. It had been decided that Dad's genius should be put to use in developing missiles launched into space, where he would tackle bigger, much more complex equations.

In July, just after school was out, we packed up our sold house and moved south to Long Beach, the center of the Military-Industrial-Aerospace Complex, which included many government agencies along with the Jet Propulsion Lab (JPL) in Pasadena, TRW in Redondo Beach, and Raytheon in El Segundo. We traded in our very cramped Livermore two-bedroom for what seemed like a hugely spacious four-bedroom home.

Not too long after our arrival, as a result of President Eisenhower's desire to further obscure the nature of IBM government associations, the Military Products Group was renamed the Federal Systems Group. New facilities for the division were built to resemble schools and churches, but with darkened windows, and group members were asked to refrain from wearing military uniforms, requiring a lot of them to wear civilian clothes now. Eisenhower had been a general and a head of the ground forces of the Allied invasion, so he was very pro-military. But he had always been leery about the "military industrial complex," and the Army and Navy now suffered under Eisenhower's "new look."

The year before, on November 7, 1957, the "Gaither Report," to ensure increased funding, had exaggerated the strength and size of Russian capabilities as greater than ours. There may have been some legitimate concern that the Russians were already far ahead of America's missile technology. That meant the United States had to increase efforts to compete and dominate the space race and missile technology.

Dad worked at the naval base in Long Beach, where the missile systems were tested, and commuted the freeways to a second launching area in El Segundo. He also spent a great deal of his time working for various government contractors that had been established along what was something of a top-secret, tech-brainpower corridor that had sprung up in the vicinity of the NASA Space Flight Center on Wilshire Boulevard just west of downtown LA. Dad was given an office at Space Systems West, a block down Wilshire from NASA, where he assisted in formulating mathematical equations used to plan high-value hits on targets in the Soviet Union.

I remember asking my mom, "Where's dad working?"

She said, "He is up on Wilshire Boulevard."

Why does Dad have to go all the way to Wilshire Boulevard? I thought. That had to be twenty or twenty-five miles from home in North Long Beach.

He was part of the NASA infrastructure and the race to space. He wasn't leaving the missile world; he was just going to another place where missiles are—space. Now they were talking about strapping a human into one of these nuclear missiles, which is basically all a rocket is—a missile without the bomb component.

While there, he would work in space operations, including the infrastructure for all missile development and NASA, Space Systems West, of which I have the IBM card. We now have pretty solid evidence (in fact, I have documented evidence) that the Federal Systems Group controlled the guidance centers for the moon walks; one could even postulate that without IBM's federal systems group, there would have been no space program, and there wouldn't have been a moon landing without IBM's machines. This is all very interesting because Dad was in Long Beach at the beginning of the space race. Remember when Kennedy said we would be the first to go to the moon by the end of the decade? Dad's expertise would now be needed on building a missile that could reach the moon.

While in Southern California, Dad worked on the development of intercontinental integrated missiles, such as the Atlas, Titan, and Thor rocket families. He was also involved with the Jupiter missile, eventually installed in Italy and Turkey. He traveled overseas quite extensively, limos sent to our house to ferry him to LAX because Mom didn't like driving the freeways.

Especially after the Bay of Pigs incident, of which he had an insider's view, Dad said the Air Force was out of control. "They put on their bomber jackets and they think they can do anything," Dad said. He was growing very concerned that things might get ugly, especially because the Air Force didn't always seem to know what they were dealing with when it came to nuclear weaponry.

This was evidenced at the Alameda Air Base near Oakland, California, when ten five-hundred-pound preignition bombs for a nuclear explosion were accidentally activated when a military plane crashed into a trailer park out in the hills. The explosion, loud enough to be heard thirty miles away, killed seven people on the ground and twelve people in the plane, including General Robert Travis. The media reported the crash, but not the bomb explosion, and the base was renamed Travis Air Force Base.

In addition to working on missiles, Dad also was involved in converting missile control systems to systems used for human space travel, more demanding in terms of accuracy and reliability, as the vehicles had to travel around the globe and then return.

Now when my Dad traveled anywhere work-related, there was always an extra guy in the backseat of the car with my dad. It was not the same one every time. They would rotate, but they were all very distinctive. I remember they were always bigger guys, very physically built, like a bodyguard.

When Dad was leaving for a trip, I always questioned why Dad's luggage was the only thing in the trunk, and the other guy, who was already in the car, never had luggage. I later found out that all of these men were security; they were never going on the trip. Dad always just said, "We are going to stop at his place next and pick his up."

When Dad came home, the other man would always get out of the limo first to make sure it looked safe, and then my dad would get out. I remember wondering, *What are they looking for?*

24

Dangerous Technology and Safe Sundays

DURING MY RESEARCH INTO DAD'S LIFE, I stumbled onto "Project Pluto," which was initially conducted at Livermore Lab. In 1957, the government created Project Pluto to develop nuclear-powered ramjet engines, made out of a fission nuclear reactor, for use in cruise missiles. This turbo-charged engine would hit speeds of 3,500 miles an hour, and could circle the world three and a half times before it ran out of nuclear fuel. The original test designs were done in Livermore, California, where my dad worked, and later moved to Nevada. But the technology had been in use since the early 1950s in lab settings.

Ramjet engines today can operate up to speeds of Mach 6 (4,600 miles per hour), and are useful in the delivery and design of missiles. (Mach is the speed of sound, so Mach 6 would be six times the speed of sound.) Two experimental ramjet engines were tested at the United States Department of Energy Nevada Test Site (NTS) in 1961 and 1964.[1] In fact, the United States utilized this ramjet technology in the

Cold War in the form of the SR-71 Blackbird, which was capable of Mach 3.5 speeds (2,685 mph):

> The SR-71, or Blackbird as you probably know it, was the pinnacle of the US military's Cold War reconnaissance efforts. Introduced in 1966, the Blackbird, with its hybrid turbojet/ramjet engines, was the fastest manned aircraft in the sky until it was retired in 1998. Despite being utterly massive—107 feet (32 meters) long with a 55-foot (17-meter) wingspan—the SR-71 only had two crew and no weapons (it was loaded up with cameras, radio antennae, and other surveillance-oriented loadout). Due to high running costs, and reallocation of funds towards other efforts such as UAVs, the SR-71 was retired after 32 years of active service. Of 32 aircraft that were built, 12 were lost in accidents—but none were ever shot down or captured by the enemy.[2]

I can just imagine somebody in the lab back in the early 1950s saying, "Wouldn't it be cool if we could develop a rocket and then have it fly at between five hundred and a thousand feet elevation, and go four times around the earth before it runs out of fuel?" Think about that—*four times around the world*. As if that weren't incredible enough, the Air Force wanted the rocket's shell to emanate radiation to contaminate the enemy. In other words, it would be like having a flying crop-dusting Chernobyl, radiating the ground below. They also wanted a way to shut off the radiation when they went over an ally country. It would even launch up to sixteen nuclear bombs. So, this thing flying 3,500 miles an hour below radar at five hundred to a thousand feet would be dropping off nuclear weapons as it circled the globe. It almost sounds as if it were out of *Star Wars*. But that was a big project at the Lawrence Livermore Lab.

The program was killed in the early 1960s when Russian radar had advanced and there weren't any soft spots—areas where we could fly undetected—anymore, so the government didn't think it could be further developed. The person who probably canned the program was Harold Brown when he became deputy secretary of the Air Force in 1965, after a year as director of the Livermore Lab. Remember my dad saying the Air Force was completely out of control? Well, this "Project Pluto" shows just how out of control it was. So, when Harold Brown gets the next promotion, so to speak, he says, "This is not going to be done."

Although Dad shared a mutual disdain with Brown for the Air Force, due to their ego trips during that time, this technology would have been right up Dad's alley because they had to shrink a lot of components for this to work, and that was Dad's forte, making things smaller. He was also gifted in figuring out when metals or compounds (ceramics) could withstand great amounts of heat, and resistance, and was often asked for input on heat resistance. This also made him a natural fit to work on space shuttle tile technology, which he did years later. Plus, he was an expert on supercharging, a component of Project Pluto.

Back at home, Dad installed a supercharger on his used white Austin-Healey Sprite, but almost immediately took it off, noting that it was far too dangerous for a family car. My brother, Bill, says Dad later put it back on again and drove it, and so did Bill, but it didn't last that long the second time either because it was "far too powerful, and dangerous." If you got hit in that thing, you were not going to fare well. The door was the thickness of sheet metal. It didn't have mass to it. I just wish they'd have let me be in the car for the test drive too! As a kid in the early 1960s, I do remember Dad talking about the power of "ramming air into an engine" for added power, which is exactly what a ramjet engine does.

After thirty-two years of active service, rather than feeling a sense of accomplishment at the technology he was helping to create, Dad felt anguish at the possibility of nuclear decimation. He revisited the debate over nuclear weapons he had joined at von Neumann's house, wondering now if the work he was doing would benefit humankind or destroy it.

Unable to sleep at night, Mom noted on many occasions that Dad would pace around the house at night. But with the details we know about Project Pluto, I can understand why. If plans were in the works to create a nuclear jet engine that could reach over three thousand miles an hour, launch nuclear bombs, and radiate the areas below it, I'm sure he was fearful for humankind. I can easily see where my dad would be thinking, *The world is going to blow itself up!*

Once a supersonic engine is put on a delivery vehicle, like a missile, the guidance system would have been so advanced that only Dad's calculations could have figured out how to maneuver accurately while flying that fast. It would have been a terrible stress for anybody to carry, even if he didn't have a faith, but for somebody like Dad whose faith was very important to him, I imagine there were many questions he asked of himself, and many talks with God. I wonder if he battled with that in his mind—*Am I doing the right thing? Or am I going against God's Word?* Knowing how all the technology worked, he knew it would either benefit humankind or destroy it.

You have to understand that Livermore Lab was so advanced and so aggressive in their research and production. A lot of positives came out of nuclear technology, such as nuclear medicine and nuclear-powered renewable energy. So, there were definite benefits, but this knowledge was so incredibly powerful that he said he was always debating with other scientists, especially those in the opposite camp, who weren't necessarily as concerned with ethics or worst-case scenarios. It was the nerds versus the military. And Harold Brown's appointment to the Air Force couldn't have come at a better time.

Plus, remember that there were thousands and thousands of these nuclear missiles around the world. Fortunately for my dad, he knew—or would be able to figure it out quickly—if any were being launched. But at the same time, you never knew if one could get released somehow, either by accident or due to sabotage. That's why Dad and his team were so particular on everyone being on their "A game," 24/7/365.

You didn't get a second chance if a missile was launched. Dad literally thought of the world blowing itself up six days of the week.

Because of that fear, having anxiously made it to the end of each week, he found solace in church, the Bible, and in prayer. He did not want Sundays to end because he was convinced that the world wouldn't blow itself up on the special day the Lord had made.

* * *

Dad taught Sunday school for young married couples at a Baptist church in Long Beach, where we lived from '58 to '62. Among some of his favorite topics to teach were the roles and strengths of husbands and wives within a marriage and within the church.

He'd missed the last two Sundays for work—he was off someplace in the Midwest, probably in a remote area of Nebraska or Colorado, working on placing the guidance systems in new silos—and the church had to get a substitute teacher. Over the two weeks of his absence, Mom said that several women had approached her while shopping at the grocery store, mentioning that they really missed Dad's teaching. His style was practical, biblical, and he presented his material in an easily digestible manner, appreciated by young couples seeking both education and encouragement.

On his next call home, Mom asked if he could be home to teach on Sunday. Dad put his group into hyperdrive to finish the job at hand. He then requested a military plane be diverted to pick him up (this act went way up the chain to be authorized), which just happened to be carrying up to four-stars of generals and their staffs.

I remember Dad saying, "There were four stars worth of generals on that plane who had to move back." What an ego deflation! Dad sat in the front of the plane. Then there was an empty row then his one security guard. Dad worked on real-time issues before pulling out his Bible and Sunday school lesson to prepare for the next day.

When landing, Dad got off with his security, never having said a word to any of the other passengers. The "nuke guys" were completely secret, and I wouldn't be surprised if a general *in the know* got wind that a "nuke guy" had been on board and told the rest of the traveling crew, "Don't even mention what happened with that last stop, because it really didn't happen."

Dad made it home in time to teach class, much to the pleasure of his eager students. But then when Monday came around, the guy vanished, off to the nuclear world he went.

25

Making Time to Be a Dad

IN 1962, WE MOVED FROM Long Beach up to San Jose, California, because Dad would begin work at the IBM lab there. My dad was still doing projects at the Livermore Lab while living in Long Beach, and toward the end of his time there, he traveled often to San Jose because he began building our house. San Jose is only an hour and twenty minutes away from the Livermore lab. And with the San Jose lab, the Rad Lab, and Stanford, there was a whole variety of Cold War companies there, and we were living in the epicenter now. Dad didn't have to travel quite as much, having his staff do that for him. So, in a way, it was as if Dad never left the Rad Lab in the first place.

Despite the incredible demands of his job and the burdens of secrecy, Dad designed the blueprints for a new four-bedroom home in a brand-new neighborhood adjacent to the brand-new seven-acre Wilcox Park. My dad did a lot of the work himself, especially the electrical, not wanting to trust that to anyone else. In his spare time, he would go to the house and wire it. There was a lot of preplanning that went into this house. Between designing, buying the land, building, and getting the whole thing done, it was a minimum of ten months or a year. My dad sketched out the whole thing, and then the builders were all prioritized. We were one of the first homes in this development next to the older part of town in San Jose.

Wilcox Park was the center of all of our activities as children and where we would play. In football season, we would play football there. In springtime and summer, we'd play baseball. And in basketball season, a lot of the neighborhood kids would come to my house. We would just kind of rotate each sport with the season. It was great fun.

To my delight, Dad's building skills included such important amenities as the solidly braced basketball hoop where I'd play basketball with my friends and all the local kids for hours after school at my house. As long as they were kids, they were welcome.

It was Shangri-la for an active child such as myself. No matter what school I was attending—from elementary through tenth grade—the last hour of class was always spent determining who was up for the afternoon sports activities. We'd go to my house, where I'd grab either the football or baseball and bats, and head for the park. Most nights we ended up playing basketball anyway.

During basketball season, we'd stay in our driveway and shoot at the hoop attached to the garage. The bracing for the backboard was classic Wallace Clauson—artistic, architectural, it was designed with nearly forty pieces of wood, structurally engineered with an elaborate maze of braces and corbels so that ten basketballs thrown at it simultaneously wouldn't phase its integrity.

If you make a shelf and then put a corbel on each end, the strength of that corbel allows you to place very heavy objects on it, and it disperses weight evenly. My dad had this elaborate bracing set up behind the basketball backboard, and it was attached through a two-by-four with big lag bolts. Nothing made my father more upset than if he saw something that wasn't sturdy. It was like an industrial-strength backboard on steroids, and was mounted to the center of the garage roof, on the edge, with big lag bolts through the trusses of the roof. He said, "Johnny, this will be able to withstand anything." No kidding. There had to be from twelve to fifteen different bracing mechanisms behind that thing.

The kids would often look at it and say, "Man, that thing is not moving." And they were right!

As we played into the early evening hours, Dad would be in the garage, tinkering away for hours in his workshop full of circuit boards and oscilloscopes and what was now an enormous collection of vacuum tubes stowed away in custom cabinets that Dad built specifically to hold his growing collection stored in 31-flavored ice-cream drums, organized by size. Anytime Dad was working on a project and needed one—even if it was at a neighbor's house, he'd say, "Johnny, go to the second row down, third one in, and bring me two of those tubes." He knew exactly which ones were where. I always had to run back to the house to get the tubes.

The only adult who routinely came to the garage was our neighbor directly across the street. His name was Rob Moore, and he was an engineer at San Jose State University. They would never go in the house, but he would casually come into the garage to watch what my dad—the ultimate tinkerer—was doing, because he was also a tinkerer.

I thought Dad seemed oblivious to the whole group of young teenagers running around, his thoughts in an entirely different dimension. But as I look back, knowing what I know now, although he was uncomfortable with adults coming over to the house, he never seemed to mind us kids hanging around with our friends, which is a bit ironic, seeing as how he never knew quite how to interact with them. Maybe he figured that as long as we were there, we weren't anywhere else, and he could at least keep an eye on us. Or maybe, just maybe, it made him feel a bit like a kid again—at least how childhood should have been.

My dad liked to hang out in the garage and watch when we played 5 on 5. He would stand there, observing, enjoying our camaraderie, and when we stopped playing, around dusk, he'd say, "Kiddos, let me show you something." He had a gigantic telescope, about ten feet long and ten inches around. I only later learned that it was homemade. He always found something in the stars.

One time he positioned the telescope on a faraway cluster of stars and told our group, "You won't see this again for eighty-six years." After viewing the object, one of the kids walked over and asked me how my dad knew that, and I said, "Go ask him."

Dad smiled at the young man and said, "It's a very simple math equation about the way the earth rotates around the sun, so it will come around again in eighty-six years." I was within earshot for the explanation and shot an eyebrow up. *How* does *Dad know that?*

Another kid in the group asked our inquisitive friend if he had found out the answer from my dad, and he said, "Well, I guess it's a math equation," and with that we started another game of 5 on 5 under the floodlights positioned at the back of the house.

On weekends, Dad would send me out into the neighborhood to determine if anyone had a broken TV. He'd spend Saturday morning tinkering with whatever needed fixing, asking nothing more for payment than a cup of coffee. Believe it or not, he also relaxed by the pool sometimes, and hit me fly balls in the park next door.

In my opinion, Dad wasn't much of an athlete. When he threw the ball, he was not very fluid—he was kind of quirky and jerky. But he was excellent at hitting fly balls. He loved it. He'd go for hours after work, hitting pop flies to all the kids in the neighborhood, and my mom would yell at him from the house, "Wallace, quit hitting those balls!" I'd get mad or tired after an hour, and I'd get lumps on my head when I missed a catch. By dinnertime, my head looked like the topography of the moon. But my dad never wanted to stop.

He even went so far as to be an assistant coach on one of my Little League teams; that practically took an act of God to make that happen, I found out later. When I was nine, Coach Walt Williams drafted me to be the catcher. Even at that young age, I was already a very accomplished catcher.

After the first few practices, when we were packing up our gear, Coach mentioned that he needed somebody to be his assistant for the team. No one was stepping forward, so one day after practice, I got all over my dad in the garage. I said, "Dad, you've got to be the assistant Little League coach!"

For him to get clearance to be the assistant coach, the decision had to go to the highest levels of the government. For some reason, permission was granted. Normally he was not to be out in public in an open field by himself. Even at practices, he said, security would surround the perimeter of the ball field at this gigantic park; they'd be stationed in cars and appear to be normal observers because they just didn't know who else could be there watching. On game days a member of security would be in each bleacher—the visiting bleacher and the home bleacher. And one person would be watching our little bug-eyed Sprite, that little white convertible sports car, to make sure no one came near it in the parking lot.

Now Dad was in completely unfamiliar territory. He had grown up on a farm. He was never able to do any of these children's activities. And he was baffled by normal boyhood behaviors. As you can imagine, my dad did not look comfortable in the dugout with thirteen kids, even though we were just doing what normal nine-, ten-, eleven-, and twelve-year-old kids do at practice or games—which is spitting sunflower seeds on the ground and throwing our gloves into the air. Dad once asked me in the dugout why I always seemed to be flicking the ears of other players next to me. I responded, "Dad, I am a baseball catcher; that's what we do."

There in the dugout, Dad just kind of sat and observed us. Usually an assistant coach, when his team was at bat, would go to first base to be in the box like a line coach. The head coach would be the third-base coach. But my dad was always in the dugout, just observing us, which I always thought was kind of odd. He would look at us as if we were some sort of psychological experiment or something. And who knows—maybe we were!

"Johnny, you're up next." All he would do during games is call out who needed to get ready to bat. At practices, though, my dad loved to hit fly balls to the team.

We were called the Santa Clara Sand and Gravel Team, named after our sponsor. We had yellow hats with black trim. At the end of the season, we took a team picture, and I remember thinking that was an anomaly because even at that age, I knew my dad did not like having photos taken of him, especially out in the open. I love that picture because I was directly below my dad. I was squatting on one knee, and my dad is above me.

I don't remember our final score—we were a good team—but I do remember that my dad never missed a single game or a practice. You have to understand: in Little League your season is only two months long, basically eight to ten weeks. My dad was at every practice and every game for that one year. And after that one season, that was it. *They* were not going to let that continue. He was quite upset because the powers that be were giving him such a hard time about wanting to be active with my sport. But if you think about it, whoever called the shots was probably thinking, *I've got to deploy all these assets now, and our "missileman" is spending his afternoons hitting little kids' fly balls? Nope. Gonna nip that in the bud.*

As an adult, I wonder how many times he would have had to stand up for me to get his higher-ups to say yes. I imagine it would have been weeks, if not months, of pleading. But I think he realized that he had been gone from our family so much of his life—and all of ours—since I'm the youngest kid, this was his last chance to be a dad.

My older brother, Bill, was a very, very competitive swimmer and held some state records. He was in phenomenal shape as a backstroker. He never played Little League, but he probably would have made the Olympic swim team had he not broken his leg in a ski accident with the church group. But because Dad was always working or traveling, he was never able to attend many of Bill's swim meets to cheer him on.

Of course, I didn't know any of the backstory then; I was just adamant about having my dad be an assistant coach. I was proud of him then. I was proud my dad came to my practices and games and hit me fly balls for hours on end. I'm even more proud of him now. But still, you'd have thought he'd have done some research on baseball before signing on as assistant coach.

If you looked at my batting average, which is the number of hits divided into the number of bats, all four years I hit exactly .500. When I was nine, I had nine hits with eighteen at bats. My last year, when I was twelve, I had thirty-one hits for sixty-two at bats. The other two years also were exactly at .500.

As much as he tried to blend in, Dad didn't understand baseball. I had fouled off a couple of hits during the season, and he said, "Johnny, I bet your batting average went down because you walked a whole bunch. You should have been penalized because you fouled off a couple of balls and left a couple of guys in scoring position when you walked."

I said, "Dad, you don't count walks against your at bats." That is a noncalculable number.

My dad didn't get upset, but he said, "That is ridiculous. Who made up this rule?"

The baseball gods, Dad.

That was how he thought the math should work, you see. But when is the last time you heard someone complain about a baseball rule?

26

Jack-of-All-Trades

DAD'S NEW JOB was at the secured IBM facility in San Jose as part of the company's ACS (Advanced Control Systems) project. His specialty now in superfast calculations, he assisted in developing the IBM 7030 Stretch supercomputers under project lead Stephen W. Dunwell.[1]

The first Stretch computer, named such because it was meant to "literally stretch IBM's capabilities in every facet of computer technology,"[2] was tested at the Livermore Rad Lab, where Dad still traveled frequently, and was used, among other things, to program the nuclear missile force, which was under installation around the world at a very steady clip. IBM would also play a part in getting NASA to the moon (and on it), another project Dad would soon be involved in.[3]

These missiles were larger, stronger, and faster than previous versions, and traveled up to five thousand miles, necessitating a complex set of controls, from tracking, to delivery, guidance, target designation, and engagement. Not only was there growth in numbers, but their yields were also increasing.

The 7030 was much slower than expected, and *PC World* magazine named Stretch as one of the biggest project management failures in IT history.[4] In spite of Stretch's failure to meet its own performance goals, it led to many of the design features of the successful IBM System/360 mainstay computer workhorse, which shipped in 1964.

Back at home, toward the end of the '60s, Dad was slowly learning to relax—a great feat, considering the world was awash in missiles, with the highest count in number in 1972. Engineering work exploded exponentially, but Dad now operated with a staff of engineers under him.

The irony of the missile build-up was that it led the country to believe a nuclear war was winnable. Messages to that effect were conveyed to the public via various mediums. Even the paint and lacquer industry produced a short, twelve-minute film around that time that depicted the expected damage of a nuclear blast on a home that was clean and tidy, versus one that was messy.[5] Less mess, less damage, the film explained.

Herman Kahn's *On Thermonuclear War* argued that a nuclear exchange could be survivable, although there would be great "human tragedy."[6] The Committee on the Present Danger, a strong political lobbying organization, was formed to emphasize that a nuclear attack was winnable, and even President John Kennedy declared in 1961 that "developments may confront us with a situation where we may desire to take the initiative" of a first strike.[7]

* * *

Dad continued to find solace in his garage and in the routine established at home. Among other devices, he created a color-changing, "home built" laser beam during those years, a remarkable feat considering no laser worked before 1961. I walked into the garage one day as he was testing out his latest adaptation; he had toned down the intensity so that the laser now worked as a laser pointer. As he put his hand in front of the light, he said, "Johnny, this technology is going to change everything." It did. It changed all sorts of medical technologies and weapons technologies. A low-intensity laser could be helpful during meetings and presentations. A strong laser beam could vaporize you.

At the end of dinner, my dad would go back to the garage, to tinker. My mom would be cleaning up. All the kids would go to their respective bedrooms, and my brother would go to the living room, and everybody had to practice their instruments for a minimum of a half hour. Music was a big part of my childhood.

My sister Nedra played the violin. My other sister, Dawn, would have the accordion going. Back in Long Beach, she'd seen a neighbor girl playing one, and thought she might like it because she could carry it with her wherever she went. When we still lived in Long Beach, Dawn was in an accordion band with about forty others, and they even had uniforms.

My brother, Bill, played the piano, like our mom, who was a very good pianist. I played the trumpet, and one of my greatest regrets is that I quit playing and focused on sports. I was number one in the orchestra and band. Even after I quit the school band, I played my trumpet quite often at church.

Because we didn't have air conditioning, we always had the windows open, so can you imagine the sound coming out of that house? You could literally hear it blocks away.

Dad also continued to showcase his woodworking skills in his spare time. He built my brother a train set that was like a city on a piece of plywood. It even had a mountain on it with a hole in the middle so the train could go through it.

When my dad built it, he and Bill didn't know where they should store it at first, so my dad figured out a pulley system so that once you finished playing with it, you could pull on a ratcheting handle and a pulley system would raise and hold it up in the ceiling, up in the sky. When you wanted it to come down, you pulled the pin out, rolled the pulley system down, landed it on the sawhorses, and played on the train set. To think about what we were living with there!

Then again, that level of effort wasn't all that surprising. Dad always gave his all with every project he worked on—for work or at home. Even during the holiday season.

Dad never smoked, but during air travel back in the '60s, the stewardesses would hand out little four- or five-pack boxes of cigarettes for each smoker's tray. Dad kept them all, and when he came home from each trip, he'd add his new cigarettes to a big satchel in his closet that probably smelled like a tobacco barn.

Each year, when we took the Christmas tree down around New Year's, my dad would cut up the tree and take all those cigarettes and light a fire. There had to be *hundreds and hundreds of cigarettes* in that fireplace box, like kindling, with as much as Dad flew, and then he would start putting parts of the very dry, dead Christmas tree on top of all those cigarettes.

You don't put a sappy Christmas tree in with five hundred cigarettes! The fire would be so big we would get a chimney fire. I would go look outside at the chimney, and it would look like a rocket engine, which is fitting, honestly. But that was his ritual, the annual cigarette tree-burning blowup. He is lucky the house didn't catch on fire, because we had a cedar shake roof.

And that wasn't all. When I was in fifth or sixth grade, my dad put in a swimming pool, with a certain concrete guy, Bob Heater. Remember: my dad was almost psychotic about concrete work, and this concrete was done so well, it almost felt like a smooth rock under foot, not abrasive at all. Although it felt like flat concrete, it was little, tiny stones. Dad designed an elaborate pool and a patio that integrated with the pool. On the far side of the pool, he had these big rocks embedded into the building of the pool on the other side.

Because we were always hitting baseballs in the backyard, they would routinely fly and land in the pool, so my dad created a mechanism where he would pull the balls out of the pool and he would put them on a drying rack. So, when we hit a ball into the pool from the park, I would go get it and put it on the drying rack. Then I would go to the stash where he was drying the ones that had gone in before, I'd get a dry one, and then take it back out to the baseball field. It was a fairly ingenious invention.

The next thing he tackled was the pool—namely, the pool's heating bill. I came home one day to see Dad up on the roof, installing solar panels that had just been delivered by a crane. *What's he doing now?* I thought. Those panels back then were big and heavy, and covered the whole backside of the roof. They had to be thirty feet wide by fifteen feet tall, the size of two rooms.

He'd gotten a bill for heating the pool and didn't like it, so he vowed he'd eliminate it. So, he converted the pool's heating source to the solar panels, which was very, very odd for back in the early '70s. I do think he was partially environmentally aware, but more than that, he loved a challenge and he didn't like to feel as though he was being taken advantage of. And it worked! He completely eliminated the pool's heating bill.

If he ever had free time, and he wasn't consumed by a home renovation project or doing something in his garage, he would come find me and say, "Let's go sift some dirt." I'm not kidding you—my dad made a dirt sifter that was about four by four feet, with mesh on it. He kept piles of dirt in the backyard near his shed where the lawn mower and edger were.

We'd place the dirt onto the sifter, and the rocks would fall to the bottom of the mesh, but the dirt would go through the holes. We always had three or four scoops of soft, clear dirt, along with rock, if we ever needed rocks for drainage.

Dad was an incredible gardener. We probably had twenty different varieties of roses in our backyard. But if my dad didn't know what to do, he went and sifted dirt. I guess it relaxed him and reminded him of farming.

27

The Perfect Saturday

EVERY SATURDAY MORNING, after my mom would make Swedish pan-cakes, I would get a haircut if I needed one—and I usually did. We got the abundant hair-growth gene in my family for sure. Dad would do the flat top on me. Then we would go mow the lawn. My dad was absolutely the most finicky guy about how he wanted the lawn to look. You had to cross-cut it, the way they do on a golf course. My dad had a powered gas edger, and you would have thought he was doing woodwork, he was so detailed and precise.

After the lawn was in pristine condition, we would go to Sears. He never went there to shop for a pair of shoes, slacks, or a sweater. But he loved seeing what new tools were coming out. Sometimes he would periodically want to see what kind of motors were going in refrigerators and freezers. Then we would leave. Those were the only two things we'd check out—tools and motors. He would buy a tool every once in a while.

My dad had three levels of tools. He had everyday grade; he had what you call "finish" grade; and then he had unbelievably sharp tools. As I mentioned before, he usually had three different grades of the *same* tool. That's how finicky he was.

After our Sears excursions, if we had enough time, we'd go look at cars. Now, I was never a big car guy, but my dad was, at least from an engineering standpoint, and I loved spending time with him. One morning we were at a Chrysler dealer showroom, and my dad told me go into the garage and get the lift. So, I dragged the lift in from the garage, and my dad started jacking a car up—in the showroom. With other people walking around. The salesmen were so shocked, they didn't say a thing.

Once it was lifted, we crawled underneath the car. Dad wanted to show me the torsion bars that were on a Chrysler product that dispersed energy. Then all of the sudden, I could see about twelve pair of shoes surrounding the car. I was afraid one of them was going to try to get into the car while we were underneath.

I said, "Dad, we should probably get out of here because somebody might get in the car and I don't want to be below it."

My dad, not reluctantly, but very pensively and quietly, got out, lowered the jack, and said, "Johnny, go return this to where you got it." No salesman ever approached him because I guess they didn't know what they were dealing with. Or maybe they were used to my dad doing that, I guess. Crazy engineer. That typifies my dad. He never wanted to see what the interior looked like or anything like that.

Another weekend, we went to the British Motor Cars retailer, to look at the new classic four-door Jaguar XJ model that had just been announced. Dad didn't care about what it looked like on the inside; instead he opened the hood, and he had a puzzled look on his face.

The salesman came up to my dad and asked, "What do you think about the engineering in the XJ?" I was sitting inside, admiring the fancy leather interior.

My dad asked, "What does XJ stand for?"

The guy said, "Experimental Jag."

In a slightly sarcastic tone, Dad said, "You know what? There is a lot of experimental engineering going on underneath this hood. I'll tell you that," my dad's dry humor passing over the salesman's head.

The Jaguar was notoriously always breaking down, but my dad didn't mind because he could fix anything.

The salesman, trying to sell my dad on a new car, said, "Can you believe the size of that engine?"

Dad was unimpressed. "I've seen engines a lot bigger than this."

Well, of course he had; he's been working on rocket engines. Now, I had no idea. I thought maybe he had seen a bigger car engine.

But the biggest treat, at least for my dad, was right next door. The business next to the Jag dealer was Western Appliance, so some days we got two stops for the price of one. When my dad walked in, they were always excited to see him, especially the service department and the sales manager. New color TVs were starting to be launched, and there was very little training given to the businesses on how to fix them. Can you imagine if you were a new high school graduate and you went to some four-week "How to Fix a Color Television" class, and now you have to go into homes and fix them?

My dad loved that kind of troubleshooting, and he built the blueprint, if you will, for how to fix the TVs, including where the exposed points were, where it could be breaking down, and how to fix the sets. My dad would read the *entire schematic*, circling every instance where there would be potential problems. If he thought a certain area would be a problem very soon, he would put a double circle around it. Those schematics were probably twenty to thirty pages in length. It was all accordionized into one gigantic sheet of paper, and he would spread the schematics out over the top of all of these TVs and stand there, looking at it, critiquing the entire TV.

Now, the reason I liked those visits to Western Appliance so much was because we didn't have a color TV at home, and they would usually be showing reruns of *Batman* and *The Green Hornet*.

Dad regularly visited Western Appliance with me from 1964 to

1969, but we didn't get our first color TV until 1969. That just sounds bizarre to even say it now—my dad was fixing TVs at the store and in our neighborhood, for free, but we had a black-and-white one at home. Finally, one met his specs after four years of looking and evaluating schematics! But it never really bothered me not having one. It's almost as if my family lived in our own world. Ignorance is bliss, after all. On a scale of 1 to 10, my childhood was about a 250. My electrical abilities, however, I'd put at a 2.

* * *

When I reached the eighth grade, Dad decided it was about time I started building my own stereo kit. I really screwed it up.

My brother, when he was a junior in high school, built a complicated model called the "AR-15" by Heathkit, which was a top-of-the-line, very complicated stereo, and it worked perfectly. So, when my dad gave me mine, he bought a real simple kit called the AD-27— it was a walnut cabinet with a turntable in it, and you had to build the amplifier from a kit.

Well, on the directions, if it says to put a transistor in where it is green, yellow, or red, you should probably do what it says. I thought to myself, *It's probably not that important.* I figured blue and yellow made green, so I'll put a green one in! Electronics doesn't work like that, and I put it together "variety-freestyle," if you will. I told my dad I was finished, he plugged it in, and the transformer inside the kit started smoking. He said, "Johnny, what have you done?!" Apparently, there were a lot of incongruent electrical currents going at the same time.

My dad quickly took it apart, looked at the circuit board, and said, "Johnny, this doesn't follow anything like the instructions say to do." He snipped all the transistors out and was able to save probably 70 percent of the connections that had enough of a stub on them that he could reconnect them. He still had to buy about a third of the new transistors.

So, after that I followed the instructions to a tee, and this time it worked, but the thing is, I gave it such a unique electrical charge that the balance knob did not work right: the knob had to be twisted hard to the right by about thirty degrees for it to be in balance. That bugged my dad because he had tested it numerous times and it all tested out perfectly. And of course, he'd been intimately involved with knob testing and balancing while in the Navy. Now he had a bonehead son who couldn't even follow simple instructions.

Sometimes at night while I was doing homework, Dad would poke his head into my room, go to the stereo, and hold that knob up. He was always trying to figure out how he could fix that. Right before he would go to bed, he would say, "Johnny, we've got to figure this out."

"Dad," I'd respond, "all you've got to do is turn the knob thirty degrees to the right and it's completely even."

He'd shake his head. "Johnny, that is not normal."

When Dad wanted to emphasize something, it was, "Johnny" or "Johnny Boy," not "John." My brother was always the serious one, so it was "William" or "Bill." I was the "Johnny Boy." My brother and I are about as different as you can get. We are on different ends of the spectrum personality-wise, as well as in mechanical ability.

Even when living in Europe, Dad would come up to my room and go to the stereo and muse over what in the world I had done to that thing. It bugged him to the day he died.

28

The Cuban Missile Crisis

DAD PAUSED TO GATHER HIS thoughts and inspect the last section of fencing we'd just hung. With the next breath he said, "Johnny, the Cuban missile crisis was a negotiated settlement. It was just as important to have the president stand down his generals as it was to stand down the Russians. It was kept classified for fifteen years that we pulled our missiles out of Turkey and Italy for the Russians to turn around their boats."

"How is it that you know so much about these nuclear missiles?" I asked.

Dad was picking up another section of fence, and from the ground he looked up at me, and said, "Johnny, who do you think put them there?"

No words would come out of my mouth, but my thoughts screamed, *Oh, my God! You put missiles . . .* You *did? What?!*

After the failed United States–backed Bay of Pigs invasion of 1961 and the United States placement of medium-range nuclear missiles in Italy and Turkey, the Soviet Union decided to respond by installing medium- and intermediate-range tactical nuclear missiles in Cuba—160 nuclear weapons that they were going to fire on America. Evidence confirming construction of Soviet launch sites within Cuba was obtained on October 14, 1962, gathered imagery taken from a U-2 spy plane overflight.

This data was presented to President Kennedy and key members of the White House staff on October 15–16, 1962. While the situation was an impending strategic threat, there was no indication from the U-2 imagery than an immediate tactical threat to the United States presently existed, as the missile sites were not yet live. The true danger lay in how the White House would respond to the Soviet overture. No contingency plans or preplanned responses had been formulated for Soviet nuclear expansion into the Western Hemisphere. No one had ever considered the scenario was possible, let alone that it could be happening without the United States' foreknowledge. The response formulated by Kennedy's White House would literally change the course of human history.[1]

The true question of the impending crisis was twofold. One, would the introduction of Soviet nuclear missiles in Cuba tip the balance of power? But more important, what would the United States' response do to the political landscape of the Cold War? As to the balance of nuclear power, there is evidence that nuclear missiles in Cuba would do little to sway the outcome of a Soviet–American nuclear exchange.[2] Politically it was a different story. Too firm a response could have effected a nuclear exchange; too soft an approach could result in a Soviet upper hand down the line in Cold War détente.

Options were bandied about, ranging from an invasion of Cuba, to airstrikes to destroy the missile sites, to pressuring the Soviets diplomatically to remove the sites, threatening Castro with an invasion if construction of the missile sites continued, to a naval blockade of Cuba ensuring no Soviet missiles could enter the country. Kennedy was opposed to a full-scale invasion of Cuba, while the Joint Chiefs of Staff advocated the action. In fact, the generals wanted to bomb the living daylights out of Cuba. Dad told me that the general who had control, specifically, Curtis LeMay of the Air Force, the one who did all the carpet bombing in Japan and Europe in World War II, was adamant about attacking Cuba. He later said what we did to resolve the Cuban missile crisis was America's "biggest defeat in our nation's history." Our saving grace was Harold Brown, who vetoed LeMay's opinion. In fact, when I asked Dad who the most important person of the Cold War was, he replied immediately that it was Harold Brown. Dad further stated, "What a crime. He will be remembered as the person who ordered the botched helicopter raid in trying to release the hostages in Iran," which happened on April 24, 1980.

By the early 1960s, Harold Brown became secretary of defense research under Robert McNamara. He was the first scientist to become secretary of defense.[3] So now, finally, a nuclear nerd, and an associate of my dad's, was part of the military. He later was director of defense research and engineering and secretary of the Air Force. And his better judgment prevailed over LeMay's desire to wipe Cuba off the map.

In the midst of this discussion, we spotted the Cuban missiles being set up—with satellite photos. But what we did not understand was how close we came then to getting nuked. Nor did we find this out until 1992, when Robert McNamara was at a conference with Fidel Castro and Khrushchev was still alive.

President Kennedy was trying to negotiate behind the scenes. Robert Kennedy, his brother, was negotiating with the Russian ambassador, Anatoly Dobrynin, behind the scenes as well. The president knew that we didn't want to go to nuclear war with the two superpowers exchanging nuclear weapons. As we know now, Cuba wouldn't have instigated; they were waiting on us to make the first move. But we were on pins and needles then.

Of course, Kennedy chose the blockade route, and a time line of the events after the initial briefing of the White House shows how the crisis evolved.

OCTOBER 18: Kennedy meets with Soviet minister of foreign affairs Andrei Gromyko, who claims any missile sites in Cuba would be for defensive purposes only. Kennedy does not tip his hand to the level of intelligence the United States has at this point.[4]

OCTOBER 19: Additional U-2 flights revealed four operational missile launch sites in Cuba. Six Army divisions are alerted, and Air Force bombers are constantly aloft and ready to strike targets in support of a blockade or invasion of Cuba.

OCTOBER 20–21: Kennedy and staffers explore options and come down to either the blockade or a full invasion as the best options. In reality, an invasion of Cuba couldn't have been pulled off properly given the Navy's lack of amphibious landing craft and other logistical concerns.[5]

OCTOBER 22: Kennedy meets with select leaders of NATO and allied countries, informing them of the situation and the response of a blockade—all of which support the United States' position. Key members of Congress are consulted and urge Kennedy for a stronger measure. The Soviets catch wind of the blockade plans. Kennedy addresses the nation that evening at 7 p.m. EST, informing the country of the missile sites in Cuba and the planned blockade. All United States military forces are placed on DEFCON (DEFense readiness CONdition) 3, and the Navy puts blockade plans into motion.[6]

OCTOBER 24: The Soviet news agency TASS reports that Khrushchev has sent a cable to Kennedy stating a blockage of Cuba:

> Such morals and laws are not to be found, because the actions of the USA in relation to Cuba are outright piracy. This, if you will, is the madness of a degenerating imperialism. Unfortunately, people of all nations, and not least the American people themselves, could suffer heavily from madness such as this, since with the appearance of modern types of weapons, the USA has completely lost its former inaccessibility.[7]

OCTOBER 25: Two United States ships attempt to intercept a tanker steaming toward Cuba. It is determined that no military materials are on aboard and it is allowed through. Intelligence reports indicate that the missile sites in Cuba are still under construction.

OCTOBER 26: Kennedy starts to change his tune on invasion, but is persuaded to take a wait-and-see approach to the blockade. Back channel communications begin with the Soviets in an attempt to deescalate tensions.[8]

OCTOBER 27: Radio Moscow broadcasts that Khrushchev has offered to table the Cuban missile program if the United States removes medium-range nuclear missiles from Italy and Turkey. Presidential advisors believe this plan is a fair trade off and neither side would lose face in such an exchange. Later in the day Khrushchev makes another overture claiming that the United States missiles in Turkey and Italy are just as bad as Cuba and repeats the previous offer. A U-2 spy plane is shot down over Cuba, killing the pilot. A number of other flash point situations happen between U.S. and Soviet forces that could potentially escalate the crisis into open conflict. Kennedy asks the Soviets to suspend work on the missile sites in Cuba while negotiations are ongoing, as a sign of good faith.[9]

OCTOBER 28: Khrushchev broadcasts on Radio Moscow that the Cuban missile program will be halted, effectively ending the Cuban missile crisis. Kennedy responds in kind by stating plans to remove U.S. nuclear missiles from Turkey. The blockade remains in place until it is clear the Soviets are keeping their end of the bargain and is totally disbanded by November 9, 1962.[10]

Now Kennedy had stood down his generals, we'd avoided nuclear war—again—and Curtis LeMay, unhappy with the decision to leave Cuba unscathed, retired in 1965. Later he was announced as George Wallace's running mate for presidency of the United States, but they lost the election in 1968 to Nixon.

Thirty years later, during an interview between Castro and McNamara, we found out just how close we came to war when McNamara, secretary of defense from 1961 to 1968, asked the dictator three questions:

1. Were you aware the nuclear warheads were in Cuba?

2. If so, would you have recommended their use?

3. If the nuclear weapons had been used, what would have been the outcome for Cuba?

Castro said, "Now, we started from the assumption that if there was an invasion of Cuba, nuclear war would erupt. We were certain of that . . . we would be forced to pay the price, that we would disappear. . . . Would I have been ready to use nuclear weapons? Yes, I would have agreed to the use of nuclear weapons."[11]

Robert McNamara was so taken aback by that and so emotionally shook up that he had to leave the room and settle down because he couldn't talk. The thought of being hit with more than a hundred nuclear weapons paralyzed his speech—literally.

Anything one thousand miles away from Cuba would have been hit with a nuclear weapon, which would have meant close to 80 percent of America's population at that time would have been annihilated. They estimate that one hundred million people could have been killed. Cuba admitted we would have blown them off the face of the earth, but they would have done as much carnage in return.

If Kennedy had followed his generals into battle, the Eastern Seaboard would be gone.

29

The Six-Day War

ON JANUARY 27, 1967, Gus Grissom died in a horrible fire while in the cockpit during a prelaunch test for the Apollo 1 mission at Cape Canaveral Air Force Station, Florida. Fellow astronauts Ed White and Roger Chaffee were also killed. The explosion was all over the news, and to save face, the government told everybody that everything had at least five backup systems, since the general population was leery of space technology after this event. In reality, there were really very few, if not limited, backup systems on those space missiles.

Dad, unaware that my brother, Bill, was nearby, was pacing after hearing the news, talking to himself, and fretting not only about the disaster, but also about the spin the government was giving it. He said, "There's no backup systems on these things," talking about NASA shuttles. That was one of the first hints to my brother that Dad wasn't a salesman, as he had told us—but it certainly wouldn't be the last.

* * *

Months later, June 5–10, 1967, the Six-Day War was fought by Israel against Egypt, Syria, Jordan, Iraq, and Lebanon. Algeria, Kuwait, Libya, Morocco, Pakistan, Sudan, and Tunisia also supported the Arab nations in the conflict. The United States was allied with Israel, and we helped them out a great deal, much to the displeasure of Egypt, which would be ruled under Egyptian president Nasser until September 28, 1970, and Russia. By the end of the conflict, Israel ended up getting 25 percent of Egypt's landmass.

The background of the Six-Day War can be traced back to the formation of the modern-day Israeli state. Arabs did not take kindly to Jews professing that, due to a feeling of divine right, and the genocide of Jews during the Second World War, they had a claim on Arab lands.

After the formation of the state of Israel, several low-level clashes happened between the newly formed country and its neighbors. On the world scene, the Arab–Israeli conflict became a proxy component of the Cold War, as Arab states, by and large, were supported by the Soviets; in comparison, the United States has always taken a pro-Israeli stance.

Most notably in the list of flash points between Israel and her Arab neighbors before the Six-Day War was the Suez Crisis of 1956, when Israel, the UK, and France invaded Egypt to seize control of the Suez Canal. Technically the invasion was a military success, but it turned into a political nightmare for Israel and her allies.

Both the United States and the Soviet Union put pressure on Israel to cease aggressions, as the conflict made the Suez Canal useless to either of the powerhouses in the Cold War. The end result was the United Nations confirming that the Suez Canal was owned by the Egyptian state and therefore the Egyptians had sovereign rights over the canal. A United Nations peacekeeping force was stationed in the Sinai Desert to enforce the 1949 Armistice Agreements that solidified Israel as a nation.[1] There was no clear peace accord to the Suez Crisis, and the lack thereof festered for ten years, boiling over into the Six-Day War.

A number of mutual defense pacts between Arab countries between

1966 and 1967 and false reports by the Soviets to the Egyptians that Israel was amassing troops on the Syrian border in May 1967 was the fuse for the Six-Day War. The match lighting of the ensuring skirmish was Nasser's reaction by closing shipping lanes in the Straits of Tiran to Israeli shipping. As far back as 1956, the Israelis had stated that such an action would be considered an act of aggression and acted accordingly.[2]

On June 5, 1967, Israel launched a massive air attack against Egyptian air bases, effectively destroying the Egyptian air force and ensuring Israeli air superiority throughout the rest of the conflict. From there, the Israelis (for lack of a better term) let all hell break loose with ground attacks on contended lands inside and outside of Israel.[3]

Without going into the stunning military tactics and performance of the Israeli military (of which there were many), by June 10, 1967, the Israelis had increased the size of their country by four times its size before the Six-Day War.[4] Israel captured the Gaza Strip, the Sinai Peninsula (up to the eastern bank of the Suez Canal), the West Bank of the Jordan River, and the Golan Heights.[5]

Russia claimed that because the United States helped Israel so much, they should do the same for Egypt if something were to happen again. So when the Six-Day War ended with the new boundaries set, Russia was furious and decided to help Egypt out the way the United States had helped Israel.

There has been debate in the years since regarding the level of United States and Soviet involvement in the conflict. One U.S. electronic intelligence-gathering ship, the USS *Liberty*, was sunk by the Israelis. According to the Israelis, the *Liberty* was mistaken for an Egyptian ship. Some believe the *Liberty* was sunk because it was gathering intelligence on Soviet, NATO, and home-brewed Israeli equipment used in the theater.[6] What is for sure is that both superpowers were intensely interested in how equipment performed under true battlefield conditions. For example, the Six-Day War held the largest tank battles ever fought since the end of World War II. Real-world data on performance of tanks and aircraft was invaluable to both powers in the Cold War.[7]

As a parting note on how the Six-Day War played into the greater drama of the Cold War, at any time the Soviets or Americans could have stepped in with direct military support for their allies. This, of course, could have led to an outright Soviet–American clash and is therefore considered one of the many decision/flash points in the Cold War.[8] Finally, the Egyptians closed the Suez Canal from the end of the Six-Day War to June 1975, which affected military logistics of both the Soviets and Americans.[9]

The war was over—at least on paper. But the bitter feelings between countries only festered. My dad would soon be in the middle of this fight, and our family would be uprooted again under the guise of a new sales position, this time in Switzerland . . . or so we thought.

30

The Curious Case of
the Water Dam

ON JUNE 14, 1967, we got a call that Marjorie, Mom's sister, had died at the age of forty-two. She'd married a man who was also in a wheelchair, and she and her husband had lived in Phoenix, Arizona, where they raised dachshunds and got by on disability, so their life had not been easy. Mom had always felt so bad that she was healthy and Marjorie was not. She knew she was so blessed to have four healthy kids, and although she never questioned why Marjorie's accident had happened, I know she thought it was unfair for such a good person to experience such unfortunate circumstances that ultimately led to an early death. If she could have somehow undone Marjorie's illness, she would have.

When Mom and Dad returned from the funeral, Mom was now mourning both the loss of her sister and the stark reality of suddenly being an only child. Although her father was still in relatively good health, he had never remarried, and she wasn't able to visit him as much as she would have liked. The distance now seemed magnified by loss. And without a support system of close friends, other than her friends at church, Mom had to grieve alone. Dad's mood was very somber during that time; he was no doubt deeply saddened to see his wife in so much pain.

My sister Dawn, in town for a visit a few weeks after the funeral, walked into Mom's bedroom and found her crying. It was understandable, of course. Her only sister had left the earth. Tears needed to flow, but it was still a shock since we'd never really seen Mom cry before.

Dawn said, "Mom, what's the matter?"

Mom couldn't even lift her face from her hands. Between sobs, she managed to squeak out, "I just miss my mom and my sister." If you've lost a loved one, especially a parent or sibling, you know sometimes there are no words that can comfort a broken heart.

Dawn hurried over to Mom's bedside and gave her a big hug, sitting with her until her body was no longer shaking from the intensity of the sadness. Mom's whole life was family, and a piece of her heart had been taken away.

She would recover, though, and soon be back to the same jovial woman we all knew.

Looking back, it was a miracle Mom was able to be so positive all the time. Perhaps it was a gift from God that her default mode was one of peace and happiness. We'd need that strength more than ever—especially Dad—over the next few years.

As another conflict brewing on the world stage led to Dad's next assignment, our lives were about to be uprooted again.

* * *

Beginning in the spring of 1970, Russia moved nearly twenty thousand military personnel, including advisers, technicians, air defense crews, and Soviet pilots, as well as large numbers of aircraft and defense missiles, into Egypt under Nasser.[1] They had never been happy with how the Six-Day War ended nearly three years before and were determined to do something about it.

Our U.S. spy satellites counted up to six hundred surface-to-air missiles (SAMs) set up in Egypt, pointed at Israel. Now, you don't set up six hundred surface-to-air missiles by happenstance. It was clear they were going to invade. They also knew that the Israelis would send their air force, and with all these surface-to-air missiles, they could pick off the Israeli air force.

We know that the Russians were very adept at the manufacture of surface-to-air missiles. In Vietnam, that's what knocked John McCain out of the sky—Russian missiles that were supplied to Vietnam. Just to show how accurate these missiles were under the correct training, during the Vietnam conflict the Americans lost more than 2,000 aircraft; the Vietnamese lost just 131 planes.[2]

At that point in the Israeli–Egyptian conflict, in March 1970—the same month that Iran signed their final ratifications for the Non-Proliferation Treaty (NPT)—my dad moved to Switzerland, and rather suddenly, under the guise of working on a water dam in Iran. We as a family, as usual, never thought to question why a salesman would be sent to Switzerland to work on a water dam in Iran. The only thought I honestly entertained about his announcement was that since I knew my dad could fix anything, I figured he'd probably know how to fix a water dam too.

I know, I know. It sounds like the most fantastical excuse. And while it was, as I said, it was all we'd ever known. He'd send for us once he was established in Switzerland, and we'd move once again.

* * *

Our relationship with Iran was not always as contemptuous as it is today. For twenty-six years, Iran was so close to the United States that in many ways, it was treated as the fifty-first state of America. Iran, at that time, was our ally—America's watchdog of the Middle East and Israel's greatest ally.

In 1953 the United States sponsored a coup to overthrow the democratically elected Iranian president Mohammad Mosaddeq. It was led by the grandson of Theodore Roosevelt and authorized by the president of the United States, General Eisenhower, along with the

British government. Initially the United States gave $1 million to overturn the Iranian president, which eventually became $5 million in aid to the CIA. We wanted the shah back in power—it worked. We also wanted to ensure that Communist-leaning tendencies were thwarted, and that the Iranian monarchy would safeguard Western oil interests.[3] Mosaddeq's overthrow consolidated the shah's rule for the next twenty-six years until the 1979 Islamic revolution.[4]

Iran had first signed the NPT, along with quite a few other countries, in London, in July 1968, and the treaty was closed for signature. It came into force on March 5, 1970. Now the United States could supply Iran with nuclear fuel, as long as they used it for peaceful purposes. There's a loophole in the treaty that says that if a country that has signed the NPT feels threatened, it can use the nuclear fuel however it wants, enrich uranium, and sneak in nuclear missiles—and it's based on *opinion*. What's more, later in 1974, when Gerald Ford became president, America *wanted Iran to become a nuclear* power because, as Donald Rumsfeld put it, Iran was eventually going to run out of oil as fuel.[5] Of course, twenty years later, he was saying the opposite about Iran needing nuclear power.

Instead of working on some water dam, my dad was really going to install missiles in Iran in case Russia became involved. The United States also knew Egypt had all those missiles pointed toward Israel, and we had to defend Israel. So, for two years, my dad shuttled in and out of Iran from our home in Switzerland with all those SAMs. And the components of the missiles Dad was in charge of had been made in the United States (and possibly Switzerland), and then transported to Iran to assemble, install, and program.

If the words "Switzerland" and "missile" in the same sentence make you raise an eyebrow, you're likely not alone. However, Switzerland, seen as the world's most neutral country, does export a lot of arms—after all, Glock, the pistol company—is Swiss, and the country has also had the capability to enrich uranium through reactors.

The moral of the story is, things are not always as they appear.

31

No Attention to Detail

"DAD, WHY DID WE MOVE TO ZURICH?" I asked as I reached for a water bottle. We were the only ones in the yard, and Dad wasn't worried about anyone else overhearing our conversation. He swigged down another small box of juice.

"Because I was helping run missiles into Iran," he answered. "Zurich is where we were building the missiles. You got lucky, going to school over there."

I nodded, trying to hide my deer-in-the-headlights look while imagining my dad as a glorified gunrunner. It had been a great experience for me to go through my last two years of high school in Switzerland. Weird at times. But great.

"Of course, you didn't make the move real easy," Dad continued. "Those shenanigans you pulled the night before you left upset a lot of people."

Research suggests that most, if not all, individuals with "sudden savant syndrome," have the gift (or curse) of an incredible memory. And I can attest to that on my dad's behalf. When my dad first told me that I was being followed in the early 1970s when we lived in Switzerland, he was telling me this in 1989—*nearly twenty years after the fact*—yet, he was recalling names of people, streets I drove down, and when—he didn't miss a beat. And let me tell you, it was a shock to my system!

Upon recalling the folly of my youth, I stopped in my tracks, stunned that Dad knew about the wild night I'd had before we'd left for Europe. I'd driven up to San Francisco with a couple of my church buddies. We had two cars, and we'd taken a ride down Lombard Street going the wrong direction at midnight.

By 2 or 3 a.m., we were running streetlights on Van Ness Avenue and Geary Boulevard, living it up and acting as though we owned the streets. It was basically the equivalent of the night before a guy ships off to the military, when his friends take him out and get him trashed—minus the booze or drugs. Of course, we were pleasantly surprised that we weren't pulled over for acting like idiots and for running at least twenty stoplights. But now I was hearing that we were followed the entire night!

Dad said, "Going through all those stoplights and driving the wrong way on Lombard Street . . . Johnny, we couldn't figure out what you were doing."

Now he really had my attention.

"I knew where you were the whole time. I was watching you from Zurich," Dad said matter-of-factly. "We had the cops trailing you 'til around nine. After that, we took over jurisdiction."

"We? Who's *we*?" My eyes must have been as big as saucers. *How did he know?* I'd never told him what my friends and I had done on that crazy night.

"The Feds."

My head was spinning again. I wasn't quite getting it. "Why didn't they pull us over?"

"They were there to make sure you *didn't* get pulled over," he countered. "You had to get on that plane to Europe the next morning. It was a matter of national security."

Me getting on a plane a matter of national security? Now I'd heard everything.

"My team was taking nuclear warheads into Iran for the U.S. government illegally. Any kind of breach would have been a disaster. Do you remember where you sat on that plane?"

I nodded, remembering the flight we'd taken to Zurich. "We flew first class."

I remember it vividly, because all three of us were on the right-hand side, with Nedra and Mom sitting together three or four rows ahead, and I was by myself in the last row of first class, surrounded by at least twenty-five empty seats. That meant I could look back behind a curtain at the rest of the packed plane—scanning the faces for someone I could bring to join me and help ease my boredom.

Dad explained that the entire first row of coach behind the curtain was security. I vividly remember asking various stewardesses why kids my age could not come up front. They just said no, politely. But at least I didn't have to stay in my seat. First class had a lounge upstairs, and I remember drinking at least five cans of Pepsi while talking to six different stewardesses over the course of the long flight. I'm sure that at least some of them were working with security as well.

"Do you remember who else was in first class?" Dad asked, knowing the answer already.

"No one. We were alone."

"That's right. They cleared it, took everyone else off. The TWA hijacking out of Zurich had just happened, and they weren't taking any chances. You remember anything about a couple of guys dressed in suits who were in the first row of coach?"

I didn't remember.

"That was your detail."

"My detail?"

"They followed you everywhere you went for two years. They lived next door to us, and watched everything."

I was stunned at that.

"That's how I know you never did drugs. I knew a lot of your friends did, but you always seemed to be able to walk away from it."

Now I was horrified. *Oh, God, what else did he see?* What else had I done?

Of course, there was that one time I did hash and Dad saved my bacon, but I never did any *hard* drugs, even when a lot of my friends were heavy into drugs. And because I was being watched, he knew I always said no to drugs, except that one time.

I was a senior in high school in Zurich, and on a Friday afternoon after school, I finally decided I was going to try smoking hash out of a pipe with my friend. I'm not sure what sparked my interest that day, but I wasn't far from the house, and it was something different, and apparently, I had nothing else to do.

Dad's security team found out immediately and notified him before I'd even driven all the way home on my moped. I was feeling woozy and drowsy, and when I got home, I stumbled into the garage. Mom, hearing me pull in, came out to the garage and immediately asked me, "John, what's wrong with your eyes?"

My dad came into the garage and oddly enough, he defended and protected me. He turned to Mom and said, "Mary, that's just the wind from being on his motor scooter." Then he told me to go shower up. So, I did. And in the middle of my shower, my friend called me to make sure I got home safely, but still completely out of it, I came downstairs completely nude to get the phone. Dad walked up and said, "Johnny, get off the phone and get to bed." But he never said a word to me about it. Still, I was so lit up that entire weekend that even the church music sounded good on Sunday.

Dad knew this wasn't normal for me. His security team kept him apprised of my behavior and my friends' behavior, so he knew I was around drugs and that my friends did drugs, but I'd never expressed an interest in it, always passing up offers and walking away from drug deals. So, I guess he thought he didn't have anything to worry about. He was right. That one experience scared me so much that I didn't try it again until a year later, when I was back in the States—and that was it.

That story made me recall another instance when he knew about something else I'd done before I even made it home. One Monday afternoon while leaving the Carlton Elite Hotel, where students and parents often went to watch previously recorded NFL games and highlights, Dad drove ahead of me (and now I know the detail followed me on my scooter). I had strapped a cassette player onto the handlebars and was jamming out to a Uriah Heep album.

I was a very animated singer, and I noticed close to me in traffic, a mother kept glancing over with an uneasy expression on her face; her two daughters in the back seat were staring out the window at me. The mom locked the doors, probably thinking I was nuts. To be fair, with my long blonde hair, athletic build, and passionate scooter performance, I probably looked more than a little intimidating.

It was lightly snowing and as we came upon a construction zone. Two undersized Italians in a small car behind me kept honking their horn. Traffic wasn't moving, and I was having trouble hearing my music over the noise. I got off my scooter, approached the car, and told them to stop honking. As I walked in front of the car, they honked again, so I walked back to the car and promptly punched a dent into the car's roof. They stopped honking, and soon the traffic was moving.

A few hours later at the dinner table, Dad offered a helpful bit of information, namely that people should never approach a car with other cars around. Of course, the detail had already informed him of what happened. I never put two and two together, but responded, "Dad, I am always careful but there were these two jerks who had to stop honking."

At Dad's next question, I snapped back to reality. "When you landed in Switzerland that first time and showed them your passport, do you remember what happened?" he asked.

"We didn't go through customs."

"That's right. You were already cleared to enter the country. We didn't want anyone to see you come in."

"They never stamped our passport the whole time we lived there," I suddenly recalled, remembering feeling cheated by that somehow.

"That was in case we had to leave in a hurry," Dad explained. "They didn't want any trace we'd ever been there."

Suddenly, my mind flashed back to the trips where I had accompanied Dad back to the States. While waiting for the plane at the Zurich Airport, he would hand me a few francs, tell me to buy a *Sports Illustrated*, and then go off by himself until it was time to board the plane.

"Why'd you always disappear at the Zurich Airport?" I asked.

"I'd go get the flight manifest from the Interpol office," he explained. "I'd check the nationalities of the passengers, where they were going, that kind of thing. Remember how I used to make us wait until everyone else was on the plane before boarding?"

I did remember. I never understood why we had to do that. Now I finally realized it was because Dad wouldn't get on the plane until he knew that everyone else on it was safe. I also recall that not a single adult visited us when we lived in Switzerland. Dad said he couldn't trust anybody.

"Johnny, there were people in the world who didn't appreciate what I was doing," he said.

32

Moving to Switzerland

DAD CAME HOME ONE DAY from work in early February 1970 and announced at the dinner table that he was moving to Switzerland because he was working for the shah of Iran on a water dam project in the north. Of course, that was just fiction.

At his proclamation, we all just kind of looked at each other. My mom said, "Oh, really, Wallace?" He said we'd all be moving there too, as soon as he was settled and sent for us.

You've got to understand: our family doesn't really show a lot of emotion. My first thought was, *Where is Switzerland?*

I knew Iran was a very old country; my thoughts morphed into trying to create an explanation that would make sense: *Why did it take them thousands of years to figure out that they needed to bring my dad to build a dam to drink water? That's a long time to wait.* That should have been an indication that something was haywire, and I did question it. But have I mentioned that I was oblivious? To be fair, he virtually was a one-stop problem-solving shop. He could fix engines, repair electronics, do woodwork, and garden, so when he said, "I'm going to build a water dam," I thought, *Gosh, maybe he knows how to do that too.*

I had only been between California and Iowa and all the states in between, because we often would drive it. My sophomore year in high school was almost over, and I had a carefree attitude about most everything. *Sounds good to me, Dad!*

He was out of the house within a week. "I'll let you know when you guys can arrive," he said. And then he was gone.

I remember my mom being anxious because she had to pack up the garage and the whole house with the movers, and she had to determine which items were going to stay in storage and which would go overseas, because my dad just vanished. We'd been living there for eight years by then, and we had a full house.

We didn't hear from him until May, when I, not my mom, received a postcard from him. My mom ran back into the house one day after getting the mail with the biggest smile on her face, and said, "Johnny, you got a postcard from Wallace!" She was so excited.

The postcard told me that Dad was in Zurich. Dad wrote, "Johnny Boy, we are going to go to this restaurant called Silberkugel (Silver Ball). You're going to enjoy this when you come here." That restaurant was famous for making little mini burgers. Then he said he would let us know when the family could come over to Switzerland too.

A few days later, he called the house, and Mom just lit up like a high school girl getting a call from her crush: "Oh, Wallace, thanks for calling!" she cooed into the phone.

* * *

America's involvement with Iran had changed course somewhat after the 1967 Six-Day War between Israel and the Arabs ended unfavorably for the Arab side. The Soviet Union, recognizing the intense U.S. support of Israel with money and arms, and aware that Israel was about to be supplied with America's F-4 Phantom jets, decided to weigh in more heavily on the Arab side. The Soviets sent twenty thousand advisers to Egypt and Syria, along with an arsenal of tanks and a variety of surface-to-air missiles, including the Scud, with a two-hundred-mile range.

To counter this threat, the United States began supplying Iran under the guise of Iranian deals with third-party countries. Iran eagerly bought up F-14s and large numbers of military and defense products from the United States. Moving Iran toward nuclear capability, the United States sold to Mohammad Reza Shah Pahlavi something he'd been requesting from America for quite some time—a 5-megawatt nuclear research reactor that is still functioning and still operational in Tehran, along with weapons-grade enriched uranium as fuel for that reactor.[1]

Iran's new Nuclear Research Center (TNRC), located at Tehran University and run by the Atomic Energy Organization of Iran (AEOI), opened a short time before the country signed the International Non-Proliferation Treaty in 1968. Ratified by the Mailes, the Iranian congress, in 1970, the treaty recognized Iran's right to research, produce, and use nuclear energy for peaceful purposes.

As soon as the treaty was ratified, the BBC Brown Boveri company was among those, including companies from Germany and France, who were contracted to construct up to twenty-two nuclear reactors around Iran. Dating back to the late nineteenth century, the Swiss firm was considered one of the premier power generation companies on the planet. Electrification efforts in Third World countries provided them with substantial profits, the company eventually merging with ASEA, a Swedish firm with a board of directors that at one time included Donald Rumsfeld, former Secretary of Defense, to form ASEA Brown Boveri (ABB Group).

Although the building of these reactors was common knowledge, what wasn't as well-known was America's determination to place nuclear warheads in Iran as a deterrent to the destruction of Israel. Back then, Israel and Iran were great allies: "Iran had formally launched a peaceful nuclear program in 1957, with the announcement of plans for cooperation with the US 'in research in the peaceful uses of atomic energy.' Iran opened a nuclear research center in Tehran a decade later, with a US-supplied research reactor. They signed the Nuclear Non-Proliferation Treaty (NPT) in 1968 and ratified it in March 1970."[2] It was no coincidence that this was the same month my father moved to Switzerland.

IBM at this point was securely tied into the U.S. government. Harold Brown, who had been the director of the Lawrence Radiation Lab in Livermore, and was deputy secretary of defense, and then secretary of the Air Force under President Lyndon Johnson, sat on the IBM board of directors. So did Cyrus Vance, the deputy secretary of defense in the Johnson administration, and later secretary of state during the Carter years. IBM was also securely tied into most other Western governments, as any country that had a military had contracted with the company to supply and run the computers for its weapons systems.

For quite some time, Dad had been traveling around the world, helping install nuclear missiles in trouble spots where the United States felt at least somewhat threatened. When the Non-Proliferation Treaty was ratified in Tehran, he was recruited to be part of the team that would sneak missiles and nuclear fuel into that country under the guise of the legal nuclear technology, and supposedly for peaceful purposes. Specifically, Dad was in charge of installing the process controls in the silos where the weapons were housed.

Similar in some ways to military bunkers, the silos were dug into the dirt. Each has a thick concrete shield across the top that can open up so operators can fire off a missile out of a tube. A few years back, I went to a missile site that you can tour outside of Tucson, and you literally go down six floors into a big silo with a missile. There's a computer thirty feet away where operators sit at a desk to fire the missile. Two separate operators have to have matching keys to access a sealed code against which they must compare the authorization code given in the launch order. The codes must match in order to launch the missile. The missile is so well insulated, with sometimes ten feet of concrete, that after operators fire a missile, they literally have to ask if it fired because you can't hear it even if you are sitting thirty feet away. There are thousands of silos all over the world.

In Dad's case, the home base for the project was Zurich; the missiles were manufactured by Brown Boveri, a company with a huge history in the nuclear space, including generators and reactors, in the nearby town of Turgi. Brown Boveri would have hired IBM, and thus my father, to help facilitate their work. As mentioned earlier, Brown Boveri was later bought out by a Swedish company named ASEA—the biggest nuclear reactor manufacturer in the world.

* * *

Dad lived in Zurich alone for six months before it was time for us to move there after my tenth grade year. I was fifteen and thought it sounded like a fun adventure. My sister Dawn was in college, and my brother, Bill, was in medical school. Nedra had graduated from high school in San Jose, but she decided to take a semester off before going to college in Seattle in January 1971, so she could spend time in Switzerland with us and help Mom acclimate to a foreign country.

Mom wasn't too keen on the move. She liked San Jose and didn't want to leave the home we'd built there. She also had some issues with her health at that time; she'd had congestive heart failure—and her doctors advised her not to travel. When Dad suggested that she obtain a second opinion from an IBM-referred physician, the IBM doc went against her personal doctor's orders and gave her a green light. Good wife that she was, Mom returned to Europe with Dad to find a home for us, and then came back to San Jose. Nedra and I were on our own for several weeks but managed to survive just fine.

Shortly thereafter, my dad called to say, "I am going to be in San Jose on July 20, and we have to finalize your passport. Pack up as if you are ready to leave, but you are not coming yet."

I said, "Where am I going?"

He said, "You are going to live with your respected brother, who is in medical school in San Francisco." Nedra and Mom would stay in our home in San Jose until given further instructions. So, I got my suitcase ready and my mom packed up all my clothes and had them shipped over. The whole house basically got put in storage, because we had to rent all furniture, all beds, virtually everything, while we were in Switzerland.

So, that's what I did. And just as promised, Dad came home on July 16, 1970, and we went to the Swiss consulate's office in San Francisco to get my passport and a Visa stamp for Switzerland.

On the drive there, I asked, "Why do I have to go to the consulate to get a passport?" My dad gave me some vague answer then. But during our fence-building project decades later, he said that it went to a very high level of the Swiss government to allow him into the country due to the high-security aspect of what he was doing. The government had to allow him to enter, because we never *formally*, *legally* entered the country. My dad said, "Johnny, if we had to leave in a hurry, I could leave no trace."

My passport picture makes me look like I'm about six. And it should have been stamped with some notification that I was going to Switzerland. Except that my passport was so uniquely stamped that I couldn't see it had a stamp of any kind. Now I know that whatever markings there were signaled to whomever in Switzerland: There was to be no trace that I ever entered the country. There was to be no trace that I ever entered the country.

After that was taken care of, my dad drove me to the Haight-Ashbury area of San Francisco, where my brother had an apartment. He literally stopped at the Haight-Ashbury intersection, which was surrounded by groups of hippies, looked at his watch, and said, "Johnny, I've got to get to the airport." He basically told me to get out of the car, take my suitcase and my baseball glove, and walk to my brother's place, which was two or three blocks away. He pointed as he said, "Go down to this street, you'll come to Stanyan Street, go up two blocks, and there is Parnassus." Then he gave me the address on Stanyan, right next to a firehouse. Now, my mom and sister were in San Jose. But for some reason he wanted me to be with my brother.

So, I walked, carrying my suitcase and glove, and found my brother's apartment.

Dad's basketball team in 1940. He is third from the right. This is the team he was on when he had to leave basketball practice for the recruitment interview with the NDRC where he took the math test at the Kiron Café.

Dad and Mom's graduating class of 1940 from Kiron High School. Lynell and Lloyd Baker were pulled out of school because "chores were more important than education," said their father.

NAME Clauson, Wallace William

Fresh. Comp.	Engl. 102	3	Fₓₓ				
College Alg.	Math. 101	5	F	0			
Theory of Proj.Draw.	EDr. 132	3	C	6			
Engr. Prob.	GenE. 104	1	Fₓₓ				
Basic – Engr.	Mil. 102	1	C	2			
Phys. Ed.	P.E. 102	R	B				
Orientation	Engr. 115	R	A				
Library Instruction	Lib. 106c	R	C				
27-21- 2,741 4-17-41				17	0.47	8	

Dad's Iowa State transcript for his freshman year. Note how they have him "flunking" Math 101 and Algebra in the Winter of 1941. There was to be no hint of a mathematical genius in him, and he was to appear as the "village idiot." His GPA for his first year is just over 1.

NAME		CURRICULUM	
Clauson, Wallace William		M. E.	

RACE Caucasian   ANCESTRY Swedish   COLOR White
DATE OF BIRTH Nov. 16, 1922   PLACE Deloit, Iowa
PAR. xxxx. Eldon Clauson   ADD. Kiron, Iowa
FATHER'S OCCUP. Laborer   STUDENT'S CHURCH PREF. Baptist
PAID $10.00 7-'40 B

Dropped indefinitely – Sch Comm
Reinstated – Ho[...] 3-15-46   6-13-41
OFFICIAL TRANSCRIPT – Self 3-15-46

F 1940 math 5
calculated in term
totals, not cum totals

W 1941 E grade
treated as F grade

S 1941 chem 102A,
Engl 102
Gen E 104
courses treated as
Designated Repeat of
W 1941 courses

This report card notes that class W1941 E grade treated as F grade. Then it further notes that classes Chem 102A, Engl 102, and Gen E 104 courses treated as designated repeat of W1941—which are considered F grades. Plus, this report card is "reinstated in 3-15-46" as he prepares to enter the University of Minnesota.

Dad on the farm with his first son, Bill, where he is to act and behave like a farmer. He does secret mathematical calculations in the farmhouse attic, waiting for his release after they determine if a mole is trying to turn him.

Dad was aways smiling when in uniform. Here he is (left) at the Jacksonville Naval Air Station in Florida where thousands of microwave radar sets were placed on submarines, airplanes, and ships to find German U-boats.

Dad at Philco radar center, in Philadelphia, PA, where they designed and manufactured microwave radar sets to capture German U-boats. Dad is back row, third from the right—ever smiling in uniform.

Dad is supposedly studying the 701 computer in Poughkeepsie, New York, as noted on the back of the picture.

His note reads: "Me—as if I were studying—Picture taken by window I pointed out to you on previous pictures I sent you."

Dad's identification badge to enter the Rad Lab in Livermore. Note it states that he has met the citizenship requirements to enter.

After driving the massive 704 computer across the country in three 18-wheelers to the IBM Livermore Rad Lab, Dad is assembling the computer. Then he will program the machine—the world's first thermonuclear computer.

This is a crop-dusting (radiation over land) nuclear reactor. It could fly thirty-five hundred miles an hour and throw off up to twelve nuclear bombs. It could fly four times around the world before running out of energy. Designed in Livermore and then tested in 1964 in Nevada, the Air Force had five on order but cancelled the order in 1965, as dad put it, "when one of us got into the upper echelons of the Air Force."

Harold Brown, who my father said was the most important person of the Cold War. Without him, the world certainly would have "blown itself up." "What a shame, Johnny, for he will be remembered as the one who ordered the botched helicopter raid to free the hostages in Iran. He was the one who got control of the Air Force. Finally, one of us was inside," Dad said. (Photo courtesy of www.media.defense.gov.)

One of the most relaxed pictures that I have of my dad. This is in our living room in Thalwil, Switzerland.

This picture was taken at the Lawrence Livermore Lab. It was printed in a 2011 *New York Times* article "Laid-Back in the Lab." They were testing a detonator for nuclear bombs. Dad is driving the station wagon. The article also notes the advanced Polaris missile calculations were done there as well. (Courtesy of the Lawrence Livermore National Laboratory Archives, reprinted at http://www.nytimes.com/2011/07/05/science/05bomb.html?_r=1.)

Me in my bedroom. The top hat on the hall is part of the album cover of Dave Mason's first album; I played it every night. We had an ongoing discussion to help me make it through those two years. The album is titled *Alone Together*, and man were we!

Dad playing solitaire. This is how he spent 90 percent of his evenings before going to bed. This was his solace, without friends. Very sad to me.

Here I am with my Moped at the end of our driveway in Thalwil, Switzerland.

High up in the Alps, I was wearing my farmer overalls that I also wore when working on our farm in Iowa.

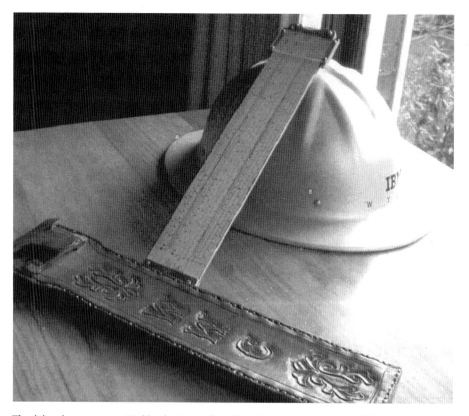

The slide rule was given to Dad by the Man, Albert Einstein, in the living room of John von Neumann during the nights of the great debate. His hard hat was from IBM when working in the missile silos.

We were far enough apart age-wise that I barely saw my brother while I was there because he was very involved at UCSF Medical School and his own social network. I would just hang out at the park or go listen to music and come home. I slept in the living room on a mattress on the floor, a small black and white TV next to the mattress, with my baseball glove always nearby.

I spent my days at Golden Gate Park, playing Frisbee baseball with opponents who were higher than the kites that were flying around. Lucky no one had to worry about getting hit by a ball, but the majority of the players were so out of it, they likely wouldn't have noticed any bruising until the next day anyway.

I spent my nights and weekends going to free concerts at Golden Gate Park and the now-torn-down Winterland Ballroom (which was initially an ice-skating rink in San Francisco). I saw at least two concerts a week, and probably passed a thousand joints, but never once tried it, or even had a beer.

I drank my six-pack of Pepsi by day, and a quart bottle of Collins Mix at night, no alcohol added, out behind a liquor store, where the drunks of San Francisco could drink in the open. I went there every night to read the sports page, because I didn't want to spend the money for a paper. That was quite a time back then.

I stayed at Bill's for eight weeks until we got a phone call from Mom to meet everybody at the airport in San Francisco on September 8, 1970.

33

An American Teenager in Zurich

ZURICH LEFT A LASTING IMPRESSION ON ME. It wasn't only that it was my first trip to Europe, and that we'd been the only passengers in first class on a 747. It was also how we traveled to our new home once we left the airport. As soon as we stepped off the plane, people were lined up to go through customs.

I said, "Hey, we've got to wait for our bags," but my dad, who had just popped his head through a side door, was very anxious.

"We've got to get out of here," he said. Somehow, we got shoved out the side door, and my dad was motioning to us to get into his Ford Cortina, parked right outside, with a sense of urgency. We bypassed immigration and didn't even stop to get our luggage, Dad reassuring us that it would be delivered.

We must have driven twenty miles without hitting a single red light. I do remember wondering how that could be possible. Now I know Dad arranged for that to happen. He had also arranged for the detail in front of his car and behind it, just in case.

Since the PLO had hijacked an airplane less than a week before, my dad was scared to death that they were going to come after his family, because he thought his "project" had been exposed. He was defending Israel, and obviously, the PLO wanted nothing to do with Israel. That is why there was so much security on that airplane flight into Zurich, and why Dad was so anxious on the drive home.

What I also didn't realize at the time was that our new home was perfect for a family living clandestinely. It was in Thalwil on Alsenmattstrasse, a very quiet road marked with Private Street signs at either end of the block. The house itself had very thick walls made of concrete, and was attached to a second home that sat in front of it. From the street, it was impossible to see that the structure included two residences.

On the house tour, Dad pointed at an open door and said, "Johnny, this is your bedroom"—he pointed at a second door—"and this is where Nedra is going to be." Then we went down to the basement. At the back wall of the basement there was a thick metal door with a gigantic lever on it and a chain. My dad said, "Johnny, don't go in this. This is where the owner keeps his gardening tools." I fell for it. I never once tried to go in that door by moving that lever. I never even touched it. I didn't have any interest in gardening, like my dad did. What was really behind that door was a walkway that went down underneath both houses and led to a private meeting area. Before any of us arrived, Dad had already solidified the elaborate security precautions with the police and other federal agents who would shadow us through the secret escape tunnel in the house, if need be.

In 2013, I went back to Switzerland for a party to celebrate our school's fiftieth year of existence. I showed up at the house with my closest teacher, who has been very helpful with my research, and one of my best friends from high school and his wife. I knocked on the door, not knowing who lived there now, and I said, "I used to live here from 1970 to 1972. Can we go down and look at the metal door?" The owner, who works for Nestlé, was very outgoing and welcoming and led us to the basement.

On the way through, he showed me how he had remodeled the house. When we got downstairs to the metal door and went inside, I could tell all new concrete had been poured, there was a legitimate safety exit window above, and the floor had been filled with pebbles. You see, when the Cold War ended, a lot of Cold War relics were either sold off or completely torn down.

Something else I didn't know was that the neighbor who lived in the house in front, a fellow named Herr Siemen, who presented himself as a Swiss watch salesman, was in fact a member of our security detail. He did speak a variety of languages, and my sister Nedra thought he was from Indonesia.

I found it odd when I graduated and was given a very nice, exclusive Heuer watch, that my dad didn't get it from him. You would think that if he had a neighbor friend who was a Swiss watch salesman, he'd buy a watch from him. Guess not. *Especially if he wasn't really a Swiss watch salesman.*

I also didn't realize that the reason Dad never parked his Ford Cortina in the garage was because he wanted it watched at all times. That explained why my scooter always had the entire two-car structure to itself. Whenever I went out on the scooter, someone from either the house in front or the third house in our complex would come out and follow at a distance. The third house had numerous windows facing our home so everything could be watched. We shared our long parallel driveway with the home that watched ours. What is also peculiar is that when Dad parked his car, he always backed down our driveway and left the car next to the front door. Why? If he had to leave in a hurry, he could pull straight out!

Dad was working with the Brown Boveri Company in a town called Turgi, but neither Mom nor I ever visited him. We never gave a thought to the fact that the IBM science research facility was just two miles away from our house, much closer than Turgi, but that Dad never worked there.

We never questioned why Dad insisted on driving a car with no radio either. At the time, we bought his excuse that he didn't care for the way the Cortina radio was built. In truth, he was afraid it was too easy to adapt it with a transponder that would give off a location signal. And that probably sounds far-fetched, except that Dad knew this was possible because the Austin-Healey Sprite that my older brother was now driving while in medical school was tagged with such a device.

Around five o'clock one morning, Bill's little Sprite was stolen. He called the police to report it, and magically, about an hour later, the police "found it" ten miles away, in another city, inside a double-locked garage. Well, the only way you can do that is if you have a hidden GPS transmitter. Now, the military had that technology before they ever released it for public use, so I can only assume Dad had that vehicle tagged and could watch it while he was in Switzerland and Iran and Bill was back in the States.

Bill's a smart guy, and I'm sure that event made him raise an eyebrow. But now that he had the car back, he didn't find the need to ask questions . . . until the next time the GPS came in handy.

Months later, Bill had just exited the Golden Gate Bridge off to Sausalito, headed to medical school, and on the approach to the tunnel, he ran out of gas in the Sprite while going uphill. He knew he was in trouble because the car was going seventy-five or eighty miles an hour, and there was no place to turn off. It would have been a matchbox against the other cars whizzing by.

Bill carefully got out of the car, and only forty-five seconds to a minute later, a gigantic military vehicle pulled up behind him with lights flashing. Out jumped a guy with a five-gallon can of gas. He threw the gas can at Bill and yelled, "Clauson, get going!"

Bill was thinking, *How do you know who I am? What's going on here?* Obviously, the car was being tracked. He told me about it back in the mid-'70s, and we both sat for a moment, thinking about how strange that was, and what a coincidence. Now it's pretty clear that Dad had to strike a deal, and the deal was this: If you want me to protect the country and lay down my life for the country, I will do that, but you've got to protect my family, and especially my kids. That's the deal. Russia was famous for kidnapping and poisoning, and Dad was always watching his back—and ours.

* * *

Just two days after our arrival in Switzerland, I began my studies at the American International School of Zurich (AISZ), which looked like a French chateau sitting on a hill. It was considered one of the top private high schools of all of Europe. A good portion of the students were in the same situation I was in—many whose parents worked for companies or governments who were defending Israel, like my dad. They graded so tough there that they warned college admission boards that a C in Switzerland was equivalent to a B in the States. As a bonified jock, I was about to have my world rocked.

Before we went inside to register, my dad pulled a list of ten books out of his pocket, including works by Kafka and Kierkegaard, and I was supposed to have at least read one over the previous summer. My dad had the list for a while but had forgotten to give it to me, so I hadn't read anything on it. The only thing I was reading regularly was *Sports Illustrated.*

That morning in orientation, when the teacher asked me what I had read over the summer, I said, "I read the Mickey Mantle story on the airplane."

In his heavy British accent, the teacher responded: "What is a Mickey Mantle?"

Nope. I'm definitely not in America anymore.

I found myself thinking that just a few days before, I was in San Francisco listening to music, playing Frisbee, and attending concerts at Winterland. I said under my breath: "Boy, this is going to be a long two years." Indeed, I was a California kid wearing a T-shirt and blue jeans in a school with a British-based curriculum, professorial lectures, and what seemed like endless homework. I wanted to go home.

Initially I had a very difficult time acclimating to that school. Everyone spoke a foreign language, but spoke English while at school. The TV programs were all German; there were no English shows.

Although English was the primary language at school, German came easily to me, as it did to my mother and sister. Dad was another story. He was better off having someone translate for him. Once, when he thought he was ordering fish in a restaurant, a fish head came in a champagne carafe of boiling water. He quickly ordered spaghetti.

Life improved as I made friends. One day after school, I heard someone in a group of kids ask, "Have you heard the Buffalo Springfield album?" It had not yet made it to Switzerland. I responded that I had a copy of the record at home. I was soon invited to my first party, provided Buffalo Springfield came along with me. From that day on, I had as many friends as I needed. That album was the icebreaker for me.

In fact, music was such an integral part of my life that I couldn't imagine even going a day without it. It was especially important in Switzerland, as I was the new kid in a foreign country, and that familiar outlet provided me great comfort.

Lee Michaels was an iconic rock star with a cult following back in the Haight-Ashbury district of San Francisco. He sang and played the Hammond organ, and his drummer was an oversized guy known as Frosty. I used to sing along to his songs, especially "Stormy Monday," where he sings about how rough the week has been, then playing on Saturday and praying on your knees on Sunday. In hindsight, it sounded a lot like my dad's life—minus all the playing.

Lee unleashes these screaming howls at the end—so, of course, I did too. The first time my dad heard me yell, I'm sure he thought something was wrong, but he soon got used to it because I played the song so often. And when I wasn't screaming to songs, I was playing my trumpet to the bands Chicago and Blood, Sweat and Tears. I wonder which of my musical talents dad preferred more.

Then there was Dave Mason, formerly of the band Traffic, whose album *Alone Together* I played literally every night. The song "Only You

Know and I Know" was my absolute favorite. The original psychedelic album cover hung on my wall, and I had an ongoing conversation with Dave to help me get through the two years in Switzerland.

While I now had plenty of friends, it took me a couple of months to adjust to the educational requirements. There was *so much homework*. It was vastly different from the public schools of California, where I was a typical jock. I was still the jock in Switzerland, but academics were now of prime importance. In the States, I was a solid B student. I was lucky to have a C or C– in Switzerland, and I was studying for three or four hours every night. It was unbelievable.

One time I got a C– on a report, and the teacher wrote, "Christmas has come early for you, John."

I also had to write a thesis just to graduate, and I had to have three different editions of it because the reading committee critiqued it throughout the whole senior year. If you didn't write a thesis, you didn't graduate.

My thesis was on Al Capone and the mob, and I got a B– on it. It was a minimum of thirty-five pages, *typed*, and for a high school kid, that was a lot of work. But let me tell you, going to that high school made college easy for me. While in college I had to do a big report on the automobile and in particular, the dangers of the American automobile, and I got an A. I was only able to do that because I had written that paper about Al Capone.

Joining the soccer team improved my social life. It afforded me the opportunity to see more of Europe, the team traveling to Italy and Holland, where I participated in the international finals at The Hague, where we lost in the finals. I was involved in some sort of sport every day after school, and if it wasn't soccer, it was volleyball, hockey, basketball, or skiing.

Nedra soon left for college in the States. With me at school every day and Dad off working in either Turgi or Tehran, Mom lived a rather isolated life in Switzerland. She spent her time shopping, going to the grocery store twice a day. She went to the mailbox twice a day too, looking for news from the States.

As usual, what social contact Mom did have was with the American Protestant Church, fifteen miles outside of Thalwil, right smack in the middle of downtown Zurich, but because of the high-security nature of the situation, she wasn't able to invite church members to our home, and she wasn't allowed to accept their invitations either. We were known as a private family that kept mostly to ourselves, even though we were not normally that way at all. Dad's one exception was to load up the car with as many of my friends as possible for church on Sunday mornings. Once Dad realized that I was awake on Sunday morning, he would come in and ask who we were picking up to go to Sunday school with us. He was adamant about filling up that car.

For relaxation, Mom and Dad ventured to health spas in the area. Although generally Mom liked to go to the movies, Dad didn't, but he agreed to go because it gave him a chance to hear English. And he probably felt a little guilty that his wife wasn't allowed to have many friends, do any socializing, or lead a normal life due to his career. Of course, anytime he was in a theater, he would go check behind the curtains to see where the doors were and who was around. He was always watching.

Now that I know the truth, I understand why Dad, while a casual sports fan, showed little or no interest in my athletic activities while we were in Switzerland. I played five sports in high school, and he only attended the first half of one ice hockey game . . . and then left. I used to think he'd just lost interest—I was the fourth child, after all. But when we were building the fence, I found out otherwise. Dad would have had to obtain approval from his superiors for anything like that. And most likely, the superiors wouldn't have granted it anyway.

Mom could never understand the reason for the social restrictions. She thought perhaps it was just a phase Dad was going through. The entire two years we lived in Switzerland, not a single adult was ever over to socialize. But sometimes Dad would venture out on his own.

* * *

While in Zurich, Dad loved going into town to the main cathedral, where Huldrych Zwingli had lived five centuries before. Zwingli, Martin Luther, and John Calvin are the three big names from the Reformation in central Europe. One day Dad walked in five minutes before five. They were closing the church down, but my dad didn't want to leave. The rector said, "Well, I see you seem to enjoy learning. Would you like to see Zwingli's private room?"

My dad replied, "Oh, yes!"

The rector locked the cathedral doors and led Dad to the belfry tower, at least twelve stories up. At the top, they found that the door was locked. The rector said, "I guess we haven't opened this in decades. Let me see if I can find the key."

He left Dad there, went down into the crypts below the church, and came back up with an iron key ring; each key probably weighed ten pounds. The two of them held the ring, trying the keys in the door, and finally found one that worked.

It was just sunset as they walked into the tiny room where Zwingli himself had slept, and the rector opened up the two window shutters. In streamed the sun-setting light, Dad could see there was one short table, a small bed, and two little chairs on opposite sides. Up near the ceiling was a carved wooden plate sitting on the ledge; that was the very first Communion plate that had ever been used after Zwingli inaugurated Communion.

The rector sat down with his back to the sunlight streaming in, and my dad sat opposite him. The rector looked my dad in the eyes and said, "You really enjoy this stuff, don't you?"

My dad, lost in the history of the room and the surreal setting, said, "Yes."

"Well, would you like to meet Zwingli?"

My dad didn't know what to say to that—Zwingli had died five hundred years before.

The rector followed with, "You can if you want to," and then proceeded to evangelize my Dad, telling him how to be saved, unaware that my dad was already a Christian. But Dad never corrected him. The rector likely hadn't had a chance to share that room for quite a while to somebody who was actually interested. And Dad certainly was, and had been, since his miracle second chance at life as a kid in a cornfield.

Actually, in the 1940s, thirty years before meeting Zwingli in a tiny belfry, Dad had had another life-changing experience in Chicago. In Dad's Bible, nearly every single sentence is underlined ten times. He knew Romans very well, because he had heard it taught at Moody Church in Chicago by Henry Ironside, probably the most famous Bible teacher in the country at that time.

The '40s were a pivotal time for Dad for solidifying his faith because he was rubbing shoulders with famous people, such as Einstein and others, who had a different view of faith and science. Dad had to make a decision: *Do I trust the Bible or do I believe in nothing but science?* He chose the former, and it was reflected in his attitude toward his own superintelligence and skill. Dad understood that there was no place for boasting because everything he had was a gift from God. And he'd remain humble until the day he died, always choosing to defer any praise given.

Thankfully, in at least a few instances, a paper trail proves Dad's accomplishments.

34

Secret Meetings and Broken Promises

DURING OUR YEARS IN SWITZERLAND, Dad spent at least 40 percent of his time in Iran, and we often didn't know when he'd be gone or when he'd be back. I'll always remember Dad's phone call on a Friday afternoon to say he not only wasn't coming home for the weekend, but that he wouldn't be home for six days due to a "huge sandstorm in Saudi Arabia." I remember wondering how he could possibly know the exact duration of a windstorm, but I never considered checking up on his claims. Dad knew we'd believe him because we always believed him. He always came back home at some point, so we had no reason to doubt him.

Working so closely with the Iranian military, Dad became acquainted with the shah, as well as with many of his officers. Dad was invited to the palace, where he met the Pahlavi family. The shah gave him a gold Swiss clock made by Turler, as well as a gigantic silver bowl and a plate. Engraved on the clock are the words "IBM Switzerland to W. W. Clauson for outstanding contribution to the BBC-IRAN Project." The "project" referred to was a nuclear program. Like the Manhattan Project.

Because Dad was the shah's right-hand man for missiles, in 1971 the shah invited Dad to a huge celebration planned to mark twenty-five hundred years of Persian history and to highlight Iran's new status as a nuclear power on the world stage. That's the only reason Dad would have been invited to that big, fancy party in the desert. Not all world leaders were invited, so my dad had to have some sort of unique quality, and it wasn't a knack for wine drinking or partying.

Guests from all over the planet, from Haile Selassie to Marshall Tito to Princess Grace and Spiro Agnew, flew in to Tehran, crowding the 160-acre tent city set up for the event, complete with Baccarat crystal, Limoges china, Persian carpets, and bidets. The 165 chefs the shah brought in from Paris cooked with 7,700 pounds of meat; 8,000 pounds of butter and cheese, and 1,000 pints of cream. French hairdressers were also available; 300 wigs and 240 pounds of hairpins were shipped in for the affair. At a time when the per capita income in Iran was $350 a year, the shah's weeklong "Disneyland-in-the-desert," as it was called, cost $250 million. It was labeled "the most expensive party" the world has ever thrown. That fact held true at least as far as 2012.

Dad didn't really see anything wrong with it, if that's what the shah wanted to do, although personally he thought it was something of a waste of money.

* * *

Dad's nervous condition, resulting from his childhood injury, grew worse while in Zurich. The worrying he had been doing for years intensified even further because we were in a foreign country and he was working on a project with such high stakes. The possibility of a kidnapping was never far from his mind.

Once, on a Saturday night, when I accompanied a bunch of friends into the mountains for a party above Wädenswil, we apparently lost my detail on the switchbacks, leaving Dad, back at home, extremely anxious. A couple of older guys were handing out pills, and I felt uncomfortable, so I called home and asked Dad to come fetch me. I was surprised at how happy he was to hear from me, even before I told him the reason for the call. He hopped in his car and quickly came out to get me, waking up his detail to follow him.

I told them I would meet them at a flat landing underneath a train trestle in that town. I grabbed my good friend Kenny, who had been drinking pretty heavily. I had to get him dressed because he was in the back room with a gal. I said, "Kenny, we're getting out of here." We stumbled down to the clearing by the trestle, and there was my dad's car. My mom came too. Completely unbeknownst to me, another car was there that was security detail, and they were fully prepared with weapons. Since I mentioned the guys at the party were handing out pills, perhaps Dad was worried I'd be poisoned and kidnapped.

Halfway home, Kenny had to throw up, so I said, "Dad, stop the car—Kenny's gonna blow!" He threw up on the side of the road, while my mom and dad just sat in the car, quietly. I took my shirt off and wrapped it around Kenny. Now I didn't have a shirt on, but at least I wasn't drunk.

Back home, I led Kenny to the spare bedroom so he could sleep it off. Then I went to my room, and to bed.

On Sunday, like clockwork, my dad got me up for church. Mom had already washed Kenny's shirt and stitched it up where he'd torn it while coming down the switchbacks to the landing area. When Kenny stumbled down the stairs with an incredible hangover, my mom smiled and said, "Oh, Kenny, I've got your shirt here for ya! It's all clean and I've fixed it." Then she and Dad asked him if he'd like to go to church with us. He was in no shape to do anything. He just wanted to get to the train station and go home, so my parents offered to drop him off at home.

While walking out to the car, Kenny asked, "You've got the strangest parents. My mom would be yelling at me, and here your mom has already washed, pressed, and stitched my shirt. Is she a saint?"

As for the party and my late-night distress call, Mom and Dad never said a word about it.

But when my dad did speak, you listened. So, years before, when he'd told me, "If you are uncomfortable in any situation, call me," I knew he meant it—and he knew when I called that *I* meant it.

When Dad wasn't worried about kidnapping, he worried that his calculations might be off, that the missiles wouldn't launch correctly if ever activated, or that they'd launch at the wrong time, causing a nuclear catastrophe. Of course, there was the political situation too. The Egyptians were fast at work building up their missiles and weaponry, as was Israel. Dad wondered if the world was now so firmly on the path toward Armageddon that there was no chance of stopping it.

And there was always the secrecy element, for added pressure, constant scenarios playing through Dad's mind about what would happen if the Soviets learned that nuclear missiles were going into Iran. Once, he took me with him to Dachau, the concentration camp outside of Munich, where I had to spend a full day and a half pacing while he was in secret meetings between the Israelis, the Iranians, and the United States concerning how they were going to defend Israel. Later that night, I had to do homework, but I kept crying because I had seen horrible things in the glass cases at the Dachau Museum. That was not at all how I wanted to spend time with my dad, but maybe it was easier that day to take me with him.

Dad had to be on constant alert. And as an American, teenaged boy in a new country, I was doing my part to keep him on his toes.

* * *

In spring 1972, I climbed the second-highest peak in Switzerland, the Dom, on an overnight hike—in jeans. I'd never done anything so dangerous in my life, and I had no idea what I was getting myself into. I was told it was an overnight trip and we needed crampons, but I thought we were going to be walking on snow.

My math teacher and tutor hiked frequently on the weekends, and since he knew I liked hiking and could handle the trek (I was in world-class shape back then), he invited me to come along with five of his friends.

We first hiked to a stone hut where you could look down at the Matterhorn. Sometime during the night, someone shoved a heavy rope in my backpack, but I didn't notice it. I was curious as to why my bag felt so much heavier on the final ascent.

We had to get up at 3 a.m. to continue the hike up the glacier, with crampons on our shoes for traction. When we got to the top, it was picture-perfect, so I snapped a photo with my camera; we were about one hundred meters higher than the Matterhorn peak. The leader opened my backpack to get the rope out, and we tied ourselves together for the descent. Then he said, "Whatever you do, nobody fall." One misstep could have pulled the whole group off the mountain. It was so overwhelming that I couldn't afford to get scared! Nearing the peak where we ascended, there were seven crosses of people who had died on our exact route.

Another time I was hitchhiking home at 4:00 a.m., after spending time away. About two or three miles from the house, the driver grabbed my knee as if he wanted me to have a relationship with him. "If you don't stop this car, I will beat you up!" I said.

He stopped the car.

Unfortunately, I had my luggage in his little VW Bug, and now I wondered how I was going to carry it the rest of the way home.

As it turned out, I threw the luggage in a bush a couple of miles from the house, thinking no one would find it. When I got home I took a nap.

Upon waking, Dad said to me, "Johnny, I understand you had an interesting night last night." He had kind of a quirky smile on his face. I am absolutely positive that the detail saw that I had gotten out and was quite upset and had to stash my luggage (which I picked up later).

One day, while riding my moped back to our house, I was forced to navigate past a stretch Mercedes 600 parked in our driveway, curtains pulled across the windows. Inside, the occupants were discussing NATO strategy, unbeknownst to me. When I went to the kitchen for my usual after-school chocolate candy bar, Mom told me Dad was meeting in the car with someone named Cyrus. We both laughed at the name Cyrus. It sounded funny. But I also remember wondering why they were meeting in the car when we had a perfectly nice living room—perfect because no one ever used it.

That evening, Cyrus—who, incidentally, was a director at IBM, was involved with missile planning and deployment, and had been deputy director of defense—was taking my parents out for a formal dinner. I didn't go because I wasn't invited. I wasn't even introduced to our guest, and that fueled my teenage angst a little. I remembered looking out the side window of our kitchen and seeing the curtains pulled in the limo. I said to Mom, "Dad is with a man named *Cyrus*. Dad's not a homo, is he?"

Mom immediately responded, "I can assure you he is not. And never use the term *homo*, but homosexual, because they are humans too."

When I left to go to Zurich on my moped a half hour later, I had to pass the parked Cortina, and the big Mercedes. And as I passed the limo, I pounded on the roof. "Thanks for the introduction, Dad!" I shouted as I drove off.

Now I know that Dad's meeting with Cyrus Vance was held in the limousine because it was more secure than the house, which could have been bugged.

Later that night, after they'd returned from dinner and I'd cooled down, Mom filled me in on their evening. Mom had felt obligated to sample the expensive bottle of wine Cyrus purchased, although she disliked alcohol as much as Dad did; she thought it tasted horrible.

Noticing the brief look of disgust on Mom's face, I tried not to break a smile. I personally didn't mind the taste of alcohol, but I kept that fact away from my father. After all, I knew how much he hated being around it. I'd heard a few stories by then about Grandpa Eldon's drinking, and one instance in particular popped into my mind.

As a small boy of maybe eight or nine, I was with Grandpa Eldon and my dad, visiting the Gustafsons' farm, where Aunt Mae, Grandpa's sister, lived. Grandpa was responsible for oiling the cow blankets. This is done by placing a pole between two trees, where it can spin, then draping a heavy blanket over the pole and slathering it in oil. The cows walk under it and get the oil on their hides, hopefully preventing flies from bothering them as much.

Aunt Mae had asked Grandpa Eldon to go oil the five blankets, and on that day, he let me drive his Plymouth, which had push buttons to activate the transmission. I couldn't see over the steering wheel, and I recall my grandfather's face was beet red—he was laughing so hard at me. I thought it was fun too! It was great hearing him laugh that way, and I was hitting every pothole on the farm, having the time of my life. I didn't realize the real culprit behind his jubilance until minutes later.

Somehow I actually drove the sedan to the correct spot and stopped it. As I stepped out of the sedan, I saw my dad. He was furious, but not at me. Grandpa Eldon was drunk.

Dad barely made eye contact with me and said, "Johnny, go inside." Then he grabbed his father by the arm and shoved him into the barn. At some point, they'd made a pact that Grandpa would never drink around me or my siblings—and he had just violated it big-time. Dad forced Grandpa to go lie down in a bedroom and sleep it off. I was halfway across the yard when my dad was closing the barn door, and I heard him say, "You promised me you would never—" With my next step, I was just out of reach to hear the rest of the broken pact.

Years later, my own drinking could have cost my dad his career.

* * *

In spring of 1972, my senior year in high school, my parents left town on a Saturday night and left me home alone. What do you do when you're home alone? I had a party at the house and invited friends, and I bought thirty-some beers for thirteen of us. A lot of my friends smoked, and while I never let them smoke in the house, the air from outside would breeze in through the door when they came back inside, just enough to leave the faint smell of cigarettes in the house. After everyone left, I frantically tried to air out the house with air fresheners, even fanning the air with my record albums, hoping to disperse the telltale sign that I'd had friends over.

On Sunday I went and returned the beer bottles to get the deposit back.

When Dad came home on Sunday he said, "Johnny, sit down in the living room."

I did as I was told, knowing from his stern tone that something was up and I was about to be in trouble.

He opened a manila folder said, "You had thirteen people over here last night." Then he started reading the arrival and departure time of each person.

"First person arrives at 11:15, leaves at 1:20." And on and on, covering each person. Now, I was thinking our Swiss neighbor had been nosy and snitched on me. Then he pulled out a picture of the beer bottles stacked outside on the front porch.

How in the world did he get that? Gosh, those neighbors sure have been monitoring me. I'm sure I looked as shocked as I felt.

Then he said, "Johnny, I'm telling you, you will never, ever have alcohol on this property again. Do you hear me?" Turns out, he wasn't yelling at me for having a party; it was for bringing alcohol onto the property, because with tensions high during the Cold War, that picture could have been used against him, if given to the right person in a high-level government position.

You can imagine the scenario: "So, what is your top nuke guy doing with thirty bottles of beer on his porch?" During the fence-building project, Dad told me he was more worried about someone, maybe even the Russians, somehow using that picture to blackmail him. Remember: Dad's group was on call 24/7/365. If you got caught with one drink, you were gone. My ignorant teenage actions could have gotten my dad fired.

* * *

Dad's general high anxiety was sometimes relieved by a game of Solitaire—or by watching football. On Monday, autumn evenings, we'd head to the Carlton Elite Hotel in downtown Zurich to attend screenings of NFL highlights. Of course, Dad would always refuse to stay for the appetizers afterwards. Every week he'd have a different excuse why. We'd always leave discreetly out the back exit.

I believe my high school friends were also something of a distraction for Dad. Once, when one of my two best friends told a joke in our living room, Dad went into a barrel laugh he couldn't stop and slipped off his chair. The joke was funny, but not *that* funny, Dad clearly using it to release built-up tension. I remember Mom coming downstairs wondering what was going on.

Of course, Dad's big relief of the week was Sundays. Man, did my dad love Sunday. It was as if it were his birthday, Christmas, and an anniversary all rolled into one, and he would always wear a suit on Sunday, all day long. When I was growing up, Dad often quoted a Bible verse in saying that "Sunday is the 'day that the LORD has made; we will rejoice and be glad in it" (Psalm 118:24 MEV).

One Saturday night, while we were sitting on the couch after the earthquake, Dad said he always figured that Armageddon wasn't going to happen on Sunday because God would never allow it.

I challenged him, saying, "Dad, it could be Sunday in Tokyo, and it could be Monday where you are. You can't be everywhere in the world."

He quickly responded, "I always felt I would be living in the dangerous areas of the world."

But on Sunday mornings, no matter where we lived, he always asked which of my friends we could pick up to accompany us to church. Afterward, we would go to some remote place for a very nice afternoon meal. In the Midwest on Sundays, the midday meal is the big meal of the day.

While in Switzerland, we drove all over the Zurich area to eat at big chalets and restaurants. Obviously, Dad had scoped these things out ahead of time. We would be gone until usually three or four in the afternoon. Then he would come back and sit in the living room in his Sunday best, with his tie still on, until eight, nine, even ten o'clock at night, playing hymns and not wanting Sunday to end. At about ten, he would call it a night and go to bed, already looking forward to the next Sunday, when the world was safe again. He could relax on Sunday. The other six nights he was nervous.

During the rest of the week, Dad ended his days by pulling out a deck of cards and playing gin rummy or solitaire by himself at the living room table. On rare occasions he would watch TV, including once when the Beatles were on *The Ed Sullivan Show*. He also liked to watch the Oakland Raiders play football. And once, in England, I remember him watching *The Benny Hill Show*.

But these breaks from his overwhelming anxiety were never enough. Usually, he'd work into the night and then go to bed for a serious bout of sleeplessness, falling into a vicious cycle of worry and fitful sleep. He finally turned to Librium, the precursor to Valium, which seemed to make things better for him. And when things were better for him, they were better for the rest of us—at least somewhat.

35

The Invalid Valedictorian

I WAS IN ZURICH FOR TWO YEARS, and I wasn't even a legal resident. The school was tied in with the government, which made it easier for our family, at least on paper.

Years later, when we were going over details of Zurich and my passport lacking a stamp for Switzerland, I asked my dad, "How can it possibly be that I didn't enter the country? I went to high school there and I have a diploma."

He said, "Johnny, we can make anything disappear when we want it to."

* * *

In my last semester of my senior year, the school allowed the senior students to pick who was going to be valedictorian. Now, normally this is reserved for the person with the best grades. A lot of my fellow classmates were very hyped up to go to Cambridge or Oxford. Academia was their whole existence and their source of status, and I was about the opposite. I was popular, sure, but I had a C or C– average. Yet, instead of choosing someone more deserving—the class voted for me. They thought that was hilarious. *Let's watch this knucklehead get in front of the group and try to give a speech.*

My father blew a head gasket when he heard I had been chosen for valedictorian. Remember: my mom was valedictorian for her class, and both my parents held that position in high respect. My brother was valedictorian of his large, five-hundred-student senior class. Then to have me chosen? What a joke!

Dad didn't like the fact that they had downplayed or joked about the position, so he told my mom to call the school up to complain. Before Mom could actually make the phone call, a parent of a fellow student called my mom and let her know that she had complained to the school that I had been elected. Mom said, "Thank you, because I was getting ready to call them too!"

Because I knew it was kind of a joke, I wasn't bothered when the title was stripped from me. I thought, *Thank God I don't have to prepare for that!* I wouldn't have a clue what to say.

I graduated from high school in Zurich in 1972. It's easy to remember the date, June 17, because it was also the day of the break-in at the Watergate Hotel in Washington. I remember hearing that on Armed Forces Radio. I also remember the date because hours later, my dad walked out on my graduation ceremony.

I remember Dad sitting by himself in the very back of the pews. With all the students and their families, there were probably 250 people in the small sanctuary. He was still there in his seat when I was named Athlete of the Year—but not, as I related in an earlier chapter—when I attempted to introduce him.

He was gone.

Following the ceremony, I searched for him everywhere, finally locating him in a shed behind the church, where my friends would often smoke. He was picking up cigarette butts with a wired contraption he'd made with a stick. "Can't your friends learn how to throw these away?" he asked.

I began to let into him about never wanting to meet my friends, two years of built-up frustration finally bursting loose.

He interrupted me, not wanting to hear it. "John, you can't be introducing me to people I don't know!" he said firmly. I remember my confusion, but Dad didn't elaborate . . . at least not then.

Soon after my graduation in June 1972, we moved back to the States, Mom and Dad to our home in San Jose, and me to Seattle, where I followed in my sisters' footsteps at Seattle Pacific College.

On orientation day, the speaker was giving an award to the parents with the most children in attendance at the school, and Dad had three—me, Nedra, and Dawn. When they said, "Who are the parents here with three?" I stood up and said, "This guy right here—my dad." My dad gave me a look that could have melted frozen butter but walking out on me at my high school award ceremony had deeply hurt me, so I wasn't going to let him get away with it again.

My older sister Dawn and her husband, Dave, were married in 1971 at the same Baptist church in Kiron as had our parents, and we'd all flown back to the States for the event. Dave was an engineer and mathematician, like Dad, and at twenty-one, when he married my sister, he was somewhat intimidating to me. Yet, it always seemed to Dave, just as it did to all of us, that no matter how much he knew about any particular subject, Dad always knew more. It wasn't an ego thing with Dad; it was just the way it was. He seemed to know everything about everything.

Dave's presence did present a particular problem for Dad, however. Because Dave spoke his language—mathematics and engineering—it was more difficult for Dad to get away with his secretiveness. In an attempt to bond with his father-in-law, Dave would frequently probe Dad about his work. Dad would be challenged to come up with an answer that made some kind of sense, but of course wasn't true. He repeatedly told Dave that as a market researcher for IBM, his goal was to find practical applications for new technologies. But anytime Dave asked him to elaborate, the answers would always be vague.

Despite the fact that he was back in California, Iran was on Dad's mind. He was fearful that the military build-up in the Middle East might explode.

36

The Yom Kippur War

IN MANY REGARDS, THE SIX-DAY WAR never really ended until the Yom Kippur War in 1973 (October 6–25). The Yom Kippur War—another not-so-simple-to-cover conflict involving the melding of Arab-Israeli politics in the Cold War backdrop—was fought between Israel against Egypt and Syria. And just like the Six-Day War, there was a ton of meddling from both the Soviets and Americans in this conflict.

The outcome of the Six-Day War had left many of the Arab nation defenders in a precarious position. Demoralized by both the military and the territory losses, Arab nations took a hard line against any peaceful overtures by the Israelis. Negotiations were stymied by both sides wishing to impose preconditions to any negotiations.

For example, in 1970 the Egyptians wouldn't come to the negotiating table without the Israelis withdrawing from the Sinai. The matter of the Sinai was of utmost importance strategically and economically to the Egyptians. With the closure of the Suez Canal after the Six-Day

War, the Egyptian government had lost a huge revenue stream for fees charged to ships passing through the canal, and ancillary industries that supported canal shipping.[1] With their national pride wounded and facing stark new economic realities, the Egyptians considered a military expedition to take back the Sinai and reopen the Suez Canal, an attractive option.[2]

In the spring of 1973, the Egyptians partnered with the Syrians in a plan to invade Israeli holdings. The Israelis caught wind of a potential invasion, but their intelligence estimates indicated that the likelihood of an offensive was low. To further muddy the waters from an Israeli intelligence standpoint, on July 18, 1973, following Russia's refusal to increase aid to Egypt, the Egyptians expelled all Soviet military advisors out to the country—twenty thousand of them. After all, you can't attack Israel with twenty thousand Russians in your backyard. That would look like Russia was invading Israel.

Anwar Sadat threw them out because he wanted to have a better relationship with the United States. He hoped that once that war was finished, Egypt could negotiate with the United States. Once they attacked Israel and tried to redraw the line, it would be easier to negotiate with Israel with the United States being a negotiator versus Russia. But the Egyptian government was playing a double bluff with the move.

First, the move confounded Mossad (the Israeli equivalent of the CIA) into believing Egypt would never pull off an invasion without Soviet support.[3] Second, Egypt was playing hardball with the Soviets to obtain weapon systems. Expulsion of Soviet advisors was the first part of a double-dog dare to the Soviets, warning that if they did not sell Egypt key weapons systems, the Egyptian government would become pro-American.[4] The move did not work, and the Soviets did not supply the Egyptians with any advanced weapons systems.

To further stymie Israeli intelligence, the Egyptians went ahead with the plans for the offensive and staged a weeklong training exercise on their side of the Suez Canal at the end of September 1973.[5] The Syrians also began deploying troops toward their border with Israel during the same time frame.[6]

Israeli intelligence did not interpret these actions as a threat to their national security until the day before the beginning of the offensive, on October 6, 1973.[7] Immense pressure from the United States kept Israel in a defensive posture for the Egyptian–Syrian assault. The United States had hoped back-channel negotiations with the Soviets would stay the hand of the Egyptian–Syrian coalition, and should the offensive occur, Israel would appear to be the victim of Arab aggression.

Secretary of State Henry Kissinger went as far as to say that should Israel conduct preemptive strikes; they would not receive "so much as a nail"[8] in support from the United States. Israel's military had always taken the stance that preemptive assaults were the best way to halt military incursions into Israeli territory. With the offensive option off the table, the best the Israelis could do was wait for the balloon to go up.[9]

On October 6 of that year, war began when Egypt and Syria advanced across the Suez Canal and attacked Israel on the Jewish holiday of Yom Kippur,[10] or Day of Atonement. This day harks back to biblical times, when the high priest would sacrifice animals at the tabernacle to wash away the sins of Israel for the previous year. Today, Jews observe Yom Kippur with fasting, prayer services, ritual baths, and other rituals, depending on the flavor of Judaism one observes. It signals the end of the High Holy Days, which begin with the Jewish New Year celebration of Rosh Hashanah.[11]

Needless to say, the Egyptians' attack on this day was both strategic and politically motivated. Imagine launching an offensive on a Christian country on a holiday that was the equivalent of Christmas and Easter combined. That's how important Yom Kippur is to the Jews. Strategically, it was like Washington crossing the Delaware on Christmas night for a surprise attack on Hessian troops.

Israel incurred huge losses in the first few days of the war, with more than 2,000 dead, 340 captured, 49 planes downed, and 500 tanks destroyed. Anwar Sadat, the third president of Egypt, was being very vocal about needing emergency supplies, blood supplies, and medical attention for his troops.

Over the objections of Secretary of Defense Arthur Schlesinger, as well as of Secretary of State Henry Kissinger, who feared an Arab oil embargo and possible Soviet intervention, President Richard Nixon approved massive airlifts to the Israelis of up to two hundred tons per day of supplies. Nixon eventually asked Congress to authorize $2.2 billion of emergency aid for Israel.

On October 13, the United Nations passed a resolution for a cease-fire based on an earlier UN resolution, UN 232. Just two days later, Israel turned a blind eye, crossing the Suez to attack Egypt. Although Israel lost a good chunk of their air force, they figured out how to go around the SAMs and attack from a different angle.

The Soviets, very much in support of the October 13 cease-fire plan, developed a second plan, but this was again ignored by Israel. War hero Ariel Sharon was in the midst of attempting to trap the Egyptian Third Corps of thirty-five thousand soldiers on the East Bank, isolating Suez City. Kissinger was sent to the Middle East to attempt to negotiate a peace settlement, yet war raged on.

Skipping all of the battlefield actions that happened during the main portion of the conflict, a cease-fire was brokered by the Americans and Soviets, ratified by a United Nations Security Council Resolution, on October 22, 1973.[12] By that date, the Israelis had crossed far to the west of the Suez Canal and were making strides in taking Port Said, the point where the Suez Canal meets the Mediterranean Sea.

On October 24, furious with Israel's continued aggression, President Brezhnev wrote a poignant letter to Nixon, demanding that the cease-fire be enforced with Russian and American intervention. If the United States refused, Brezhnev said, the Soviets would go it alone.

There was a whole sequence of communications over a three-day period between Brezhnev and Nixon and Kissinger that sounded as if we were going tit for tat.

First, the Egyptian side was ready to do a cease-fire.

Then Russia claimed that Israel was in complete violation. Brezhnev had information that the Israelis were out of control. They were not abiding to the treaty.

Nixon said, "No, it's not the Israelis who are in violation; the Egyptians are."

Israel had flagrantly violated the cease-fire.

With each pass, things got a little more intense, neither country wanting to back down.

Then Russia went on military alert, resupplying Egypt with Scud missiles and bringing in nuclear warheads as well.

We made it clear that any unilateral invasion by the Soviets was wholly unacceptable. But in response, as a precaution, we had undertaken alert measures. President Nixon raised the nuclear alert level to DEFCON 3 (two levels below nuclear war), and Kissinger sent a memo advising NATO countries to do the same. We could be going to war. We told our allies and NATO—and Europe, even—to spike it up.

Kissinger's memo noted that this specific report was so classified and top secret that if it got into the wrong hands, it could be perceived that we wanted to have a confrontation with our enemy. Nixon didn't want to go to war against Russia, but if the memo got out, it could have been interpreted as such. Unfortunately, due to a mole at a high level in our government, probably out of West Germany, Russia quickly heard about the memo anyway.

But before Kissinger's ink had dried, Dad said, "A memo from the highest levels of the government sent me back to Iran." Dad was briefed on the memo that was about to be sent out to NATO command to heighten their nuclear alert. Then he was given an urgent summons to return to the missile silos in Iran to ensure that proper system controls were in place to meet this new threat, because Russia said they were going to attack Israel. Iran, at that time, was the largest purchaser of defense mechanisms from the United States, with nineteen nuclear reactors slated to be built.

Dad ran home to pack. Realizing he'd inadvertently allowed his passport to expire, he made a call and requested that a new one be waiting for him at the airport the next morning. During this time, Brezhnev sends a warning to Nixon that if Israel's aggression doesn't switch to a ceasefire in the *next few hours*, they were going to attack!

The United States was on pins and needles for a while. Finally, Israel backed off and abided by the cease-fire. That's when Brezhnev wrote another memo to Nixon, basically saying, *By the way, you know that memo you sent out, going up to military alert readiness? We knew about that within twenty-four hours.*

To add fuel to the flame, there was a peace conference we'd agreed to attend a month before with Russia. We were acting as though we wanted to work toward peace, so Brezhnev brought up the conference discussion he'd previously had with the United States, asking, *Why would you go up on military readiness?*

Nixon just about dropped his jaw on the floor. He wrote back to Brezhnev and said that the United States took Russia's threat very seriously when they said they were going to go in to Israel alone, so the United States did what we had to do. I thought Nixon handled that very diplomatically.

Dad left for Iran the next morning, on October 25, 1973, and had to fly commercially to Iran though he'd let his passport expire. He called one of his handlers and said, "You've got to have a new passport for me, and I'll be landing in five hours," so his team had to make a drop at JFK with an updated passport.

He was nervous because up to that point, for a period of years, he was flying around in secret military planes and hadn't needed his passport when he'd left the country. He never wanted to be checked in to flights because that would have obviously been a record of his location. He was like a vanishing entity.

But as planned, his team was able to make a drop for him in a restroom at the JFK airport. To do that, Dad told me, you take a newspaper, like they do in the movies—a guy or a gal walks up with a newspaper and what's in it slides out and goes into your newspaper. *They really do that.*

Dad would stay in Iran for over a month, waiting for an attack. I can't even imagine the pressure.

While the Soviet alert ended on October 26 with a new UN resolution to create a buffer zone force composed of forces from nonnuclear countries, tensions remained high, so Dad stayed on in Iran for several more weeks. It was as if he were babysitting his missiles, and all of their controls, switches, and computers. He was constantly on edge, wondering if the Soviets would invade and staring at all the process controls, praying it would all work in the event of a launch.

Sporadic battles kept cropping up until October 28. Field commanders on both sides were distrustful of each other keeping the terms of the cease-fire, and acted on tactical levels as threats were perceived. At the end of the conflict, Israeli forces had pushed within sixty-five miles of Cairo and likely could have taken the city had peace not broken out.[13]

The end result of the conflict, from a land-grab standpoint, was a wash. Both sides went back to post–Six-Day War territorial borders.[14]

From a political standpoint, Israel had shown the Arab world that screwing with God's chosen people is not a good idea.

* * *

My dad came back to the States from the silos several weeks later, in early December. When you go up on military readiness, you don't just turn the switch down and then go have coffee and tea. You go up, it is incredibly intense, and you slowly come down.

Soon after that, during the December 1973 holiday break in my sophomore year at Seattle Pacific, I brought Celeste, then my girlfriend, to visit my parents in California. We'd met in my second quarter of my first year at school at an off-campus party on January 10, 1973, and I was fascinated and intrigued—as I still am—with her. Back then, my long blond hair was cropped on top, like Rod Stewart's, and I'd been wearing wooden shoes ever since I lived in Europe. Apparently, she was intrigued by me as well.

I hadn't seen Dad in several months at that point, and he seemed distracted, to say the least. After all, he had been in the Iranian missile silos—an underground command control center—for probably six weeks. I remember my dad was just jittery, climbing the walls, and more agitated than I'd ever seen him. After being involved in a potential missile crisis, the last thing he wanted to see was me with my goofy haircut and lace shirt.

He was sitting in the living room with my mother when I walked in and said, "Hey, Mom, I'd like to introduce you to my girlfriend, Celeste."

Mom hugged Celeste, said hello, and then walked into the kitchen. Then I introduced Celeste to my dad.

My dad wasn't rude, but he sure wasn't friendly or engaging either. He said, "Hi. How are you doing?" but it was clear he wasn't asking to become engaged in a conversation. Then he took a look at me in my hip outfit with my long blond hair. His expression was a look of absolute puzzlement.

Confused about his behavior, I walked into the kitchen, where my mom was making dinner. Celeste followed me, not wanting to feel more uncomfortable by being left alone with my agitated father. I said, "Mom, what's wrong with Dad?"

She said, "Oh, I wondered the same thing. He tells me he doesn't like his new boss."

"You mean Dad's got a boss?" I asked.

He'd never mentioned any of his coworkers before, or a company hierarchy, and he certainly never mentioned having a boss. But I bought it.

37

The World's Greatest Hot Plate

WE HAD JUST FINISHED UP the fence that evening, and it was perfect: level, expertly constructed, a thing of beauty. It was a visible reminder of a project completed with Dad. By the time nine thirty rolled around, I began to feel my exhaustion from the heavy labor over the last two days. I went to bed, marveling at the fact that Dad had gone back out to the yard to inspect our work yet again.

"I've never seen your dad so talkative," Celeste said, looking up from the crossword puzzle she was completing as I climbed into bed. I nodded. "What's he been talking about?" she asked.

I told her that he'd been discussing his career, but I offered no further details.

She turned back to her crossword puzzle. "What's a seven-letter word for 'philanderer'?" she asked.

"H-U-S-B-A-N-D," I answered.

"Funny," she replied, not bothering to look up.

It wasn't that I wanted to keep Celeste in the dark; it was just that I hadn't come even close to dealing with two very big issues. First, I hadn't quite wrapped my brain around the fact that Dad was soon to die. And second, it was entirely out of character for him to be telling me a story like this—to be telling me anything at all, in fact. I was having trouble believing it could even be true.

I already felt like a fish out of water back in New Jersey, with a new house, a new job, and limited friends and family in the area. Now I'd discovered I didn't even know my own father. I didn't know if I even knew myself anymore. I was very on edge, and the feeling would stay with me in the months that followed.

* * *

During the late 1970s and early 1980s, Dad worked at the IBM facility in San Jose, participating in a wide range of projects, including the space shuttle. In fact, IBM computers played a key role in each shuttle mission, from lift-off to landing, and IBM's Federal Systems Division developed the initial shuttle orbiter avionics data processing system. I remember Dad bringing home a shuttle tile. When he handed it to me, it felt like chalk. It was two by two by twelve inches, similar to the shape of a brick. I said, "What is this, Dad?"

He said, "Johnny, that's the world's greatest hot plate holder." Those space shuttle tiles are what kept the shuttle from burning up, and my dad actually had a piece of that at the house in San Jose. I'm sure that was classified . . . you don't walk around with space shuttle tiles in the early 1970s, unless you're my dad.

He had personal projects at home too, such as the 1974 Ford van he converted into something of a camper, personally customized with a wood frame chair he designed that would fold out into a bed. It had walnut wood paneling, nice thick carpets, and customized captain's chairs. He also converted the engine to run on natural gas, a rarity at the time, because he was frustrated with the long gas lines from the embargo. Even better, he could switch between gas and natural gas. He spent so much time on that van that Mom began to call herself a van widow. Dad even customized Bill's van.

Sometimes Dad would still work into the night at his walnut desk. He told Dawn's husband, Dave, as well as my brother, Bill, that he was developing "bubble technology" to enable the storage of large volumes of data, although he never described the project in any concrete way. He told Mom he was doing a follow-up on IBM customers to measure customer satisfaction, and that the report he was writing was equivalent in magnitude to a PhD thesis.

What Dad was really doing, of course, was far more than that. He was calculating the coordinates for the installation of cruise and Pershing nuclear missiles that were to be sent to England under Jimmy Carter. The Soviets had installed their SS-20 missiles in silos all over eastern Europe in 1979 and 1980, making it imperative that the new cruise and Pershings be placed in western Europe as rapidly as possible.

Harold Brown (whom I contacted and got an e-mail response from, saying he wasn't able to add anything to my story) was Carter's secretary of defense. He knew my dad was not only capable of bringing missiles to England, but was also competent enough to do the job. (First you've got to program them, and then you install the guidance on them.)

Once Reagan took office in January 1981, he was not shy about sharing his military plans publicly to move missiles to Europe. So, while my dad is in England, looking for a house for him and Mom ahead of the move, half a million people were rioting and marching because they knew the United States was going to put Pershing II IRBMs (intermediate-range ballistic missiles) in West Germany. These missiles were capable of destroying Soviet hard targets, and their flight time from Germany to targets in Russia was only four to six minutes.[1] That meant the Soviets could be attacked at any time, and would have to consider being proactive and striking our U.S. missile sites first, if threatened.

Meanwhile the United States also placed cruise missiles in England, and the public knew about that too, because of Reagan's admission. Russia had already brought in mobile SS-20 (surface-to-surface) Pioneer nuclear missiles all along the Eastern Bloc countries. They're very hard to spot because they're mobile, they launch from a mobile firing platform, and they're very accurate. Europe didn't want to be the war playground for two superpowers.

The political climate in the United States was certainly ripe for a build-up. Winning a landslide victory against Jimmy Carter in 1980 partially based on his commitment to focus on national security, Ronald Reagan assumed the presidency in January 1981 and soon turned investment in defense into a new offensive strategy. Reagan's advisors, many of whom once sat on the hawkish Committee on Present Danger, had convinced him that it was of utmost importance for the United States to be prepared to initiate nuclear war and succeed, and that any nuclear exchange could be contained before it spread into general war, and could last as long as six months.

The trillion dollars per year that were invested during Reagan's tenure, far more than the Soviets could ever match, made the Pentagon's every wish a reality. This included a new MX missile, the continued production of the formerly discontinued B-1 bomber, and new aircraft carriers, as well as a build-up of the naval fleet to six hundred ships. The spending spree also allowed for the development of the stealth bomber, the Trident II missile, and the deeply controversial Strategic Defense Initiative, or Star Wars. All of this meant my dad would be traveling more often.

38

Moving to England

CELESTE AND I GOT MARRIED at the Magnolia Presbyterian Church, followed by a reception at the Military Officer's Club in my community on November 26, 1976. Apart from avoiding the alcohol and trying to be personable, Dad spent the majority of the time trying to hack into the Muzak system to play better music through the speakers at the Officer's Club. Because it was proprietary software and output, he couldn't tap into the system. It is the only time I ever saw him get frustrated by something electronic that he couldn't figure out.

I still remember him sitting on the ground, trying to tap into that amplifier that wouldn't allow his tape recorder to be played. He had his tools out. He had opened the whole thing up. We finally resorted to a portable cassette player and we played music in the background.

* * *

In the late 1970s, Dad had also begun traveling extensively to the UK, where 160 missiles were to be located. In the fall of 1982, with the actual installation of the missiles about to take place, it was time for Dad, now sixty, to move to the UK.

He told us that he was given a position in Romsey, in southwest England near Southampton, and would need to move there to be close to the Hursley Lab, which is the primary communications hub for NATO. Hursley Lab is a gigantic estate with what looks like a British castle on it. Dad positioned this move as if it were his last hurrah: "I think they are putting me out to pasture, but there is this new technology project they want me to work on, so I need to take it." He told us they were basically forcing him to retire afterwards. But that was just an excuse.

However, as it turned out, that's exactly what would happen.

To convince Mom to go along with the program, he told her that although he wasn't looking forward to retiring, he was bored at his job in San Jose and that he'd been pushed to the back burner. He told her he desperately needed the challenge of a new job in Europe to get himself on track again. We were so agreeable as a family to whatever Dad told us.

Dad also kept a diary from that two-and-a-half-year period in England—the only diary he ever kept, to my knowledge—beginning on April 2, 1982. The majority of the entries are vague and seemingly mundane—and very brief. One full year's worth of living condensed into thirty-six pages, and scribbled in pencil. Starting with graph paper and later, lined notebook paper, each entry takes up only three or four lines, five at the most, covering such details as what he ate for breakfast, what the weather was like, where he went that day, or who he saw, generally noted by the person's initials. His first entry, on April 2 says, "In Rochester with planning meeting, then stayed in good old Midway, and sensitivity about project." *No kidding.*

Later on, in his first week there, on April 4, he wrote, "Arr. London 9:35. 1/13 hrs late to a bright day left all the bad weather behind. Arr. at Lanniston House 12:00 noon off to bed, slept 15 min. Swan nat. got me up for a car delivery, stopped by O'Kanes—had sandwich. Bed felt good at 10 PM. By the way, stopped by Baptist Church, church service over, welcome back for Easter service. Off to bed with coco and sandwich."

Later that month, he wrote, "Off to Salisbury shopping for the day. Big crowd. Home by 2 p.m." His other entries, earlier and later, are utterly prosaic accounts of the weather, his meals, travels here and there, and whether the trains were slow or the roads crowded, meetings he attended, car repairs, and so forth. Some are charmingly humorous, like his entry from April 20: "Horrible show on TV last night, more screwing scenes than I could count."

Made harder to decipher due to his chicken scratch and the many abbreviations and code words he used, any clues about what he was actually doing and why he'd have kept a brief diary for that time period are difficult to interpret. I have often wondered if the government told him to do that for some reason, but I can't figure out why that would be. There are a hundred scenarios that might be feasible. Maybe he was worried something was going to happen to him, and he wanted to leave a diary so we would have something to read. Maybe it was a way to document this kind of secret life he had to live. Maybe he had to keep a log of activities for his employer. He certainly wasn't practicing his handwriting, his small cursive script often difficult to read.

Mom was reluctant to move to England but finally relented. But before the move, to make sure Dad moved back to the States eventually, she insisted on buying a home in Seattle, where they would live when they returned from Britain. She told him on a call one night, "Wallace, if I am going to move to England, I am going to first buy a house in a suburb of Seattle to make sure that when you do retire, you will move back to where I want to live." She house-hunted in Bellevue and purchased a home there after Dad had already been in England for several weeks, Dad somewhat annoyed that he wasn't part of the process since he'd never seen the new house. He was more annoyed that there was a common easement walkway on the side of his lot, where strangers could walk by routinely. His whole life had been spent being wary of strangers, and now he lived next to a common area on the side of his lot. He would always say to my mom, "Boy, I wish I would have looked at this house before you bought it, Marilyn."

He may have also been a little annoyed at the extensive use of her favorite color, purple, in the decorating. I would say 80 to 90 percent of her wardrobe had shades of purple in it. My mom, left to her own devices, put in the most obnoxious purple carpets in that house. The builder forced my mom to pay up front for the carpets because he told her, "If for some reason you don't close on this house, there is not another person alive who would want carpets this color."

Meanwhile, Dad was living in a hotel called the Potter Herron until Mom arrived and they bought a house. When Dad lived there, the bartender and restaurant worker was a young woman who had a ton of boyfriends. She had two children who couldn't have been more than five or six, and she had never been married. When he'd go downstairs for dinner each night, he would see the kids running around, and he'd see her with a different guy all the time.

One night he approached her and said, "I would like to ask a favor."

"What men don't want favors?" she replied.

I'm quite sure she'd never had a man ask about what Dad had in mind. He wanted to pick up her sons each week and take them to Sunday school when my mom arrived.

Flustered and grateful, she said yes.

Mom didn't know when she was going to be summoned to join him, so she didn't mention the impending move when I came to visit her one day. I was at the house in San Jose for a visit two just days before the move, and Mom didn't say anything at all. The night I left, the movers came and packed up the entire place. Two days later, when I was at a Sheraton Hotel in Montana on business, I received a phone call from Dad telling me that he and Mom were now living in a rented town house in Romsey, seventy miles south of London. Needless to say, I was shocked. I was also surprised that Dad had found me to tell me about it. No one knew I was staying in this particular hotel. "Oh, I just took a guess," he said when I asked him about it. "Mom said you were going to Montana, and salesmen always stay at Sheratons." When we were building the fence, he told me it was always easy for him to know where I was because I used a credit card and he had the ability to trace authorizations.

Making good on Dad's promise, my parents would go pick up the bartender's kids on Sundays and take them to Sunday school and then go out for a nice meal. Years later we found the card the kids gave my parents when they learned they were leaving to come back to the States. It says, "We are going to miss you." One of the kids drew a face with tears streaming down. It was signed by the two boys and their mother.

I think Dad wanted that mother to see a different side of a guy than one who just wanted a sexual favor. *He* wanted to get her kids to church. You don't find too many strangers, even foreigners from another country, who would take your kids to church, but he wanted her little guys to have a chance to go.

* * *

While in the UK, Dad worked at the Hursley Lab, on a one-hundred-acre parcel of land that was once the heart of an extensive manor owned by the Cromwell family. The town of Hursley, once part of the manor, was a typical English village consisting of a high street with two pubs, a beauty shop, a post office, an auto body shop, and a small market. Behind the church graveyard and down a path through a thick grove of trees lay the IBM facility, where intelligence reports came in from the United States via satellite. But Hursley Lab isn't too keen to talk about their past.

When I was doing research and had shared Dad's time at Hursley Lab, a friend of mine was in that area and told me, "Since I'm here, I might as well spend some time in there." He said they were initially very gracious to him at Hursley, and then he started asking a lot of questions about the Cold War, specifically, whether they knew of any missile projects going on, or if they knew of a Wallace Clauson. When he didn't get any answers, he went to lunch, where he continued asking around to see if anybody knew who my father was.

After lunch he went back to the lab and was told, "If you don't get off the grounds, you'll get arrested." So, he had to leave. Obviously, some of the projects going on there were of a sensitive nature, and asking questions was not to be tolerated. They would have loved Mom.

Never one to ask questions—or at least too many, once again, Mom was in a foreign country where she knew no one. Thankfully, once she moved to England, she really did enjoy her time there. She loved to window-shop, and there were plenty of stores to keep her interest—she loved to look at grocery stores and clothing. And she did make a few close friends there while attending the church, especially the Barbers, an elderly couple who doted on Mom as if she were their own daughter.

Hursley was a warm and friendly IBM community, famous for its lavish employee Christmas gatherings, complete with Santa and personalized gifts for all the children. They also had an annual Open Day, where company employees and Hursley townspeople were invited to bring their families into the facility. There were annual Halloween parties, and a huge fireworks display on the grounds every Guy Fawkes Day, November 5. The Hursley IBM Club was a bustling hub of employee social and athletic activity, sponsoring a slew of cricket games and teams. Although Mom and Dad attended various dinners at the IBM Club, most of their social interaction, as usual, revolved around Romsey's Baptist Church.

Life at the Hursley Lab presented some minor irritations for Dad. Despite the fact that it was very much a "dry" company, and that possession of alcohol at a worksite was considered a dismissible offense, the Hursley programmers and other facility employees had a tradition of drinking their lunch at the Dolphin Inn, one of the two local pubs. On Fridays, they'd stay all afternoon, crowding up the place. Other days, they'd return to the lab, but were much more inclined to take a nap than to do any constructive work. Many would find the most comfortable position possible at their desks and sleep away the afternoon. A committed teetotaler, Dad found this practice somewhat difficult to take.

Because he never knew when he or his team might be needed

in an emergency situation, none of the employees under his direct supervision were ever allowed to drink. In relaying that story, my dad said, "You never could have been a part of my team because you were drinking in high school. I ended a lot of careers due to the nineteenth hole." That included drinking on your own time. That was a no-go. You would never know when you could be called in to work, and he had no tolerance.

Back to his routine, Dad wrote in his diary, "Comfortable bed. Good ham sandwich. Good Bible study class tonight. A car broke down. Had to buy a new tire."

Several days later: "Bad accident on the side of the road. Flowers are pretty."

The day Brezhnev died, November 10, 1982, Dad wrote, "News this morning on way to work Brezhnev has died. Now the inner power struggle is on again. At 75 he passes on into the oblivion of history." When I first read that entry in his diary, I thought, *That is very opinionated for a guy who is talking about Bible studies and that bran flakes are good, and then all of the sudden he is talking about the oblivion of the history of Brezhnev.*

But if you think about it, Brezhnev made his life hell for decades.

39

The Evil Empire

BY 1983, A YEAR AFTER DAD'S ARRIVAL IN HURSLEY, ten thousand nuclear warheads were aimed at the Soviet Union, and the Soviets were deploying SS-20s by the dozens, something that clearly disturbed NATO. Then in March of that year, Reagan introduced his administration's new term for the Soviet Union, calling it "the Evil Empire" while making his most aggressive speech of the Cold War, written and delivered with the primary goal of offending the Kremlin. The Soviet leadership was indeed very disturbed by the tone of the address, as well as by Reagan's terminology, stoking their fears of nuclear attack.

Two weeks later, on March 23, Reagan announced the Strategic Defense Initiative, Star Wars, accelerating Soviet fears, as it would leave them defenseless, with no way to strike first and no way to retaliate, giving the Soviets another reason to suspect Americans were preparing for nuclear war. The fact that this represented the creation of a technological gap between the countries that was far greater than anything else that heretofore existed, served to make things worse. So did the impending arrival of the Pershing IIs in Europe.

Dad began working around the clock to install as many missiles as possible and to again, as in Iran, ensure that all of the process controls were in place in case of engagement, and that the missiles would reach their various targets in Russia.

Reagan grew increasingly bombastic, taking on an evangelical tone that described the situation in apocalyptic terms, most likely based on his fixation with the book of Revelation. He had publicly and repeatedly put forth his view that it was possible that Armageddon was soon to occur. This not only convinced Americans that nuclear war was possible; it put the Europeans on edge as well.

The European public protested across the continent. In the UK, the Women's Peace Camp formed outside Greenham Common, a U.S. Air Force base twenty miles north of Hursley, where a great number of the cruise missiles were undergoing installation. Dad had to travel there often. And although he sympathized with the women's cause—like them, he felt that Armageddon may be imminent—he also believed that the allies had no choice in the matter, given the Soviets' actions.

Dad would try to arrive at the base as early in the morning as possible, always in a windowless armored vehicle, when the contingent of angry female protestors was at its lowest point of the day in terms of numbers. He always entered through a very private, secured entrance where the protesters weren't allowed to congregate, so he would not be seen.

At home, he continued to keep records of his seemingly average day. "Comfortable bed. Nice sandwich today. Off to fly to Miami, then Minneapolis, then back." Later on he wrote, "Bill was able to come visit us in England," and "I was able to see John's kids." Maybe it was a release for him, a small routine he could keep each day, and even though he couldn't even tell his wife what he was doing, confiding in a piece of paper made him feel a little lighter.

The Soviets felt that their worst nightmare was approaching. Ever since the tragic, casualty-laden surprise Nazi invasion of Russia in

1941 had shocked the nation, the fear of another surprise attack was embedded in the Soviet psyche. Added to this was Russia's awareness that the United States had used nuclear weapons before, destroying two Japanese cities.

But because of America's widespread ignorance of this mind-set, as well as an inability to see itself as an aggressor nation capable of an overt nuclear strike, the United States was unaware of the Soviet apprehension. They were completely clueless when it came to the determination on the part of Russian premier Yuri Andropov, a paranoid world leader who rarely appeared in public and who had never visited the West, to take every possible measure to guarantee that the Soviets would never be the victims of a surprise attack again.

The Soviets amped up their worldwide surveillance activities, Soviet agents collecting "warning signs" that could possibly signal a move toward a nuclear strike on the part of the allies. From stockpile levels of such commodities as oil and meat, to the price of blood, to the movement of diplomatic vehicles in Washington and other Western capitals, even the smallest of variations from the norm were reported back to the very paranoid and vehemently anti-American Yuri Andropov, the one-time head of the KGB in Moscow, and later General Secretary.

Andropov and other Soviet leaders knew that the United States would need an excuse to launch an attack. That excuse came on August 31, 1983, when a Korean Airlines 747 flew into Soviet airspace over the Sakhalin peninsula, heading toward a sensitive military base. At that time, it was common for spy planes on both sides to fly sensitive reconnaissance missions, venturing as far as the pilot dared to go to collect as much data as possible before making a quick retreat to international airspace.

Detecting the airliner, the Soviets sent out radio signals, but the pilots did not answer. They then sent up scramblers, but the airliner continued on its course toward the military base. When the Soviets fired warning shots, the airliner finally made a turn to international airspace. Nevertheless, the Russian commander in charge gave the order to shoot the plane down. All 296 passengers on board were killed, 50 Americans, including a U.S. Congressman, among them.

The Russians tried to deny their involvement, but in the face of tremendous world condemnation, they eventually admitted they had shot the plane down by accident. Despite the fact that the U.S. administration was aware that the incident was largely a result of a misunderstanding, Reagan's rhetoric intensified, and it allowed the National Security Council, long opposed to arms control negotiations, to recommend suspension of all dialogue on this matter.

On September 26, 1983, with the Soviets now suspecting that the United States had its excuse to launch an attack, an incident occurred that heightened Soviet anxiety even further. In an early-warning bunker south of Moscow, Officer Stanislav Petrov, monitoring a Soviet satellite taking surveillance photos over North America, was shocked when alarms began to signal that a missile aimed at the USSR from a silo in the American Midwest had just been launched. With no evidence of any malfunction, and the impossibility of examining photographic images because the Midwest was now in shadow, Petrov knew that if the missile were indeed heading toward the USSR, it would be in Soviet airspace within twenty-five minutes.

Petrov, unable to confirm that the missile had been launched, felt instinctively that the report was in error, and convinced his superiors to sign on to his opinion. He consequently overrode the automatic response attack that would have annihilated half of humankind.

But then alarm signals went off again, meaning a second missile had launched. News of the incident had by now reached Andropov, the powers that be agreeing with Petrov to override again. This was followed by the supposed launch of three more missiles, all overridden because of a lack of confirmation. It was now just two minutes and counting before the first two missiles would be entering Soviet airspace, if in fact the first report had been correct. Petrov sweated it out, and was finally proven right. It was later discovered that the satellite's sensors had been triggered by the reflection of high-altitude clouds.

Had a less cautious individual than Petrov been manning the decks that night, the result might have been very different. Two weeks later, Petrov was fired, no doubt to keep him quiet, and the incident was kept secret for years to come.

October 1983 was one of the tensest months of the Cold War. With the imminent arrival of more cruise and Pershing missiles in Europe, the nuclear disarmament campaign intensified, with protests staged around the globe. Soviet anxiety was building due to the fact that the Pershings could reach their airspace within eight minutes.

Dad was growing increasingly worried, wondering if we were truly on the brink of Armageddon. He spent extra time in church on Sundays, praying for humanity. But to my family, it simply looked as if he were in mourning.

Grandpa Albin had died two months before, on August 29, 1983, at the ripe old age of ninety-three, in Denison, Crawford County, Iowa. Mom was heartbroken, of course, as were we all. Grandpa Albin had spent the last few years in a nursing home after we finally convinced him he shouldn't live on the farm alone anymore. He'd gotten to the point where he could no longer drive. He couldn't lift his right leg to put it on the brake, so he had to reach down and grab his leg with both hands to move it over and push the brake, likely steering with his knee. As you can imagine, that wasn't the safest driving technique. But it was a small town, so people smiled and moved out of his way until he finally stopped driving altogether.

He never remarried after Grandma Sadie died, and Mom wasn't able to check on him as much as she liked. While he initially protested, he grew to like the nursing home. He was quite popular with the ladies and still had a sharp mind. He also still had all his hair—beautiful, wavy, and thick—and had to get it cut every seven to ten days. It wasn't uncommon for women to crawl in bed with him, wanting to get cozy. Grandpa would just say, "No, honey."

Although he was the epitome of stoic in his younger years, he had a wonderful sense of humor as well, and kept up on all the latest news and movies. He'd also continued to eat well, exercise, and play chess with the local college students—all activities undoubtedly pointing to why he lived such a long life.

Dad no doubt grew to love him and look up to him as a father figure, even if they weren't openly communicative about things like that. Dad's own father had passed away in July 1967 at the age of sixty-seven in a hospital in Minnesota, and while they had repaired their strained relationship—for the most part—Grandpa Albin no doubt had a special place in Dad's heart, and was a healthy role model of what hard work and a loving parent looks like. After all, Dad hadn't had that example with *either* of his parents.

While Dad was able to mend his relationship with his father, it was his mother, Dorothy, whom he had continued to have issues with. Grandpa Eldon, knowing Dorothy favored Dolores over my dad, for whatever reason, told his wife—in front of witnesses—to make sure she left them an equal inheritance once she passed away. Grandpa Eldon was expecting for her to live longer—and rightfully so, thanks to decades of heavy drinking on his part.

When Dorothy died in 1981, while she didn't leave a large inheritance, she left it all—around $25,000—to Dolores. Unable to understand why his mother loved Dolores more than him, he was haunted by that final act of favoritism until his death.

Now, in the wake of his last parental role model passing on, we watched Dad struggle over the fall of 1983, growing more and more nervous, but never knowing the source of his true anxiety.

* * *

On October 10, 1983, Reagan organized a private screening of *The Day After,* a TV movie depicting the effect of a nuclear strike on the town of Lawrence, Kansas. Reagan was deeply disturbed by the film, writing in his diary that it was "very effective and left me greatly depressed."[1] Coincidentally, just days later, he was briefed by Robert McFarlane, the national security adviser, on possible scenarios in the event of nuclear war. Reagan was pained as well as sobered by the estimate that 150 million American lives would be lost, even if the United States were victorious in the conflict. He was also just as surprised that the Russians actually believed the United States would launch an attack on them. That meant they were ready for war.

Then, on October 23, 1983, a massive suicide bomb exploded on the U.S. Marine base in Beirut, killing 241 soldiers. America went on high alert, another sign to the Soviets that something horrendous might be coming their way.

A day after the bombing, U.S. Marines landed on Grenada, a British protectorate, to overthrow the island's nascent Communist regime. Unfortunately, the U.S. administration had neglected to inform the British, greatly angering prime minister Margaret Thatcher—the equivalent of Britain invading the U.S. Virgin islands and forgetting to inform the president of the United States.

A swirl of diplomatic communications ensued between Washington and London, the Soviets taking this as *another sign* that something was imminent. With all of this action, and no explanation, it is a wonder the Russians didn't take action. But the worst was right around the corner.

40

Able Archer

TEN DAYS LATER, EARLY IN THE MORNING, Dad was picked up by a car and taken to Gatwick, where a plane was waiting to fly him and several other IBM'ers to the Supreme Headquarters Allied Powers Europe (SHAPE) command center in Casteau, Belgium, for the ten-day annual exercise with NATO—the North Atlantic Treaty Organization. The code name for the intricate allied war games was "Able Archer 83" and during the ten days, the United States, in addition to other NATO forces throughout western Europe, replicated a period of conflict resulting in a simulated DEFCON 1 coordinated nuclear attack. The exercise practiced "command and control procedures with particular emphasis on the transition from purely conventional operations to chemical, nuclear and conventional operations" during a time of war.[1]

My dad had been invited to participate, and his job—from an underground bunker near NATO headquarters—was the coordination of the nuclear "launch." Making one calculation after another in order to read the earth's topography, he was responsible for keeping the low-tracking missiles on track. He also had to ensure that if the computers were going to be used to simulate war, they were unhooked from active systems. As he said, "I had to make sure we deactivated them, but were still able to launch them." You don't want to simulate war and realize one computer is still live.

In the exercise, the conflict began as a skirmish and then slowly escalated. Despite the fact that all communiqués were labeled "EXERCISE," and although the Soviets had monitored these kinds of war games many times before, the political and diplomatic climate of the time made them very shaky.

Because of the situation in Beirut, NATO forces were put on a higher state of alert than during any previous war game exercise, code and radio frequencies changed as alert status switched to "nuclear." This further frazzled the Soviets. And soon after Ronald Reagan became president in January '81, Russia saw Reagan as a cowboy with a six-shooter, riding on a horse. They were absolutely convinced that Reagan was going to nuke them. Remember: we were the only country that had actually dropped an atomic bomb on people, and at that time, Ronald Reagan was not openly discussing anything with Russia.

The Able Archer exercise also introduced several elements not seen in previous years, including a unique format of coded communication, radio silences, and the participation of heads of government. Already paranoid because of the events over the previous months, the Soviets believed that Able Archer 83 was simply a ruse, and a genuine nuclear first strike was in preparation.[2] Deciding to put Soviet nuclear forces on a level footing with the movement of the NATO forces, the Soviets had made extreme preparations and were expecting to get hit with a nuclear weapon. Runways in the USSR and eastern Europe went into full alert status and were lined with bombers on standby. Nuclear submarines in the Arctic went into hiding under the ice, missile-launch ready.

"But no one noticed," Dad told me while building the fence. "We were too busy with the exercise." In fact, Dad was working virtually around the clock, called here and there for help with mathematical calculations. He was definitely starting to feel the effects of the long days, and he hadn't been feeling all that well anyway.

By the evening of Saturday, November 5, the war game script had the Soviets resorting to chemical warfare, the NATO forces preparing for a "retaliatory nuclear strike." Nuclear planners began to identify twenty-five targets to strike in the Soviet Union, the "request" transmitted to Washington and London, the transmission picked up by the Soviets.

In the event of a nuclear strike by the United States, the order must come from the president. Dad and some of the others involved in the exercises began to worry that perhaps the Soviets would grow alarmed if Reagan were to make the decision to launch an attack during these games. They went to a commanding officer and pleaded their case—it would be better if the president was taken off this job. The powers that be agreed, and national security adviser Bud McFarland convinced President Reagan that he should be out of the exercise and instead travel to Japan. Nevertheless, the Soviets took this as a ruse as well. Meanwhile, Reagan continued to think about Able Archer and about the devastation he saw in the screening of *The Day After*.

With Reagan out of the picture, the Soviets began to truly panic, nearly convinced that the 350 missiles about to be launched at them were real, not imaginary. They suspected that the attack would come on their November 7 holiday, Revolution Day, when they would be most vulnerable. Seventy-five mobile missiles were dispersed into the field around the USSR, the country going into DEFCOM 2 status (preparation for responding to a nuclear attack) for the first and only time in history.

On days nine and ten of Able Archer, it was nuclear war as planned. But as soon as the missiles were "launched," all Able Archer communications went dead, and Soviet radar picked up absolutely nothing flying toward their airspace. The exercise—and the panic—was finally over. But the backlash would soon begin.

There's a BBC documentary called "Able Archer 1983: The Brink of Apocalypse,"[3] in which a mole is interviewed about Able Archer 83. He was taking copies of classified documents from NATO and sending them to Russia. This should have contained the information proving that Able Archer was simply a routine exercise, but the Russians *still* thought it was a trick.

Consider that eight months before, in March 1983, President Ronald Reagan, in a speech at an evangelical ministers convention in Florida, called the Soviet Union "the focus of evil in the world," and "the evil empire."[4] And in October of that year, just a month before the Able Archer exercise, Deputy Secretary of State Kenneth Dam delivered a speech on "superpower relations emphasizing the immediate threat posed by the Soviet Union."[5] So it was no secret that the United States' stance toward Russia wasn't a positive one.

Days after the Able Archer exercise had ended, William Casey, head of the CIA under Ronald Reagan, found the president sitting at his desk in the Oval office, back to business as usual. Casey, no doubt spinning with adrenaline, told Reagan that he had just about gotten the world nuked. In the meantime, it appears that Bud McFarlane, the NSC adviser, also told Reagan about the threat shortly after it happened, either confirming Casey's intelligence or having the distinct honor of shocking the president first.

Reagan had no idea what Casey was talking about, completely unaware that the Russians had taken Able Archer seriously. Casey admitted that a spy named Oleg Antonovich Gordievsky had informed him that Russia had gone to DEFCON 2 during the exercise. Gordievsky was an ex-KGB officer and Soviet double agent; he was later called "the West's sole source of information on the Soviet war scare during the early 1980s."[6]

Upon learning how close we came to nuclear war—that his enemy had spent ten days expecting a nuclear attack when the United States wasn't even thinking about going to war, nor were we ready—Reagan was livid because he'd gone out of his way to make sure he and the U.S. military had followed all precautions and guidelines during Able

Archer. He was also stunned that the Russians could actually believe that America would be capable of committing such an obscene act of nuclear destruction.

Trying to save face, Reagan's immediate staff tried to downplay Casey's newly received intelligence and label that information as classified. People such as Caspar Weinberger, Reagan's secretary of defense from 1981 to 1987, and George P. Shultz, then secretary of state, didn't want this news to be made public.

Surprisingly, that document, among many others related to the Able Archer 83 incident, was declassified in October 2015, thanks to twelve years of constant pressure from author Nate Jones, director of the Freedom of Information Act Project for the National Security Archive. Although there are likely thousands of documents about Able Archer 83 that are still classified, those that have been released completely verify everything my dad told me about the Able Archer exercise.

When Dad found out what happened, he was not only stunned, but he was angry that the U.S. government had pushed things, and risked the nation, as they had. Later, when my dad told me that, he was so visibly upset that he said to me, "Johnny, I could have been vaporized." His expression turned incredulous and he stared into the yard.

Dad said he later came to believe that the events surrounding the Able Archer exercises were what finally brought an end to the Cold War.

But first, Reagan's tone had to soften considerably.

On November 18, Reagan wrote in his diary:[7]

George Shultz & I had a talk mainly about setting up a little in house group of experts on the Soviet U. to help us in setting up some channels. I feel the Soviets are so defense minded, so paranoid about being attacked that without being soft on them we ought to tell them no one here has any intention of doing anything like that. What the h—l have they got that anyone would want[?]

On November 19, President Reagan met with Casey, Weinberger, Bush, and McFarlane to create an agenda in dealing with the Russians:[8]

1. Reduce use and threat of force in international disputes;

2. Lower high levels of armaments by equitable and verifiable agreements; and

3. Establish minimal level of trust to facilitate the first two objectives, including:

   a. Compliance with past agreements;

   b. Human rights performance;

   c. Specific confidence-building measures;

   d. Bilateral ties when mutually beneficial.

After Reagan's camp had so openly chastised the Soviets, Reagan would now have to quickly begin to back-channel, and he did so as early as December.[9] On January 16, 1984, Ronald Reagan himself gave a speech that marked a dramatic shift in policy, focusing now on "common concerns, the mutual desire for peace and the urgent need to address 'dangerous misunderstandings' between Moscow and Washington."[10] The aggressive rhetoric so evident in Reagan's first term was now replaced with a friendlier tone. Suddenly the Russians weren't evil after all and Reagan was willing to negotiate. All the while, he was desperately trying to relay to the Soviet government that he wasn't crazy, he wasn't going to nuke Russia, and he was certainly not as ruthless as Hitler, as was suggested in recent months by the powers in Moscow.[11]

Sixteen months later, in March 1985, Gorbachev was elected as the first executive president of the Soviet Union, and over time, the U.S.–Russian relations were much improved, both presidents working to end the Cold War and developing a warm friendship in the process.[12] He never again referred to the Soviets as an evil empire. There would, however, be uncomfortable reminders along the way of the not-too-distant past.

Several years later, on May 31, 1988, Reagan was visiting Gorbachev at the Kremlin, and a reporter, no doubt hoping for a marketable sound bite, asked Reagan if he still considered the Soviet Union to be "the evil empire." Reagan shook his head and answered no, and after a brief pause, told the reporter, "You are talking about another time, another era."[13]

In 1990, Gorbachev won the Nobel Peace Prize for helping to end the Cold War.[14] As we now know, the Cold War could have easily ended in a different way—it could have been a *hot war*, and neither of us—you nor I—might be around to read the words on this page.

41

The Deadly Diagnosis

WITHIN A FEW SHORT MONTHS IN 1984, Yuri Andropov passed away.

Mikhail Gorbachev took over and invoked glasnost—government transparency.

And Dad was diagnosed with colon cancer.

I'd spent a week there, visiting my parents in the spring of '84, and although he didn't express any sort of concern that there was something wrong with him, you could tell he was very distracted. Of course, he'd just lived through Able Archer and learning Russia had gone to at DEFCON 2. But he was about to meet his biggest enemy yet.

In late summer of 1984, Nedra and her kids had gone to visit Mom and Dad for six weeks, and she noticed he was pale and he was tired a lot. In the fall of '84 Dad finally went to the doctor after he got awfully bloated and uncomfortable. Sadly, he was diagnosed with cancer again.

His doctor had found cancerous polyps in the 1960s. After surgery to remove them, Dad never followed up. Flexible scopes are used these days, but back then the procedure only covered the lower part of the colon because the instrument was rigid—it was just a metal rod with a scope on the end, and it couldn't bend and go into your intestine—and left the patient very uncomfortable afterwards. As smart as the man was, and in the health environment in which he lived, I'll never know why he didn't stay on top of his suggested visits. But for whatever reason, Dad never went in for another scope and it's likely that another polyp progressed to colon cancer.

I was at my brother's house when Dad and Mom called with the news. They thought at first it was Crohn's disease. The next call was that they thought it was cancer, and it was a large tumor that had metastasized to his liver and obstructed his bowel. Doctors surmised that it had probably been growing for twenty years. The next day, the lymph biopsy came back positive. The cancer had progressed more than they thought.

On a phone call with Mom soon after the diagnosis, Nedra said, "Mom are you worried?"

Mom said, "No, Nedra. I'm just concerned. What can you worry about?"

Dad was going to jump on the Concord airplane and have surgery in New York, but the doctors wouldn't let him get on a plane because his tumor could rupture at any time, so instead he had emergency surgery for a bowel obstruction there in southern England. The doctors believed the surgery was successful.

For someone who was used to always being in control, Dad did very well with accepting the fact that all he could do was fight it. He did that valiantly.

Thankfully, they were in a great church in England then, and his church family took over when we couldn't be there. Mom said she felt so loved by the church there; they got her through that hard time.

* * *

On August 31, 1984, Dad retired from IBM, and he and Mom moved back to the San Jose area days after. Dad would go through a grueling series of exit interviews in Los Gatos, California—several weeks long—made more arduous by the fact that he was still going through cancer treatments.

Exit interviews from your typical corporate job might take thirty minutes to an hour, maybe two at the most, depending on how chatty the conversation becomes, or if there's a more pressing topic to be covered, such as pay or transferring company documents. But my dad's exit interview sounded more like an interrogation. After all, he'd spent almost forty-five years working for the government in some capacity, and his exit interviewers would have had to go back to the early 1940s, when he was recruited by the NDRC. There's no telling how large his file was after forty-four years of service and having been involved in an incredible amount of clandestine operations. They'd have likely wanted to review each and every project he ever touched, reminding him of what he could and couldn't talk about once he was retired.

This sounds grueling in and of itself, but was made even more difficult by Dad's cancer treatments, which made him nauseated and tired. He often had to excuse himself to the men's room and get sick. Still, he was held in a room for hours each day, day after day, being told again and again, "You can't talk about X project, Y project, or Z project."

It's probable that some of that time during the exit interviews would have been spent in counterintelligence, with Dad being asked who he'd come in contact with while in Switzerland or Iran, and with interviewers showing him pictures of people, places, and items to see if any of them rang a bell and therefore needed to be discussed further. It's common practice for the military to debrief their members after tours of duty, and it's also common practice in the intelligence community.

For example, when John Steinbeck and playwright Edward Albee returned from a 1963 goodwill tour in the Soviet Union, each man was individually debriefed by State Department personnel.[1] Albee's debriefing lasted a single day. Steinbeck, who had requested to perform duties abroad for the CIA, was grilled for three days over the trip.[2] One can imagine that if a two-month trip to Russia required a three-day examination, a forty-four-year career dealing with nuclear secrets debriefing would take some months.

I am sure Dad was fully debriefed when he left Switzerland in '72, after each trip home from Iran, and after the Able Archer 83 exercise. But now, upon his rather forced retirement, his last forty-five years were paraded in front of him on paper and film. I can only imagine it would be similar to the oft-repeated cliché of your whole life flashing before your eyes.

I always wondered why my dad felt he was being forced out and if he'd have taken retirement eventually anyway. People like my dad have to stay busy at all times. And maybe he was worried that he'd have nothing to do once he left IBM. Of course, he quickly found a hundred projects to tackle around the house, and I genuinely believe he seemed much happier and relaxed upon retirement. But it's not uncommon for people who've been blessed with lengthy careers to in many ways define themselves—and their life's purpose—by that one job.

I also considered a more gracious thought, more to ease my mind than anything else: If the government knew Dad was dying of cancer, they may have let him go simply due to psychological pressures. Perhaps they'd actually had compassion and resolved that a man with terminal cancer should spend his remaining time with family instead of pacing the floors at work until one day he drops dead at his desk. He'd spent his whole career being loyal, and having a terminal colon cancer diagnosis, including ruptured organs, it would have been tough to remain on the cutting edge of missiles. But from what it sounded like, the exit process was brutal and he was spared no niceties.

On the day of his retirement, he wrote, "Friday Aug 31st, 1984. A milestone date. Up early and in office before 8 A as I've done for so many years. Cleaned out desk and packed up. Called a few for final fairwell [sic]. It is with very mixed emotions I sign out at 33 years 9 mo's of service which has for a vast majority of time been very rewarding."

Dad knew he was finished—both career-wise and health-wise, as he was at the near expiration of his time on earth. He knew that he was an integral part of the Cold War. And the Cold War was nearly over.

Dad's 103-page diary concludes with an ominous note. On November 14, 1984, Dad wrote, "To office for couple of hours. New medical plan major changes. Painted in garage & some edge plastering—Eve N/D were here for dinner—clear & cold."

One Sunday morning in late summer of '84, once Dad's awful exit interviews were complete and just before my parents moved back to Seattle, they attended the 9:30 service at Menlo Park Presbyterian Church with my brother Bill.

When service ended at 10:30, a guy jogged over to my dad in the parking lot and put his arm around him. It was Gene Amdahl, a physicist and computer scientist who had worked with Dad on many projects at IBM, including the Stretch computer and the IBM 360. It had probably been fifteen years since they had seen each other, but instead of a heartfelt hello, what followed was an awkward conversation and a refusal of more money than I'd have known what to do with.

"Wally, it's been so long since I've seen you! I have all these companies, big super computer companies, bigger than the one IBM is making, really massive computers, very complex," Gene said. "I need someone to manage these companies, to be the head. It's beyond me. I need someone."

Dad simply said, "Oh, I'm fine. I don't need anything."

Gene kept pressing; Bill was standing right between them, trying to figure out what was going on. Finally, Gene says, "Wally, *stop resisting.* Everybody knows that you know more about computers than anybody in the world. Write your check. I don't care if it is seven or eight figures! Take the money and manage these things. I need help."

Still, my dad said, "I can't do it right now. Thank you." And Dad started walking toward his car, a stunned son and dutiful wife following behind. Bill had already begun to suspect there was more to Dad's "sales" career than he'd been letting on, but even he was stunned to hear someone so casually mention that Dad knew more about computers than anybody in the world.

I don't know if Dad was still under a noncompete contract from IBM, which prevented him from doing work with another computer company. It's also possible that he suspected he might have to deal with cancer again, and he didn't want to take on a second career with possible health issues ahead. Then again, he might have really settled on the idea of retirement, but I doubt that. All I can say is if someone approached me soon after retirement and offered me what amounted to an open-ended salary to run a business in an area of my zone of genius, I'd have to think long and hard before turning it down.

Finally free of his job, and cancer treatments, he enjoyed a few good years with Mom in Seattle, traveling to his children's homes to see his grandkids and building whatever needed building, trying to act like a retiree. He enjoyed reading and getting outdoors. A hobby he'd picked up in Zurich, power walking was something at which he excelled.

One time in Europe, he walked so fast in front of Mom that he lost her. Another time, while walking on Zurich's busy Bahnhofstrasse, he walked so fast he hit a moving car. He just bounced right off it and kept walking.

Now in Seattle, he was slowly learning how to relax and enjoy a life without daily distractions of national importance. But he could never completely distance himself from world politics, no matter how much he may have wanted to.

On one occasion, when I went to visit him and Mom, we were watching a news conference on the Iran–Contra hearings where some panel member was drilling Oliver North. My dad, wearing his Mister Rogers sweater, walked up to the TV set and shut it off as though he had been personally offended.

I was smart-alecky, and said, "Come on, Dad. What do you know about Iranian stuff like this? All you did was build a water dam in Iran."

My dad looked at me and he said, "Johnny, I know a little bit more about Iran than that. Let's have our soup and lunch now, and let's pray." That's all he said. He didn't elaborate, but it shut me up.

Now that he was no longer responsible for saving the world from nuclear disaster, his perspective seemed to change during those years. Surprisingly, he had a peace about this new chapter in life that I didn't quite understand.

* * *

In November of 1984, still woefully unaware of Dad's incredible mathematical talent, I gave him a HP 41C pocket calculator for his birthday. It was very sophisticated at that time, more like a mini computer. But instead of acting excited, or even the least bit interested, he looked at it and gave me this smirk. I'll never forget that look—like I was a day late and a dollar short. Back then I didn't understand his sly smile, but now I know it meant, *I don't need this, Johnny.*

My dad had spent forty years calculating equations that could power supercomputers, launch missiles, and helped put a man on the moon. And I gave him a pocket calculator for his birthday. He never even played with it! Instead he put it in his desk drawer and that's where it stayed.

Dad had another surgery in late 1985 and began BCG treatments under his doctor's care to boost his immune abilities. After surgery Dad also had nasogastric intubation, which requires inserting a plastic tube through the nose, past the throat, and down into the stomach. My sister Nedra said Dad hated the NG tube in his nose. Even though we learned soon after that his cancer was in remission, I think he knew it would win in the end.

His appreciation of his family growing, he wanted to spend more time with us. He said that his one regret in life was having spent too much time pursuing career and financial success.

Ever since the big reveal, I've always found it ironic that the Cold War icon in the media is James Bond. The paradox is that in reality the Cold War was won, not at the barrel of a gun, but with the barrel of a missile as a threat, and with computers. In reality, Dad was the secret James Bond without a gun.

But not even James Bond can live forever.

42

Searching for a Miracle Cure

THE NEXT MORNING, HAVING FINISHED my fence, Dad broke ground on the flower bed he'd talked about for the front yard, and he found a few other small repair projects to keep himself occupied before I had to take him to the airport at noon for his return to Seattle.

Just as we were leaving for the airport, the phone rang. It was the girls he'd tutored at the hardware store two days before. Dad was already in the car and didn't want to return into the house, so I spoke to them. They'd aced the test, they said, and Dad got most of the credit. They said he was the most amazing math teacher or tutor they'd ever had. I was happy for them, wished them luck, and told them I'd pass along the good news.

When I got into the car and told Dad what they'd said, he just shrugged as if his brilliance in math, and teaching it, was something he just accepted. I was expecting a bit more of a response from him, but when it didn't come, I decided maybe the girls' amazement was enough.

There's really not a higher compliment, after all.

When we said good-bye at the airport, I gave him a big hug, and he said, "See you soon, Johnny Boy," as he walked away. I knew the next time I saw him, he might look quite different. It was a very strange feeling. First my father's identity had left him. Now his body was going to follow.

It was a quiet drive back home. I found myself wondering why he'd chosen me to hear his story.

Now, after years of asking myself this question, I have concluded that perhaps it was because I was the *least* like him, because I was someone he considered to be a "regular guy." Perhaps he sensed that as the most stubborn of all his children, I had the commitment and dogged persistence it might take to tell his story to the world.

* * *

Six months after Dad's visit to New Jersey, I was laid off from my job when the division I was with merged with another division of Johnson & Johnson, but immediately after that, a different division of J&J picked me up. They kept me at a job in New Jersey, but I kept thinking, *Man, John, you are vulnerable.* I have this big home on three and a half acres, and I am one job away from being unemployed.

Soon after that, I got a promotion to become the corporate business manager for Johnson & Johnson in Chicago.

Gosh, again? We had just gotten settled in this house, and I had just experienced the scare of being laid off and hired again. The house was being packed up in New Jersey, and the kids were crying, and I didn't want to move either, and we wouldn't be if I could have kept my regular job, but it didn't exist any longer. J&J bought my home, and we were now on full corporate relocation to the Chicagoland area.

Once again, I was leaving my dad's handiwork behind for someone else to enjoy for years to come. That made this move all the more bittersweet. The next house we bought—wherever that was—would be the first house I'd ever live in that didn't benefit from Dad's craftsmanship.

Now there was only one thing left in the house, which was the phone, and just as I was about to walk out the door, it rang. It was the owner of a medical distribution company in Seattle called Biddle & Crowther. "John, this is Berk Biddle. I understand you are moving to the Chicagoland area.

"The board of directors has voted that they want you to come in and run the company," he said.

"Who in the heck are the board of directors?" I asked.

He said, "You are speaking to him." Berk has a very unique sense of humor. He added, "Whatever you do, don't buy a house in Chicago, because I am going to bring you back to Seattle."

As you can imagine, Celeste was none too pleased with any of it. But it was an incredible opportunity, so we both agreed that I needed to consider it. So, I moved to Chicago under the guise of being a long-term employee in the Chicagoland area, but I had no intention of doing that. And as it turned out, this guy had already called a Group Company Chairman high up in corporate in HQ in New Brunswick, New Jersey, and worked it out with him because Biddle & Crowther was a large Johnson & Johnson distributor.

Over a stretch of several months, I took numerous trips to Seattle to work out the details, always visiting Mom and Dad for a day or two. Each trip, Dad's condition worsened as he grew thinner and more frail. Mom knew what was happening, and expected the worst.

Dad's cancer had progressed just as predicted. My sisters were taking Dad to many of his appointments since Mom didn't like to drive. His doctor, Dr. Warner, had a huge practice, and for some reason, the Washington state board discredited his license, and he went out of business. Dad felt better when on his BCG treatments, but when they stopped, he became desperate. Searching for a possible last-minute cure, he and Mom traveled to Mexico in the fall of 1990 for an experimental drug therapy. By this time, having finished all medical therapies in the United States, he had that jaundiced look that typifies liver cancer.

My parents were in Mexico for a week, trying any trick in the book, and it was an absolute fiasco. Dad was really getting sick by now; the plane was delayed in San Diego on the way back home, and he got sick at the airport. They had to wait around in the airport for half a day to get home. My mom said it was a miserable time for both of them.

Today BCG drugs are now approved for certain types of bladder cancer therapy. But that was Dad's last hope. Now he seemed to be going quickly downhill, despite the benefit from the earlier treatments, and he couldn't stay in Mexico forever.

Needing to get back to Seattle as soon as possible, I accepted a new position as director of marketing, then as COO of Biddle & Crowther, and I moved back to Seattle in December 1990. My family left before me, and I packed up the house for the movers, marveling at all the times my mother had been in charge of packing up the houses over our many moves growing up.

We temporarily moved into my mother-in-law's house on the water as we searched for a house. The rush was on for several reasons, and thankfully I found a great house not too long after—it's the home I still live in today—because I wanted Dad to at least see the kind of house I was moving into.

I picked him up from his home in Bellevue, and we drove the fifteen miles into Seattle without a word. He was so sick, all he did was walk in, look around for less than a full minute, and walk out. He didn't even make a comment. But at least he'd seen it and physically stood in the house, and in some way, that was enough of a blessing.

43

The Last Goodbye

I BEGAN MY NEW POSITION on January 1, 1991. I visited Dad as much as I could, but by now he was largely unable to participate in the conversation. So, I told him about how much his grandkids loved playing in the fenced-in backyard, how everyone was doing in school, about my job and Celeste's, and I made obligatory commentary on the weather. Only once did I consider wanting to talk about the story he'd told me, but I couldn't bring myself there. He was fighting for his life. The last thing I wanted to do was to bring up those memories again and cause him more stress. Plus, I had just started a new job with a thousand distractions. And subconsciously, I was still in a place where I didn't want to believe it anyway.

By then he looked emaciated. My dad had always been a fit guy, but now he was noticeably very thin in the waist. His cheekbones were protruding, and the cancer had colored his face a pale yellow. He could walk, but was very unstable, and it was hard to watch. Basically, after Mexico, he knew—we all knew—that he was going to die.

We watched him shrink and shrivel away, and he ended up just skin and bones. Bill asked him at the end, "Dad, what do you think about this cancer that is just eating you alive?"

He said, "Bill, this is the very best thing that has ever happened to me in my whole life."

That was obviously not the answer my brother expected. Bill looked at him in disbelief and said, "What?"

Dad said, "For the first time, I can just rest and relax and lay in the arms of Jesus."

I guess, in the most positive way to see such bleak circumstances, this the very first time in his life he was privileged to relax. He never ever felt he could do that before. The government had inducted him as a teenager, deprived him of a normal life, used him for their purposes—and ultimately God's—but he was exhausted. He'd had a horrendous schedule his entire career. Most people today cannot comprehend the magnitude of the tension of the Cold War, when school drills anticipated bombs dropping nearby and taught children how to get under their desks. Many older homes have bomb shelters as basements, especially if they were built in the 1950s. Back then it was a legitimate worry. Now it is just a spider haven.

So, in the midst of all the pain of that cancer, that he could say it was the best thing that had ever happened to him was a miracle. For the first time he didn't have to deal with the stress of worrying about the world.

Years before, he had heard a man named Paul Anderson speak soon after he received a cancer diagnosis. Paul had such a sense of peace with whatever happened, and my dad really admired it. Now, in the face of death, Dad said he understood how Paul felt. "I do have peace," Dad said. "Whatever happens to me, I am a winner either way."

So, toward the very end, when Dad grew tired of getting blood transfusions, he said to Bill, "No more transfusions. That's enough."

Bill said, "Are you sure, Dad? You know what that means."

He said, "Yep, no more."

"Well, what's your thinking?"

Dad confidently answered, "Well, you're not prolonging my life by doing this. You're just prolonging my death. I'm happy to go."

He was right—we weren't extending his happy, functional life; we were just extending his death, and Dad did not believe in doing useless things.

We as a family, including Mom, with her now faintly purple hair, agreed that we wouldn't push for any more transfusions.

On April 30, 1991, Dawn picked Dad up for his almost-daily doctor's appointment. He said, "This is the last time I'm going to this doctor."

Dawn said, "What do you mean? We are battling this, Dad."

Turns out, he was right.

* * *

On May 1, 1991, Dad was admitted to hospice care.

On May 2, I left work early and went home to grab my sons, Joey and Chris. I said, "We are going to have to say good-bye to Grandpa." My wife had taken my daughter the day before, and since Caitlyn had already said good-bye, it was now the boys' turn.

I remember wrestling with my boys in the hallway of Dad's new nursing home. We did mock wrestling, like they do on TV, and I let my boys beat me up, pinning my shoulders to "win one for Grandpa." Dad heard the commotion and wondered what in the world was going on.

My sisters and my mom were in the room with him, and they were singing all sorts of hymns to comfort Dad during his final hours. Finally, I realized he was really looking horrible with that jaundiced cancer color. Knowing time was short, I brought my children up to his bedside so he could give them each a final kiss. I told my ten-year-old Chris to kiss Grandpa good-bye. Then I had Joey, who was six, kiss Grandpa on the nose. Joey said, "Grandpa, you don't look so good."

Now it was my turn to give him a kiss, and as I leaned toward him, I said, "Dad I need to say good-bye."

He turned his head and whispered, "Johnny boy, I have learned so much from you."

A lump immediately formed in my throat. Trying not to break down, I said, "Dad, what could you have possibly learned from me?"

"I learned about life."

That was the most heartfelt thing my dad had ever said to me. And the last time he ever looked me in the eye.

Through tears I whispered back, "I will see you in heaven."

* * *

In the car, to ease my pain, I asked Chris to get out a cassette tape and play the song "Cold Metal" by Iggy Pop, about playing tag in the auto graveyard. A good friend of mine, Ron Stirm, had made this recording with a variety of songs, which we played all the time in New Jersey.

As soon as I got the kids home, I grabbed a big can of beer and continued to play extremely loud music in the living room while sitting up against the speakers Dad helped build—those big simulated Klipsch corner horns—as if the sound would drown my sorrow and pain. Knowing I wanted to be alone, Chris went upstairs to read to Joey, and my wife was reading to my daughter, Caitlyn.

The next song was Ozzy Osbourne's "Mama, I'm Coming Home." I remember visualizing Dad going to heaven as the guitar wailed. Then, almost miraculously, when that song ended, the phone rang. It was 10 p.m. My sister Nedra sobbed, "Dad just passed." They'd been singing "Amazing Grace" in his hospice room when he stopped breathing.

I knew I needed to tell my family, but my wife somehow knew that's what the call was about. I turned the music down and walked upstairs. Caitlyn, eight years old and full of spunk, was unaware of what had just happened. As I stepped into the room, she said, "Dad, when are you going to grow up?" She was annoyed, saying my music was so loud she couldn't hear her mother read.

Celeste gently reprimanded her, and I walked over to the where the boys were reading. Caught up in the moment and in memories of my own childhood, I launched myself into the air, flying onto the bed like Superman.

44

The Funeral

THERE COULDN'T HAVE BEEN MORE THAN FIFTY to seventy people who attended Dad's memorial service in Bellevue at Covenant Church, where my parents had attended for some years now. Most were either relatives, church members, friends of mine, or my siblings' friends who knew my dad. I remember asking my mom, "Have any of Dad's workmates even called to wish you the best?" She shook her head and clutched her handkerchief to her chest.

As heartbroken as Mom was, I think she saw Dad's death as a relief because he'd been so sick. She knew it had to happen. Still, it was a difficult end to a lifelong partnership. In their decades of marriage, no matter where Dad had gone or how long he was there, he'd always come home to her. Now, somewhere in eternity, he was patiently waiting for her.

The only mention of Dad's work life in the sermon was that the family moved around a lot because of Dad's work at IBM. I was secretly hoping some of Dad's work associates would show, but no one did. I even have the register where guests who attended the funeral signed in and left messages. And there was no one listed whom I didn't recognize. In fact, *to this day*, not a single business associate has ever attempted to contact my mother.

I was very disappointed, to be honest. After nearly fifty years of honorable employment—*even if Dad had only been a salesman*—I would have expected at least a handful of associates to come and pay their respects. At the very least, they could have sent flowers or a card to my mother in her time of grief. But the fact that absolutely no one came to his funeral or even acknowledged his passing left a bitter taste in my mouth. Honestly it made me recall Dad's tone when he said IBM was moving him to England for his last hurrah. Maybe he knew it would end this way.

My brother, Bill, who worked for IBM for a couple of years in the early '60s, coincidentally, on 360 computers—the successful version after the Stretch had failed so miserably—wasn't as shocked at IBM's treatment of Dad. He thought it was simply the nature of the way big companies have transformed.

The early IBM, even before that, in the 1950s, was a big family, and they treated everybody like family. Employees would go to various events at the IBM headquarters and have cookouts. But everything changed in the late 1970s, when the computer came onto the public scene for the first time.

Now there were credit cards, and you couldn't have credit cards without computers. Companies had become oriented to the stock market and were less concerned with treating individuals like family. Dad knew everything was changing for the worse when it came to the net effect of the computer on society. Oh my goodness, was he a realist.

After we buried Dad at the location of his choice—the base of Mount Si, a high peak in the Cascades, near Snoqualmie Falls—I went back to my busy life managing a large medical distributorship and raising three children. Although I did my best to block it out of my mind, I thought about Dad's story often. I'd take out the stack of business cards he left for me under the desk and stare at them, wondering what they represented.

One of my regrets came when we were cleaning out Dad's workshop. Dad had always kept vacuum tubes—tubs of them—in every size, as I mentioned before. He used them often in projects around the house, whether he was repairing TVs or radios. I never knew how expensive they were, and since he never mentioned that I should keep them, I tossed them out at the dump in Bellevue. Now of course I know how foolish that was. Those were G-force rated to go in missiles, and they were worth between $50,000 and $200,000.

You would have thought he'd have told me to keep them, but he was dying, so he had more important things on his mind. Not knowing what they were worth, I recall thinking, *What am I going to do with these tubes?*

On a happier note, one thing I did in memory of him was buy one of the last five hundred of the original style of experimental Jag, called the XJ. You have to understand: Dad and I were looking at a brand-new car's product release in 1968, called the Jaguar XJ, when I was in seventh or eighth grade. And now, more than thirty years later, I bought one of the last models to come into the country. I found it in Texas and had it shipped up. It's white, the same as his bug-eyed Sprite. I plan on having the license plate read, "Wally" or "Wally's" or "Wallace," or maybe just abbreviate "Missileman."

My dad, when he lived in England, wanted to have a used Jaguar to drive around in, probably thinking it would break down and he could fix it! The government said no. But rebuilding something was his relaxation. He looked at that as joy. And now every time I drive mine, I think of Dad.

45

The Fifteen-Year Refusal

WHEN IBM SOLD ITS FEDERAL SYSTEMS DIVISION to Loral Corporation on January 1, 1994, for $1.58 billion with surprisingly little fanfare, I was one person who noticed.[1] At the time, I was working as a consultant just down the block from Loral's offices in Palo Alto. I would drive by the space satellite manufacturer, wondering if there were records of my father inside.

In his book, *Who Says Elephants Can't Dance? Leading a Great Enterprise through Dramatic Change*, Louis V. Gerstner Jr., the former CEO of IBM, said one of his toughest decisions was selling the federal systems group, but their cost structure no longer fit into the IBM model. Louis added, "[They] had an illustrious history of important technical breakthroughs for various national security and space programs."[2] But the Cold War had ended, and Cold War contracts had dried up.

The Cold War was dead. Dad was dead. The era was coming to a close.

I finally found myself accepting Dad's story intellectually, but still had difficulty absorbing it emotionally. Although I told myself he was forced to live a lie because it was the only way for him to do his job, I know that deep down I felt betrayed by him and angry at him. I believe this is the primary reason it took me so long to tell his story. The secondary reason was my belief that the research required to fill out the story would be a monumental task, adding unwanted stress to my already busy life.

For fifteen years I kept the story locked inside of me, and it began to consume me from the inside out. I became like Dad in that I didn't talk about it to anyone. When any talk of his IBM career came up, I immediately switched the subject. I somehow wanted the world to cling to the vision it had of my father, even if that vision was wrong. It meant that I didn't have to disrupt the status quo or explain that he, in fact, had been living a double life.

However, withholding the story had an effect on me. My beer consumption rose steadily, partly out of a need to drown my confusion and anger, partly due to a subconscious reaction to Dad's admonitions against liquor at the same time he was living a lie. You can lie to the people around you every day of your life, but you can't have a beer? I felt his opinion had been unnecessarily self-righteous.

So, in the mid-'90s, in an attempt to "ease the pain." I would grab a big can of Foster's after we had put the kids to bed, and browse through the stack of business cards that were left behind. The alcohol helped me both relax and sleep. But that nightly routine didn't help my marriage, my job performance, or my weight. I ballooned up to 285 pounds. Courtesy of beer.

Withholding the story also affected my child rearing. I began to lose patience with my children more often. I had always felt as if I'd learned patience from my dad. Again, my discovery that he'd been lying to me all those years somehow made me discount the value of what he had taught me.

Also, I had a reverse reaction when it came to involvement in my children's lives. I coached my daughter's soccer teams. I coached my son's baseball teams and traveled with him when he became a competitive tennis player. I did it all with great enthusiasm, as if *not* wanting to be like Dad.

Ultimately, I decided I couldn't sit on the story any longer. When Dawn and Dave visited Seattle in 2005, Nedra and her husband, Dirk, and I all went out to dinner, and I told Dad's story there.

Of course, it left the two couples in speechless disbelief at first. But on some level, it did make sense to them. It made sense to Dave and Dirk because of the vague answers my father would give to their questions about his work. It made sense to Nedra because of Dad's personality. He was the type of man who could do clandestine work and keep it clandestine. (Remember: from a young boy he had protected his father's moonshine-drinking habit.) And later, when I told Bill, it made sense to him because he'd experienced the two unexplainable instances with the Austin-Healey, and he'd also overheard Dad talking to himself about the space shuttle not having that many back-up systems on it when Apollo I exploded.

It was there at the restaurant that I committed to writing a book. I began to do the research, the aid of the high-speed Internet and Google's search engine spurring me along. As I drilled down, I found that the business cards Dad had left me were from companies that had been connected to the development of nuclear missiles and/or space projects, and the control systems needed to manage them.

When I was looking for all the declassified documents I needed, I didn't get much support from those who could have shed the most light. As you know, the government doesn't go out of its way to help you. So, that was frustrating, but I was determined to find out everything I could.

46

Game On

IN ADDITION TO DOING INTENSIVE RESEARCH to learn as much about the business cards as I could, including the names and the businesses listed, I visited the Advanced Institute in Princeton, looking for pictures of my dad, because my dad spent a lot of time there, since von Neumann was his closest mentor. I also met with a noted Cold War professor at Princeton when I started my research. He told me that outside of Chicago, the government trained men and women on how to live a completely separate life. That made perfect sense because if you asked my dad a question, he would never answer it. He would always ask one back. If I asked him, "How was your day, Dad?" he would respond, "Well, what did you learn today, Johnny?" He always got the other person talking. Apparently, he was professionally trained to do that.

My family has a news clipping from the 1950s saying my dad had been promoted, and it even included an actual picture of him. Remember: up until '58, IBM admits that my dad existed. So, it is in the IBM publication, but they misspelled our name, Clauson. They spelled it "Clausen," which is quite common, but now I am wondering if they did that intentionally. The photo showed all these guys who had been promoted in the Applied Science Department, which was the Cold War arm of the Federal Systems Group, which IBM does admit existed. They had a special group inside IBM that basically did projects for the Cold War. It was just very odd in the 1950s to see four or five guys who were part of this same Applied Sciences group being promoted.

I also contacted Olivia Fermi, Enrico Fermi's granddaughter, asking for her help in discovering information about my dad. She sent my query to IBM and received a response from Paul Lasewicz, the official IBM archivist at the time, which she then forwarded to me.[1] We were able to get IBM to confirm that my dad did work there, at least up until 1958, after which he simply doesn't exist any longer in their files.

> Olivia, good morning! The additional info you provided helped, as well as a little google action. A W.W. Clauson joined IBM in 1950 in St. Paul, and became a customer engineer (CE) the following year in St. Louis. In 1953 he was assigned to our Poughkeepsie plant as a CE, and from there moved to Oakland. He was promoted to Operations Assistant in District 17 (Minnesota?) in 1957, and became a Western Region Special Systems representative for our Applied Science Organization. Of note—Poughkeepsie in 1953 was the center of IBM's electronics expertise, where our best electronics thinking resided. And our Applied Science organization was an organizational structure focused on bringing advanced science to bear on current and future client scientific computing needs. Cuthbert Hurd, a PhD in Mathematics and former Oak Ridge employee who organized a centralized computing facility there, headed Applied Science, which was formed in 1949. According to Emerson Pugh in his *Building IBM*, the organization was staffed with highly qualified people, many with PhDs in math, engineering, or science. The representatives were trained in sales and automatic computing, and then assigned to branch offices to assist with sales and installation of IBM equipment

for solving scientific and engineering problems. They also provided feedback to IBM product development groups on new requirements.

I don't have any information on Clauson post-1958, although I won't rule out that a very deep, very time-consuming dive into organizational documentation might turn up additional content. But with our Centennial ongoing, I won't have the resources for that this year.

Of course, I knew better. You don't delete somebody unless there are overwhelming issues with security and you have to try to cover somebody up. My brother, Bill, saw his paychecks personally until the day he quit. He was always snooping around once he figured out that things weren't adding up.

I'd handled his estate upon his death and saw that his paychecks came with an IBM logo on the upper right-hand corner. He'd been in IBM company photos and he received IBM employee Christmas gifts. We have his slide rule, given to him by von Neumann in the presence of Einstein, and the engraved gold Swiss clock given to him by the shah of Iran in 1971. That was thirteen years after Dad's name supposedly no longer existed in IBM's files, according to the first archivist.

The next archivist confirmed that when my dad went to Iowa State, he lived in a separate apartment off campus, and I have the address for that. But we know now he wasn't in school. They just paid for his apartment.

Since then, IBM has digitized everything, so if you put the word *the* in IBM's records, it will tell you how many millions of times the word is used in their archived files. You put my dad's name in and nothing comes up. Nothing! I can only surmise the reasons why my dad would have worked at a company for almost thirty-five years but be whitewashed from public company records.

Now, in case you're wondering, somewhere along the way, I assume it would be a reasonable question for my mother to ask her husband about their finances. Especially during the year my dad was pretending to be a farmer—how was he making any money? Why was it so difficult to find a job as an engineer right out of college? But these are questions that will likely remain unanswered forever. I can only assume it was my mom's blind faith about him not being able to find a job. Obviously, he must have been getting money for his calculation work.

I don't know if my parents reviewed their finances together. I don't know that she would have ever questioned his frequent trips or his seemingly strange career jump from an engineering student to a farmer. Maybe she was content to be a wife and mother, leaving all the details to my father to sort out. Or maybe they had some early conversations that laid the ground rules for their future together—a sweeping disclaimer that he'd be traveling a lot and not to worry, and not to ask questions.

Early in their marriage, when they were living in Minnesota, Dad won an award at work and was also promoted. The notice, mentioned earlier, included an actual picture of him, with his name misspelled. Still, Mom, being the proud wife, sent a note to the Kiron hometown newspaper, to be mentioned. When Dad heard what she'd done, he nearly blew a gasket, saying, "You do not print anything about me anywhere!" Needless to say, Mom never did that again, although for years she wondered why he'd gotten so angry over her sweet gesture.

Because there was always a constant paycheck, it's safe to say he was being paid by some government entity the whole time—from his acceptance into the National Defense Research Committee as a teenager to his retirement in 1984. Perhaps IBM simply took over in the early 1950s.

What I can say *for certain* is that when you're Swedish, it is very easy to compartmentalize. You don't dig a lot into details that aren't readily offered. I think it's part of the culture of Sweden to be very nonemotional, very matter-of-fact. Those traits are part of the reason why cell phones were so popular in Finland when they first came out. Nokia exploded originally because of the Finnish people, because Finns, like Swedes, don't like to have face-to-face conversations! They want to be on the phone.

I actually had a woman file a complaint against me in HR at Johnson & Johnson because I *wouldn't* hug her. Apparently, there's an Italian thing back in Jersey—when you say hello to somebody, you

267

give them a hug. Well, when she went in for the hug, I turned sideways and patted her arm, basically blocking her hug. She complained that I was being disrespectful to her culture. When HR told me what her complaint was, I said, "Are you serious? Listen, I'm Swedish. *We just don't do that.*"

47

A Woman's Faith

WHEN I FINALLY BEGAN TO TELL MOM some details about Dad's life, it didn't seem to affect her as much as it had affected my siblings. Perhaps this was because she came from an age when a man wasn't expected to discuss his work life with his wife. Dad had come from an abusive home, in a small town, and from a culture that wasn't overly expressive or communicative. Perhaps from a very early age, Mom accepted that her friend, then husband, was quiet and secretive when it came to personal matters. She would have no doubt seen the bruises his father had inflicted on him. Whether she would have asked him about the bruises, we don't know. But she seemed to accept him as he was and not ask a lot of questions once they were married. Maybe she'd always had an inkling that Dad was doing something other than computer sales, but as his faithful wife, she'd resolved that his secret was her secret.

Or perhaps it was because she was so sick, and she was longing to be with him again.

Mom's main concern was that I not *embarrass* Dad's memory by writing about him. Although I repeatedly stressed that I wanted to celebrate his life, not embarrass him, she was initially adamant that nothing about his life should be revealed. Dad worked for IBM, and that was all anyone needed to know. Looking back, I think this was just her way of registering discomfort with the story itself.

Mom contacted my brother, Bill, who is now an anesthesiologist in the Bay Area, to complain about my writing of the book. Bill called to admonish me about it. He initially shared her view that this just wasn't a story that needed to be told, that there were "too many government unknowns that would be best kept secret," he said.

We tried reading her excerpts about my dad, but they were vague; I didn't want to upset her. Mom, finally warming up to the idea of telling his story, said, "Johnny, you have to make sure you write about how dad liked to have dinner at the shah's palace."

I asked, "Why *was* Dad having dinner with the shah of Iran?" See, my dad never told me that. Mom had me walk to her closet and pull out the old clock that the shah had given him, thanking him for his contribution to the Iran/BBC project. The story slowly began to unravel from there.

The next time I visited her, I asked, "How could you never worry about your children or your husband?"

It was her faith in Christianity that wouldn't allow her to worry. She smiled and said, "It's all God's will."

My mother, a devout Christian, was quite vocal her entire life about being pro-Israeli and never could understand why Dad would hush her while in conversation about her love for Israel, even if they were at church. I remember very vividly my dad telling my mom, "Don't talk so loud, Marilyn!" He *literally* was protecting Israel, and he didn't want her comments to bring needless attention to him.

Mom took Dad's gesture to mean that he didn't care about Israel, a thought that would have been disturbing to her. He never explained himself though, other than telling her he didn't like politics. The real reason for his discomfort at her desire to openly support Israel was that he didn't want the attention or the added stress of having to talk about the issue. He had no interest in discussing theories or sharing opinions on what should and shouldn't happen, because he was actually living the reality on a daily basis.

My dad worried all the time. That's why he had to take Librium. And Mom was the complete opposite—she had complete trust in him and was completely loyal. He'd be packing to leave and she wouldn't know where he was going or when he'd be back, but she'd say, "Wallace, when you get home, that will be great. Just let us know if you can."

I remember as a small kid, I would say, "Mom, where's Dad going?" She'd say, "Well, we don't quite know, but he'll call if he can."

When I was a kid, sometimes I'd come home from school and he'd be gone again. He would periodically call. I remember as a small boy in Long Beach having to stand on a chair to get the phone off the wall to answer it. I'd answer in my kid voice, and Dad would say, "Can I talk to Marilyn?" My mom would get this gigantic smile on her face.

When he came home, he never acted like "Hey, the chief bottle-washer is now home" and we should all acknowledge him. He kind of melted into the background, same as he did anytime we were in public. He knew Mom had to take a strong position to run the family because he wasn't really involved a lot. So, he just quietly and subtly came into the house and went about his way. Of course, we were excited to see him again, but since he wasn't overly excited and my mom wasn't overly excited, we just thought that was the way it was. If they weren't too excited, we didn't get too excited. There were never really huge euphorias or huge depressions. Everything was kind of kept in the middle. I know that sounds strange, but it is exactly the way it was.

Interestingly enough, there's a very similar dynamic with my own family. Because I travel almost as much as my dad did, my wife and I always thought this way of living was normal. When I was on a work trip, I would often spend an extra day or two visiting friends and not come home right at the end of a meeting.

Everybody at work would ask, "What are you doing hanging around here for another day or two?"

I'd say, "I'm visiting friends."

That answer seemed to shock everyone; they assumed my wife would want me to come home immediately. I'm sure I picked it up from my dad, but to me, it was normal to hang around and see my old neighborhood family friends for a day or a day and a half and then come home. When else am I going to see them?

One time, my boss cornered me about this so-called strange behavior. He said, "I want to see your airplane ticket to make sure you are actually leaving at the end of the meeting." I guess a lot of couples want to know exactly when you're coming home and why you don't come home immediately. My wife had to basically run the family, with me being gone so much. Cell phones changed a lot of that, though.

I also think I married a woman very similar in temperament to Mom. My wife is an ICU ER nurse. She is unflappable and always so calm—at least when I'm not being relocated. And that's how I always pictured my mom.

We are a very stoic Swedish family. I only remember my dad once hugging my mom or holding her hand. Only one time did I ever see outright affection. It was in San Jose, in 1965. He went up behind my mom and gave her hug in the kitchen and walked away.

Of course, you can see where growing up with that lack of affection would get me in trouble later. In fact, my wife and I got in an argument when I refused to hold her hand outside the IBM building when we were getting our marriage license. I didn't think public affection near where I worked was appropriate, and she got really upset at me. I didn't separate marriage from my work. I said, "No, you don't do that when you're near a work environment."

Some days I'm amazed she still married me.

48

A Love Reunited

WE ALWAYS THOUGHT MY MOTHER would be the first one to die, because she always had high blood pressure and diabetes, and she was off and on insulin and always tired. She ended up also having IBS and celiac disease, we found out later. But no matter how she felt, she made sure that other people took precedence over her own needs—being selfless and giving even when she should have been concerned with herself.

Nedra used to always say that it would be better that my dad go first than my mom, because my dad would have been so lost without her. He would know how to boil an egg and make popcorn if he were lucky. Mom handled all the finances. She paid the bills their whole marriage. She knew exactly what was on the table and what there was to spend. My dad handled the investments, I'm sure, but she did the day-to-day.

She could handle life. She lived so much of her life alone anyway. She was more than capable of being alone. My dad really was so dependent on her when he was here, in every way. And because he was aware of the role she had to unknowingly take on, he honored her a lot. In his later years he would so often say how thankful he was for having such a good wife.

After Dad's death, Mom missed him terribly, but she dealt with it the best she could. Fortunately, Nedra, Dawn, and I lived nearby, and Bill visited as often as he could. She moved into a three-bedroom condo, closer to Nedra and Dawn. She rebounded very well, and since Dad had made good money and IBM kept paying a pension, she had enough to live on for the next twenty years. Dad had a nice salary, and it has been said that people with secret lives have a great pension (to keep everyone quiet, even in retirement).

Finally, she decided she was going to get off all the medicines and go on her own vitamins, and I think that is what prolonged her life. We'd told her since her blood pressure was up that she needed to at least be on a blood pressure medicine. Her own mom had died of a stroke, after all. But she wouldn't do it and she stroked.

She had left-sided weakness, but she never lost her mind. Dawn brought over her knitting needles and all of her yarn, to help Mom regain the use of her hands. And sure enough, she did it. From then on, she was knitting her heart out for all the grandchildren.

* * *

Mom died in 2011 at the age of eighty-eight. She had been diagnosed with uterine cancer, and we struggled as a family to decide if we were going to let her have surgery because she was always known to get infections. Her doctor said the cancer wouldn't have killed her, but we didn't want her to be constantly uncomfortable either.

A few days after surgery, she got pneumonia, and the family was called in the middle of the night. We all rushed to the hospital, where we then learned she had contracted every sort of infection possible, including *C. diff.*

When we visited her in the ICU she said, "Tell me more about Wallace." I tried not to tell my mom anything too shocking because I only wanted to tell her when my research and this book was completely finished, which wouldn't happen for several years.

Wanting to soothe her mind and appease her request, my brother read her the part of the story where Dad was having dinner at the shah's palace. Mom was so out of it on pain medication, she likely didn't hear a word.

At one point, in immense pain, Mom regained enough strength to ask Dawn to unplug everything and let her die. Dawn started to cry and said, "Mom, I can't do that. Are you kidding me, with John and Bill and Nedra? I'm not pulling the plug." Mom never brought it up again. She died within thirty-six hours, finally reunited with her beloved husband.

At Mom's funeral, Nedra gave an incredible overview of Mom's life. As much as Dad had traveled and went around the world, Mom never worried. They were two country kids who lived off a dirt road—and who fell in love with each other.

To this day, one of my greatest regrets was not telling Mom the whole story about Dad when she asked. But at the time, I said, "Mom, there is a sliver of a chance that Dad—your husband, my father—made the world a safer place to live. We should celebrate his life, and that's what we're going to do."

I believe he did.

And we have.

* * *

In 2012, I agreed to speak about the Cold War and living in Zurich to a retiree community in Phoenix, Arizona. Six months before I spoke, Sergei Khrushchev, Nikita Khrushchev's son, gave a lecture to the Pebble Creek residents. I stayed in the casita of the director for education, in which Sergei had also stayed. I was thinking, *Dad would turn over in his grave if he knew I slept in the same bed as Nikita Khrushchevn.*

It was during the Q and A session when a man stood up and said, "John, do you remember me? I was with you in school. My dad was also an IBMer, as director of IBM's Science Research Center. You were a great athlete. So, I went home and told my dad, 'Hey, we are going to do well in school because we have an athlete here, and his name is John Clauson.'"

My old classmate said that when his father didn't immediately answer, he continued, "Do you know of his dad? He works for IBM."

And then, in front of the audience of 250 people, my old friend told me that his dad's response was this: "You are never, ever to mention that name again, ever."

Perhaps our family name was forbidden or maybe even feared in some circles back then. But nothing in this world will keep me from telling the truth—and my dad's truth.

In the end, the family decided to celebrate Dad's life and his extensive career through the Cold War. Now everyone's eager to have the story told, Dad's secret finally seeing the light of day.

Dad, you can now come in from out of the cold.

APPENDIX

Yom Kippur Cease-Fire Sequence of Documents Between Kremlin and the White House

THE FOLLOWING SEQUENCE OF EVENTS during the UN cease-fire at the end of the Yom Kippur War of October of 1973 is taken from the declassified NSA archives that became available around 2001.

PAGE 1: Egypt agreeing to cease fire if Israel does the same.

PAGES 2–3: Brezhnev to Kissinger, claiming Israel is in violation of the Security Council cease-fire agreement.

PAGE 4: Richard Nixon assures Brezhnev that Israel will honor the truce, and implicates Egypt as the aggressor.

PAGES 5–6: Brezhnev becomes upset with "treachery" being allowed by the Americans during this cease-fire. He claims that relations could be permanently altered with Israel's actions.

PAGES 7–9: Brezhnev writing to Nixon on October 24, claiming the US and Russia should combine forces and intervene with combat troops, and stop Israel. Note "if it is impossible to act jointly with us," we will "consider the question of taking appropriate steps unilaterally." Nixon takes this as a threat to invade.

PAGES 10-12: Nixon on October 25 in his reply stating, "we could in no event accept unilateral action." Says this is not the time for Russia to act "unilaterally but in harmony with cool heads."

PAGES 13-14: Kissinger also on October 25 sends memo to allies and NATO partners (LUNS and Permreps), saying that Soviets considering "unilateral intervention" is "wholly unacceptable to us." We go to a heightened level of military along with nuclear heightened prepared-ness—"certain alert measures in our military forces around the world." This memo sends my father back to the missiles in Iran. Note, that the memo says they do not want "confrontation with the Soviets," and confidentiality is of the utmost of importance. The Soviets through their "mole" in some country, have this memo within twenty-four hours and have knowledge our increased military activities. My father told me that he was very concerned for the US wanted him to fly "commercially" to Iran, with him thinking they would know he was going back to Iran.

PAGES 15-18: This memo on October 26 from Brezhnev to Nixon claims the US has just "a few hours" to resolve Sadat's request to stop aggression and allow "food, supplies, and medications, and blood." He truly is questioning US "intentions." He also states that he has knowl-edge of the Kissinger's memo in going to "bring U.S. armed forces to combat readiness."

PAGE 19: Nixon replies back the next day to Brezhnev that Israel will comply with the Security Council's cease fire and insure that key sup-plies can be delivered. Nixon rebuttals back claiming that their inten-tion of "unilateral intervention," was a serious threat and it was taken "seriously."

great translation
rec'd 5:00 pm
10/23/73

N M C C
THE NATIONAL MILITARY COMMAND CENTER
WASHINGTON, D.C. 20301

THE JOINT STAFF

TRANSLATION OF USSR 02, 231807Z October 1973.

02
USA/USSR
231807R

TOP SECRET/SENSITIVE

ESTEEMED MR. PRESIDENT: SPEC CAT "EYES ONLY"

I AM NOTIFYING YOU THAT THE EGYPTIAN SIDE IS READY TO CEASE
FIRE IMMEDIATELY IF THE ISRAELI ARMED FORCES WILL CEASE FIRE.
YOU CAN CATEGORICALLY NOTIFY THE ISRAELI GOVERNMENT OF THIS.

WE HOPE THAT THE UNDERSTANDING DISPLAYED BY YOU OF THE URGENCY
AND ACUTENESS OF THE TASK TO IMMEDIATELY CEASE FIRE WILL BE
GIVEN TO THE ISRAELIS IN THE MOST EXPLICIT FORM.

WE PROPOSE THAT THE CEASE FIRE BE IMPLEMENTED IMMEDIATELY.

WE ALSO PROPOSE THAT THE SECURITY COUNCIL BE CONVENED MOST
URGENTLY. WE ARE GIVING OUR REPRESENTATIVE IN THE COUNCIL
CORRESPONDING INSTRUCTIONS.

WE WILL BE GRATEFUL IF YOU WILL URGENTLY INSTRUCT YOUR
REPRESENTATIVE IN THE SECURITY COUNCIL IN SUCH A WAY THAT
OUR AND YOUR REPRESENTATIVES ACT CONCERTEDLY ON THE BASIS
OF THE PLAN WHICH WAS THE SUBJECT OF DISCUSSION BETWEEN THE
USSR CHARGE D'AFFAIRES AND MR. KISSINGER.

                    RESPECTFULLY,

P SECRET/SENSITIVE   L. BREZHNEV

                    SPEC CAT "EYES ONLY"

Message from Brezhnev to Secretary Kissinger as read by Minister Vorontsov to the Secretary on the telephone on October 23, 1973 at 10:40 a.m.

President Sadat has informed us that in the morning on the 23 of October Israeli forces in violation of the decision of the Security Council renewed firing on the West Coast of the Suez Canal and are moving into the southern direction. We would like to underline that Moscow has its own reliable information which proves that this is the fact and that the Israelis apparently decided to widen their bridgehead on the West Coast of the Canal. Thus Israel once again challenges the decision of the Security Council. This is absolutely unacceptable. All this looks like as a flagrant deceit on the part of the Israelis. We will express the confidence that the United States will use all the possibilities they have and its authority to bring the Israelis to order. It goes without saying that Israeli forces in this case should be withdrawn to the positions where they stayed during the acceptance of the ceasefire decision.

President Sadat suggests that the Soviet Union and the United States agree among themselves about measures which would insure physical parting of Egyptian and Israeli forces with the help of the observers of the United Nations.

Sadat suggests in particular immediate use of the United Nations observers and first of all the personnel of the United Nations which was placed previously along side the Suez Canal and which is now in Cairo. That is our point of view, Brezhnev says, that it would be really wise to do so since the personnel of the United Nations, which is in Cairo now, need only appropriate orders and they could be immediately dispatched to the place of conflict.

2

We suggest that the Soviet Union and the United States urgently submit
to the Security Council a draft of appropriate resolution to this effect. If the
United States/agrees to that the draft could look like that and follows the text
of the draft:

The Security Council referring to its resolution 338 of October 22, 1973,

(1) Confirms to its decision about immediate cessation of all fire and all
military activity and demands that the forces of the sides should be withdrawn to
the position where they were at the moment of the adoption of the decision on
ceasefire.

(2) Suggest to the Secretary General of the United Nations to immediately
take steps for immediate dispatch of the UN observers to supervise the observation
of ceasefire between the forces of Israel and Egypt, using for that purpose first
of all the personnel of the United Nations which is at present in Cairo.

Mr. Brezhnev would like to underline to Secretary Kissinger the urgency
of these matters.

Sent via hotline o/a 1:10 p. m
Tuesday, October 23, 1973.

Dear Mr. General Secretary:

I have just received your message regarding violations of
the Security Council decision on the ceasefire in the Middle East.

I want to assure you that we assume full responsibility to
bring about a complete end of hostilities on the part of Israel.
Our own information would indicate that the responsibility for the
violation of the ceasefire belongs to the Egyptian side, but this is
not the time to debate that particular issue. We have insisted with
Israel that they take immediate steps to cease hostilities, and I urge
that you take similar measures with respect to the Egyptian side.

You and I have achieved an historic settlement over this
past weekend and we will not permit it to be destroyed.

                                Sincerely,

                                RN

Serial Translation
Rec'd 5:00 RPN
10/29/73

N M C C
THE NATIONAL MILITARY COMMAND CENTER
WASHINGTON, D.C. 20301

THE JOINT STAFF

TRANSLATION OF USSR 01, 231600Z October 1973.

01
USA/USSR
231600R

TOP SECRET/SENSITIVE

WASHINGTON. THE WHITE HOUSE. **SPEC CAT**   **"EYES ONLY"**

ESTEEMED MR. PRESIDENT:

ISRAEL HAS FLAGRANTLY VIOLATED THE SECURITY COUNCIL DECISION
ON THE CEASE FIRE IN THE MIDDLE EAST. WE IN MOSCOW ARE
SHOCKED THAT THE UNDERSTANDING WHICH WAS REACHED ONLY TWO
DAYS AGO HAS IN FACT BEEN RUPTURED BY THIS ACTION BY THE
ISRAELI LEADERS. WHY THIS TREACHERY WAS ALLOWED BY ISRAEL
IS MORE OBVIOUS TO YOU.

WE SEE ONE POSSIBILITY FOR CORRECTING THE SITUATION AND
FULFILLING THE UNDERSTANDING...IN FORCING ISRAEL TO
IMMEDIATELY OBEY THE SECURITY COUNCIL DECISION. WE VOUCH
FOR THE ARABS, SINCE THE LEADERS OF EGYPT AND SYRIA HAVE
STATED THAT THEY WILL IMPLICITLY FULFILL THE SECURITY
COUNCIL DECISION.

WE PLEDGED WITH YOU, JOINTLY AS GUARANTOR-COUNTRIES, TO
ENSURE THE FULFILLMENT OF THE SECURITY COUNCIL RESOLUTION.
IN THIS CONNECTION, WE PROPOSE THAT THE MOST DECISIVE
MEASURES BE TAKEN WITHOUT DELAY BY THE SOVIET UNION AND

TOP SECRET/SENSITIVE

5

TRANSLATION OF USSR 01, 231600Z October 1973 [continued].

THE UNITED STATES OF AMERICA TO STOP THE VIOLATIONS OF
THE UNDERSTANDING REACHED AND OF THE SECURITY COUNCIL
RESOLUTION BASED ON [THIS UNDERSTANDING]. WE WOULD LIKE
TO BELIEVE THAT ON YOUR PART, ON THE PART OF THE UNITED
STATES GOVERNMENT, EVERYTHING WILL BE DONE IN ORDER THAT
THE SECURITY COUNCIL DECISION AND OUR UNDERSTANDING WITH
YOU WILL BE IMPLEMENTED. TOO MUCH IS AT STAKE, NOT ONLY
AS CONCERNS THE SITUATION IN THE MIDDLE EAST, BUT IN OUR
RELATIONS AS WELL.

WE WILL BE GRATEFUL FOR A SPEEDY RESPONSE.

RESPECTFULLY,

L. BREZHNEV

Mr. President:

I have received your letter in which you inform me that Israel ceased fighting. The facts, however, testify that Israel continues drastically to ignore the ceasefire decision of the Security Council. Thus, it is brazenly challenging both the Soviet Union and the United States since it is our agreement with you which consititutes the basis of the Security Council decision. In short, Israel simply embarked on the road to defeat.

It continues to seize new and new territory. As you know, the Israeli forces have already fought their way into Suez. It is impossible to allow such to continue. Let us together, the Soviet Union and the United States urgently dispatch to Egypt Soviet and American military contigents, with their mission the implementation of the decision of the Security Council of August 22 and 23 concerning the cessation of fire and of all military activities and also of the understanding with you on the guarantee of the implementation of the decisions of the Security Council

It is necessary to adhere with/delay. I will say it straight that if you find it impossible to act jointly with us in this matter, we should be faced with the necessity urgently to consider the question of taking appropriate steps unilaterally.

We cannot allow arbitrariness on the part of Israel. "

We have an understanding with you which we value highly--that is
to act jointly. Let us implement this understanding on a concrete
case in this complex situation. It will be a good example of our
agreed actions in the interest of peace. We have no doubt that all
those who are in favor of detente, of peace, of good relations between
the Soviet Union and the United States will only welcome such joint
action of ours. I will appreciate immediate and clear reply from you.

Respectively,

L. Brezhnev

October 25, 1973

Mr. General Secretary:

I have carefully studied your important message of this evening.
I agree with you that our understanding to act jointly for peace is of the
highest value and that we should implement that understanding in this
complex situation.

I must tell you, however, that your proposal for a particular kind
of joint action, that of sending Soviet and American military contingents
to Egypt is not appropriate in the present circumstances.

We have no information which would indicate that the ceasefire is
now being violated on any significant scale. Such violations as are taking
place can be dealt with most effectively by increased numbers of observer
teams to inform the Security Council of the true responsibility for violations.

We are prepared to take every effective step to guarantee the
implementation of the ceasefire and are already in close touch with
the Government of Israel to ensure that it abides fully by the terms of the
Security Council decisions. I assume that you are taking similar steps
with Egypt.

In these circumstances, we must view your suggestion of unilateral
action as a matter of the gravest concern involving incalculable consequences.

It is clear that the forces necessary to impose the ceasefire terms
on the two sides would be massive and would require closest coordination

so as to avoid bloodshed. This is not only clearly infeasible but is not
appropriate to the situation. In this situation the Security Council requires
accurate information about what is occurring so that it as well as each of
us can exert maximum influence in Cairo and Tel-Aviv, respectively, to
ensure compliance with the terms of the ceasefire.

To this end, I am prepared to join with you at once to augment
the present truce supervisory force by additional men and equipment. I
would be prepared to see included in such augmented truce supervisory
units a number of American and Soviet personnel, though not combat
forces. It would be understood that this is an extraordinary and temporary
step, solely for the purpose of providing adequate information concerning
compliance by both sides with the terms of the ceasefire. If this is what
you mean by contingents, we will consider it.

Mr. General Secretary, in the spirit of our agreements this is
the time for acting not unilaterally but in harmony and with cool heads.
I believe my proposal is consonant with the letter and spirit of our understandings and would ensure a prompt implementation of the ceasefire.
This would establish a base from which we could move into the negotiations
foreseen by Security Council Resolution 338 which we shall jointly sponsor.

I will await a prompt and positive reply from you on these proposals.
Meanwhile, I will order the necessary preparations for the steps I have
outlined. Upon receipt of your agreement, I will immediately designate

representatives to work out the modalities with your representatives.

You must know, however, that we could in no event accept unilateral action. This would be in violation of our understandings, of the agreed Principles we signed in Moscow in 1972 and of Article II of the Agreement on Prevention of Nuclear War. As I stated above, such action would produce incalculable consequences which would be in the interest of neither of our countries and which would end all we have striven so hard to achieve.

WH

Department of State TELEGRAM

SECRET

25 101Z OCT 73 ZFF4
FM SECSTATE WASHDC
TO USMISSION NATO FLASH 0587
BT
S E C R E T STATE 210450

NODIS

CONTROL: 7166Q
RECD: 25 OCT 73 7:30AM

E.O. 11652: XGDS
SUBJECT: MESSAGE FROM THE SECRETARY.

FOR AMBASSADOR RUMSFELD FROM THE SECRETARY

PLEASE URGENTLY INFORM LUNS AND PERMREPS ON COMPLETELY
CONFIDENTIAL BASIS AS FOLLOWS.

1. AS THEY ARE AWARE THE EGYPTIANS HAVE PROPOSED
INTRODUCTION OF US AND SOVIET FORCES IN THE AREA OF THE
CONFLICT. THE SOVIETS HAVE SUPPORTED THIS PROPOSAL.
IN ADDITION WE HAVE RECEIVED INDICATIONS THAT SOVIETS
MAY BE CONSIDERING UNILATERAL INTERVENTION.

2. WE ARE INFORMING SOVIETS THAT INTRODUCTION OF US
AND SOVIET MILITARY CONTINGENTS IS INAPPROPRIATE BUT
THAT WE ARE READY TO SUPPORT INCREASE IN SUPERVISORY
FORCE, INCLUDING, AS AN EXTRAORDINARY AND TEMPORARY
MEASURE, SOME US AND SOVIET PERSONNEL. FUNCTION WOULD
BE SOLELY SUPERVISORY AND ACQUISITION OF
ACCURATE INFORMATION REGARDING COMPLIANCE OF THE TWO
SIDES WITH THE CEASEFIRE.

3. AT THE SAME TIME, WE HAVE MADE CLEAR THAT ANY
UNILATERAL INTERVENTION BY THE SOVIETS IS WHOLLY
UNACCEPTABLE TO US.

4. AS A PRECAUTIONARY MEASURE WE HAVE UNDERTAKEN
CERTAIN ALERT MEASURES IN OUR MILITARY FORCES AROUND
THE WORLD, INCLUDING EUROPE.

5. WE ARE OF COURSE IN CLOSE TOUCH WITH ISRAELIS TO
ENSURE THEIR COMPLIANCE WITH THE CEASEFIRE AND ARE
CONFIDENT THAT OUR POSITION WILL BRING THE FIGHTING
TO A CONCLUSION.

SECRET

13

Department of State

SECRET

TELEGR

6. WE HOPE WE CAN COUNT ON FULL NATO SUPPORT FOR OUR ACTIONS IN THIS SITUATION. OUR SOLE PURPOSE IS TO END THE FIGHTING AND LAY THE BASIS FOR NEGOTIATIONS LEADING TO A SETTLEMENT AND PREVENT UNILATERAL SOVIET ACTIONS WHICH WOULD REPRESENT GRAVE THREAT TO PEACE.

7. PLEASE ENSURE THAT YOUR COLLEAGUES UNDERSTAND THAT WE DO NOT REPEAT NOT WANT A PUBLIC CONFRONTATION WITH THE SOVIETS AND THAT THEREFORE THE INFORMATION YOU HAVE CONVEYED MUST BE KEPT TOTALLY CONFIDENTIAL.

KISSINGER

DRAFTED BY: TEXT AS RECEIVED FROM WHITE HOUSE

APPROVED BY: S-THE SECRETARY

CLEARANCE: S/S-O:RMWRIGHT

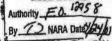

N M C C

THE NATIONAL MILITARY COMMAND CENTER
WASHINGTON, D.C. 20301

THE JOINT STAFF

TRANSLATION OF USSR 01, 270020Z October 1973.

01
USA/USSR
270020R

TOP SECRET/SENSITIVE

PAGE 1   **SPEC CAT**

"EYES ONLY"

DEAR MR. PRESIDENT:

PRESIDENT SADAT HAS JUST INFORMED US THAT HE REQUESTED
YOU TO TAKE CATEGORICAL MEASURES FOR AN UNCONDITIONAL CESSATION
OF HOSTILITIES BY ISRAEL, WHO IN VIOLATION OF ALL THE DECISIONS
ADOPTED BY THE SECURITY COUNCIL IS WAGING FIERCE BATTLES AGAINST
THE EGYPTIAN THIRD ARMY.

I MUST TELL YOU THAT SUCH ACTIONS BY ISRAEL JEOPARDIZE
THE INTERESTS OF UNIVERSAL PEACE AND ARE DETRIMENTAL TO THE
PRESTIGE OF THE SOVIET UNION AND THE UNITED STATES OF AMERICA
AS POWERS WHICH HAVE ASSUMED DEFINITE OBLIGATIONS TO
RESTORE PEACE IN THE MIDDLE EAST.

WE ALSO KNOW THAT PRESIDENT SADAT, IN ADDITION TO HIS APPEAL
TO YOU TO SEEK TO OBTAIN A CESSATION OF HOSTILITIES FROM
ISRAEL, ALSO REQUESTED THAT EGYPTIAN AIRCRAFT, HELICOPTERS OR
OTHER MEANS OF TRANSPORTATION BE GRANTED AN OPPORTUNITY TO
DELIVER NON-MILITARY CARGO UNIMPEDED -- CARGO SUCH AS FOOD
SUPPLIES, MEDICATIONS, AND BLOOD FOR THE WOUNDED IN THE THIRD
EGYPTIAN ARMY, LOCATED ON THE EASTERN BANK OF THE SUEZ CANAL.

TOP SECRET/SENSITIVE   SPEC CAT   "EYES ONLY"

TRANSLATION OF USSR-01, 270020Z October 1973 [Page 2].

PRESIDENT SADAT HAS ALSO INFORMED US THAT YOUR ANSWER TO HIM
WAS THAT YOU WILL NEED SEVERAL HOURS TO TAKE APPROPRIATE
MEASURES. NOW, WHEN I APPEAL TO YOU, SEVERAL HOURS HAVE ALREADY
PASSED. UNFORTUNATELY, HOWEVER, WE HAVE INFORMATION THAT THE
EGYPTIAN PRESIDENT'S REQUEST HAS STILL NOT MET WITH A
FAVORABLE DECISION.

I MUST TELL YOU FRANKLY THAT IF THE NEXT FEW HOURS DO NOT
BRING NEWS THAT NECESSARY MEASURES HAVE BEEN TAKEN TO RESOLVE
THE QUESTION RAISED BY PRESIDENT SADAT, THEN WE WILL HAVE THE
MOST SERIOUS DOUBTS REGARDING THE INTENTIONS OF THE AMERICAN
SIDE CONCERNING THE UNDERSTANDING RECENTLY REACHED BY US ON
AN IMMEDIATE CEASE FIRE, AND ALSO CONCERNING A CONFIDENTIAL
PORTION PERTAINING TO THE NORMALIZATION OF THE SITUATION AND
THE RESTORATION OF PEACE IN THE MIDDLE EAST.

WE STILL HOPE THAT AT THIS DIFFICULT HOUR, OUR RESPONSIBILITY
FOR THE OUTCOME OF ALL EVENTS WILL BE DISCHARGED IN THE NEXT
FEW HOURS. WE HOPE, IN PARTICULAR, THAT ON YOUR PART, EFFECTIVE
AND IMMEDIATE INFLUENCE WILL BE BROUGHT TO BEAR ON ISRAEL
CONCERNING PRESIDENT SADAT'S REQUEST.

NOW I WANT TO TOUCH ON ANOTHER MATTER, MR. PRESIDENT. FOR
TWO DAYS, WE HAVE NOT REACTED TO YOUR UNEXPECTED DECISION
TO BRING UNITED STATES ARMED FORCES, INCLUDING THOSE IN EUROPE,
TO COMBAT READINESS.

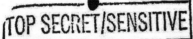

I HAVE JUST COMPLETED MY ADDRESS AT THE WORLD PEACE CONGRESS.
IN MY SPEECH, I DECIDED NOT TO TOUCH UPON THE ISSUE OF YOUR
DECISION, WHICH AS IS WELL KNOWN HAS ATTRACTED WIDESPREAD
ATTENTION THROUGHOUT THE WORLD. I DID NOT MENTION THIS
BECAUSE I HAD IN MIND DISCUSSING THIS QUESTION DIRECTLY WITH
YOU IN A CALM ATMOSPHERE. HOWEVER, ISRAEL'S CONTINUING
NON-COMPLIANCE WITH THE SECURITY COUNCIL'S DECISIONS, COMBINED
WITH THE ABOVEMENTIONED ACTIONS UNDERTAKEN BY THE U.S.A.,
UNWITTINGLY SUGGESTS THE IDEA THAT THE MEASURES UNDERTAKEN
ON THE PART OF THE UNITED STATES TO INFLUENCE ISRAEL TO
IMMEDIATELY FULFILL THE SECURITY COUNCIL'S RESOLUTIONS ARE
NOT ONLY INADEQUATE AND INEFFECTIVE, BUT, AS IS EVIDENT,
ENABLE ISRAEL TO CONTINUE ITS ADVENTURISTIC ACTIONS.

I REPEAT THAT WE ARE SURPRISED BY YOUR ORDER TO BRING U.S.
ARMED FORCES TO COMBAT READINESS. HOWEVER, THIS STEP
UNQUESTIONABLY DOES NOT PROMOTE A RELAXATION OF INTERNATIONAL
TENSION, AND WAS BY NO MEANS THE RESULT OF ANY KIND OF ACTIONS
BY THE SOVIET UNION, WHICH WOULD REPRESENT EVEN THE SLIGHTEST
VIOLATION ON OUR PART OF THE UNDERSTANDING REACHED WITH YOU.
BUT WE ARE FACED WITH THE FACT AND CANNOT BUT TAKE THIS INTO
CONSIDERATION.

IT SEEMS TO US THAT THE MEASURES TAKEN WERE CARRIED OUT AS A
MEANS OF PRESSURE ON THE SOVIET UNION. THERE HAVE BEEN OPEN
COMMENTS ON THIS IN THE AMERICAN PRESS AND EVEN AT PRESS

CONFERENCES. BUT YOU YOURSELF UNDERSTAND THAT SUCH CALCULATIONS
CANNOT INTIMIDATE US OR SHAKE OUR RESOLVE TO ACT IN THE SPIRIT
OF UNCONDITIONAL COMPLIANCE WITH ALL PORTIONS OF THE SECURITY
COUNCIL'S DECISIONS.

RETURNING TO THE SITUATION IN THE MIDDLE EAST, I WOULD LIKE TO
STRESS THAT IT IS OUR PROFOUND CONVICTION THAT THE IMMEDIATE
RESPONSIBILITY IS THE TASK OF INFLUENCING ISRAEL TO FORCE IT
TO IMMEDIATELY FULFILL THE SECURITY COUNCIL'S DECISIONS, BASED
ON OUR UNDERSTANDING WITH YOU.

I ALSO HOPE THAT PRESIDENT SADAT'S REQUEST TO YOU WILL MEET
WITH A FAVORABLE DECISION AND THAT YOUR PERSONNEL, AS WELL AS
THE OBSERVER PERSONNEL, AS DETERMINED BY THE SECURITY COUNCIL'S
DECISION, WILL WITHIN THE NEXT DAY BE DISPATCHED TO [THEIR]
DESIGNATED PLACES TO FULFILL THEIR FUNCTIONS.

                          RESPECTFULLY,

                          L. BREZHNEV

26 OCTOBER 1973
COLLATION: 3 3 26

TOP SECRET

SENSITIVE

WHITE HOUSE
SITUA... ...OM
SPECAT OCT 27 AM 2:37

DEAR MR. GENERAL SECRETARY:

WE HAVE STUDIED YOUR MOST RECENT MESSAGE CAREFULLY. I
WANT TO ASSURE YOU THAT WE STRONGLY FAVOR THE ESTABLISHMENT OF AN
EFFECTIVE CEASEFIRE AND THAT WE WILL CONTINUE TO MAKE EVERY EFFORT
TO ACHIEVE THIS FULLY, IN THE SPIRIT OF OUR MUTUAL UNDERSTANDINGS
AND IF AT ALL POSSIBLE THROUGH COOPERATIVE EFFORTS WITH YOU.

AS TO YOUR FIRST POINT, WE WILL RAISE WITH THE ISRAELI
GOVERNMENT THE ISSUE OF NON-MILITARY CARGO, INCLUDING FOOD
SUPPLIES, MEDICATIONS AND BLOOD FOR THE WOUNDED FOR THE EGYPTIAN
ARMY LOCATED ON THE EAST SIDE OF THE CANAL ON AN URGENT BASIS.
WE WILL MAKE EVERY EFFORT TO GET YOU A RESPONSE BY LATE AFTERNOON
TODAY WASHINGTON TIME.

WE AGREE ALSO THAT THE UNITED NATIONS TRUCE SUPERVISORY
ORGANIZATION PERSONNEL SHOULD BE POSITIONED PROMPTLY AND OUR
UNDERSTANDING IS THAT THIS PROCESS IS WELL IN TRAIN. WE BELIEVE
THAT THE SAME PRINCIPLE SHOULD APPLY TO THE UNTSO AS APPLIES TO
THE UN FORCE, NAMELY, THAT IT WOULD BE BETTER IF IT WAS MADE UP OF
INDIVIDUALS COMING FROM COUNTRIES WHO ARE NOT PERMANENT MEMBERS
OF THE SECURITY COUNCIL. HOWEVER, IN LIGHT OF YOUR DESIRES TO
HAVE SOVIET OBSERVERS INVOLVED, WE HAVE OFFERED A LIMITED NUMBER
OF AMERICAN PERSONNEL FOR SERVICE IN THE UNTSO. WE BELIEVE THE =

SECRETARY GENERAL IS CONSIDERING THE AUGMENTATION OF UNTSO, AND
THAT HE WILL DECIDE HOW MANY OF OUR RESPECTIVE PERSONNEL WILL BE
UTILIZED. WE CANNOT ACCEPT THAT OBSERVERS OR REPRESENTATIVES OF
ANY COUNTRY CAN BE ACTIVE OUTSIDE THE OBSERVER FRAMEWORK OF THE
UN.

AT THE SAME TIME, WE ALSO FAVOR THE EARLIEST POSSIBLE
POSITIONING OF THE UNITED NATIONS FORCE, AND WE WELCOME THE FACT
THAT SECRETARY GENERAL WALDHEIM HAS MOVED PROMPTLY AND THAT
THE FIRST CONTINGENTS OF THE UN FORCE HAVE BEEN AIRLIFTED TODAY
FROM CYPRUS TO THE AREA.

FINALLY, AS TO THE ACTIONS WHICH THE UNITED STATES TOOK AS
A RESULT OF YOUR LETTER OF OCTOBER 24, I WOULD RECALL YOUR SENTENCES
IN THAT LETTER: ''IT IS NECESSARY TO ADHERE WITHOUT DELAY. I WILL SAY
IT STRAIGHT THAT IF YOU FIND IT IMPOSSIBLE TO ACT PROMPTLY WITH US IN
THIS MATTER, WE SHOULD BE FACED WITH THE NECESSITY URGENTLY TO
CONSIDER THE QUESTION OF TAKING APPROPRIATE STEPS UNILATERALLY.''
MR. GENERAL SECRETARY, THESE ARE SERIOUS WORDS AND WERE TAKEN
SERIOUSLY HERE IN WASHINGTON. WE BELIEVE OUR JOINT SUPPORT FOR
THE ESTABLISHMENT OF THE UN FORCE INCLUDING THE PERMANENT MEMBERS
WAS A SENSIBLE COURSE IN OUR MUTUAL INTEREST. FOR OUR PART, WE
CONTINUE TO ADHERE SCRUPULOUSLY TO THE PRINCIPLE OF JOINT COOPERATION
TO HELP MAINTAIN AN EFFECTIVE CEASEFIRE LOOKING TOWARDS A FUNDAMENTAL
SETTLEMENT.

SINCERELY,

RICHARD NIXON

SENSITIVE

TOP SECRET

SPECAT

NOTES

CHAPTER 4: SECOND CHANCES AND A GIFT FROM GOD

1. Darold A. Treffert, *Extraordinary People: Understanding Savant Syndrome* (New York: Ballantine, 2006), 15.
2. Brian Fung, "Eureka! When a Blow to the Head Creates a Sudden Genius," *Atlantic*, May, 17 2012.
3. Rosa Prince, "From 'Goof' to Maths Genius Thanks to a Blow to the Head," *Telegraph* (UK), April 20, 2014, http://www.telegraph.co.uk/news/worldnews/northamerica/usa/10777222/From-goof-to-maths-genius-thanks-to-a-blow-to-the-head.html.

CHAPTER 5: THE PROBLEM SOLVER

1. David A Mindell, "Engineers, Psychologists, Administrators: Control Systems Research in Wartime, 1940–45," *IEEE Control Systems* magazine, August 1995, 92, http://ieeexplore.ieee.org/stamp/stamp.jsp?tp=&arnumber=408457.

CHAPTER 6: AN INVITATION FROM THE NDRC

1. Military-Industrial Complex Speech, Dwight D. Eisenhower, 1961, at http://coursesa.matrix.msu.edu/~hst306/documents/indust.html.
2. "Order Establishing the National Defense Research Committee," author's possession.
3. Vannevar Bush, Bushvarsion.hink,u *Atlantic Monthly*, July 1945.
4. Jerome B. Wiesner, *Vannevar Bush, 1890–1974: A Biographical Memoir* (Washington, D.C.: National Academy of Sciences of the United States, 1979), PDF e-Book, 94.95. Available online at http://www.nasonline.org/publications/biographical-memoirs/memoir-pdfs/bush-vannevar.pdf,
5. Ibid., 95i96.
6. Christoph Laucht, *Elemental Germans: Klaus Fuchs, Rudolf Peierls and the Making of British Nuclear Culture 1939–59* (Basingstoke, UK: Palgrave Macmillan, 2012), 41.
7. Newsweek Staff, "Radar," *Newsweek*, December 1, 1997, http://www.newsweek.com/radar-169944.
8. Ibid.
9. G. Pascal Zachary, *Endless Frontier: Vannevar Bush, Engineer of the American Century* (New York: Free Press, 1997), 127–29.
10. Ibid., 130–31.

CHAPTER 7: A REAL EDUCATION

1. Jack B. Copeland, Copelandshe Quaker?of Computing, Q*Stanford Encyclopedia of Philosophy*, revised June 9, 2006, http://plato.stanford.edu/entries/computing-history/.
2. Robert Slater, *Portraits in Silicon* (Cambridge: MIT Press, 1989), 54ridg
3. "John Atanasoff," TheInventors.com, http://theinventors.org/library/inventors/blatanasoff_berry.htm.

CHAPTER 8: HIDDEN GENIUS

1. David A Mindell, "Engineers, Psychologists, Administrators: Control Systems Research in Wartime, 1940–45," *IEEE Control Systems* (August 1995): 95, http://ieeexplore.ieee.org/stamp/stamp.jsp?tp=&arnumber=408457.
2. Irvin Stewart, *Organizing Scientific Research for War: The Administrative History of the Office of Scientific Research and Development* (Boston: Little, Brown, 1948), 52–78.

CHAPTER 9: THE SETUP

1. See "The Nobel Prize in Physics 1939: Ernest Lawrence," Nobelprize.org, accessed February 6, 2017, https://www.nobelprize.org/nobel_prizes/physics/laureates/1939/lawrence-bio.html.
2. Luis W. Alvarez, *Alfred Lee Loomis: 1887–1975: A Biographical Memoir* (Washington, DC: National Academy of Sciences, 1980), http://www.nasonline.org/publications/biographical-memoirs/memoir-pdfs/loomis-alfred.pdf.
3. Joe Holley, "Henry Loomis, 89; Physicist Led VOA and Public Broadcasting," *Washington Post*, November 8, 2008, http://www.washingtonpost.com/wp-dyn/content/article/2008/11/07/AR2008110703752.html.
4. Ibid.
5. Ibid.

CHAPTER 10: BOMBS AWAY

1. Times Staff and wire reports, "George Elliott, 85; Warning on Pearl Harbor Went Unheeded," *LA Times*, December 26, 2003, http://articles.latimes.com/2003/dec/26/local/me-elliott26.
2. George Elliott Jr., "There's Nothing Wrong with Our Radar!" ed. David J. Castello, PearlHarbor.com, accessed February 7, 2017, http://www.pearl-harbor.com/georgeelliott/index.html.
3. Ibid.
4. Ibid.
5. Ibid.
6. Ibid.
7. Times Staff and wire reports, "George Elliott, 85."
8. Ibid.
9. Ibid.
10. "Pearl Harbor: Day of Infamy," Military.com, accessed February 7, 2017, http://www.military.com/Resources/HistorySubmittedFileView?file=history_pearlharbor.htm.
11. Evan Thomas, *Sea of Thunder: Four Commanders and the Last Great Naval Campaign 1941–1945* (New York: Simon and Schuster, 2007), 57–59.
12. "Pearl Harbor Facts," About.com, accessed February 7, 2017, http://history1900s.about.com/od/Pearl-Harbor/a/Pearl-Harbor-Facts.htm.

13. NHHC, "Midway Operational Lesson," *Naval History Blog*, June 7, 2013, https://www.navalhistory.org/2013/06/07/midway-operational-lesson.

14. Robert Keith, "CRS Report for Congress Received through the CRS Web," Library of Congress, Congressional Research Service, September 13, 2001, https://digital.library.unt.edu/ark:/67531/metacrs7567/m1/1/high_res_d/RS21010_2001Sep13.pdf, p. 2.

15. Ibid.

16. Ibid., 2.

17. Ibid., 3.

18. Ibid., 4.

CHAPTER 11: THE PROBLEM WITH PEARL HARBOR

1. "1941 JANUARY 4 WARPLANE PRODUCTION: Interviewing Date 12/18–23/40: Survey #226-K," question #6, http://ibiblio.org/pha/Gallup/Gallup%201941.htm.

2. Harry Elmer Barnes, "Summary and Conclusions," in Harry Elmer Barnes, ed., *Perpetual War for Perpetual Peace: A Critical Examination of the Foreign Policy of Franklin Delano Roosevelt and Its Aftermath* (Caldwell, ID: Caxton Printers, 1953), 682–83.

3. Robert Higgs, "How U.S. Economic Warfare Provoked Japan's Attack on Pearl Harbor," Independent Institute, May 1, 2006, http://www.independent.org/newsroom/article.asp?id=1930.

4. Ibid.

5. George Morgenstern, "The Actual Road to Pearl Harbor," in Barnes, ed., *Perpetual War for Perpetual Peace*, 322–23, 327–28.

6. Ibid.

7. Higgs, "How U.S. Economic Warfare Provoked Japan's Attack on Pearl Harbor."

8. Morgenstern, "The Actual Road to Pearl Harbor," 384.

9. Elliott, Jr., "There's Nothing Wrong with Our Radar!"

10. Photograph in author's possession. See also the aerial view photo at https://upload.wikimedia.org/wikipedia/commons/9/95/K-25_%287609929206%29.jpg.

11. William Lanouette, with Bela Silard, *Genius in the Shadows: A Biography of Leo Szilard: The Man Behind the Bomb* (New York: Skyhorse, 2013).

12. Howard Walls, letter to Elizabeth B. Drewry, September 29, 1965, author's possession.

13. Ibid.

14. National Defense Research Committee Report for First Year of Operation, 27 Jun 40–28 Jun 41, p. 35, author's possession.

15. Alex Wellerstein, "The Price of the Manhattan Project," *The Nuclear Secrecy Blog*, May 17, 2013, http://blog.nuclearsecrecy.com/2013/05/17/the-price-of-the-manhattan-project/.

16. Ibid.

17. Ibid.

18. The SCR-535 was an IFF (identify friend or foe) set with a range of seventy-five miles.

CHAPTER 12: IN THE NAVY

1. Merton J. Peck and Frederic M. Scherer, *The Weapons Acquisition Process: An Economic Analysis* (Harvard Business School, 1962), 619.

CHAPTER 13: THE RISE OF RADAR
1. Kuang Keng Kuek Ser, "Where Did Iran Get Its Military Arms over the Last 70 Years?" PRI, June 1, 2016, https://www.pri.org/stories/2016-06-01/where-did-iran-get-its-military-arms-over-last-70-years.
2. Ibid.

CHAPTER 14: LOVE AND MARRIAGE
1. Henry De Wolf Smyth, "Atomic Energy for Military Purposes (The Smyth Report)," http://www.atomicarchive.com/Docs/SmythReport/smyth_iii.shtml.

CHAPTER 15: THE FARMER WITH AN ENGINEERING DEGREE
1. PAN, "The DDT Story," the Pesticide Action Network website, accessed February 7, 2017, http://www.panna.org/resources/ddt-story.

CHAPTER 20: AN UNLIKELY COVER
1. Michael Heale, *The United States in the Long Twentieth Century: Politics and Society since 1900*, 2nd ed. (n.p.: Bloomsbury Academic, 2015), 174.
2. E-mail from Paul Lasewicz regarding Wallace Clauson, sent to Olivia Fermi, granddaughter of Enrico Fermi, and forwarded to me May 6, 2011.
3. Ibid.

CHAPTER 21: HIRED BY IBM
1. "IBM 701," IBM Archives, accessed February 8, 2017, https://www-03.ibm.com/ibm/history/exhibits/701/701_intro.html.
2. Ibid.
3. Ibid.
4. E-mail from Paul Lasewicz regarding Wallace Clauson, sent to Olivia Fermi, and forwarded to me May 6, 2001.
5. "704 Data Processing System," IBM Archives, accessed February 8, 2017, https://www-03.ibm.com/ibm/history/exhibits/mainframe/mainframe_PP704.html.
6. Ana Swanson, "What It Would Look Like If the Hiroshima Bomb Hit Your City," *Washington Post*, August 5, 2015, https://www.washingtonpost.com/news/wonk/wp/2015/08/05/what-it-would-look-like-if-the-hiroshima-bomb-hit-your-city/?utm_term=.50a56f3d8862.
7. John Markoff, "Laid-Back in the Lab, Maybe, but They Spurred the Weapons Race," *New York Times*, July 4, 2011, http://www.nytimes.com/2011/07/05/science/05bomb.html.
8. Ibid.
9. Ibid.

CHAPTER 22: FEAR AND A FALSE ALARM
1. "Oasis Bordello Museum," RoadsideAmerica.com, accessed February 8, 2017, http://www.roadsideamerica.com/story/13039.

CHAPTER 23: NASA

1. Terrence R. Fehner and F. G. Gosling, *Battlefield of the Cold War: The Nevada Test Site*, vol. 1, *Atmospheric Nuclear Weapons Testing, 1951–1963* (Washington, D.C.: United States Department of Energy, 2006).

2. "Operation Hardtack I," Nuclear Weapon Archive, last changed November 30, 2001, http://www.nuclearweaponarchive.org/Usa/Tests/Hardtack1.html.

CHAPTER 24: DANGEROUS TECHNOLOGY AND SAFE SUNDAYS

1. "Project Pluto," The Black Vault, accessed February 8, 2017, http://www.theblackvault.com/documentarchive/project-pluto-nuclear-ramjet-engines/#.

2. Sebastian Anthony, "Lockheed Unveils SR-72 Hypersonic Mach 6 Scramjet Spy Plane," *ExtremeTech* (blog), November 6, 2013, https://www.extremetech.com/extreme/170463-lockheed-unveils-sr-72-hypersonic-mach-6-scramjet-spy-plane.

CHAPTER 26: JACK-OF-ALL-TRADES

1. See "Stephen W. Dunwell," IBM Archives, https://www-03.ibm.com/ibm/history/exhibits/builders/builders_dunwell.html.

2. Chuck Boyer, *The 360 Revolution* (Armonk, NY: IBM, 2004), ftp://ftp.software.ibm.com/eserver/zseries/misc/bookoffer/download/360revolution_040704.pdf, 16.

3. Ibid., 17.

4. Jake Widman, "Lessons Learned: IT's Biggest Project Failures," *PC World*, October 9, 2008, http://www.pcworld.com/article/152103/it_project_failures.html.

5. National Paint, Varnish and Lacquer Association, "The House in the Middle" (film), 1954, https://archive.org/details/Houseint1954.

6. Herman Kahn, *On Thermonuclear War* (Princeton University Press: 1960).

7. See Fred Kaplan, "JFK's First-Strike Plan," *Atlantic*, October 2001, https://www.theatlantic.com/magazine/archive/2001/10/jfks-first-strike-plan/376432/.

CHAPTER 28: THE CUBAN MISSILE CRISIS

1. "Cuban Missile Crisis," John F. Kennedy Presidential Library and Museum website, accessed September 4, 2016, https://www.jfklibrary.org/JFK/JFK-in-History/Cuban-Missile-Crisis.aspx.

2. James G. Blight and David A. Welch, *On the Brink: Americans and Soviets Reexamine the Cuban Missile Crisis* (New York: Hill and Wang, 1989), 200–1.

3. "The Nation: Childe Harold Comes of Age," *Time*, January 3, 1977, http://content.time.com/time/magazine/article/0,9171,947797,00.html.

4. Blight and Welch, *On the Brink*, 440.

5. Ibid., 465.

6. Ibid., 4, 16, 20, 144, 335.

7. Nikita Khrushvhev, "Khruschev Letter to President Kennedy October 24, 1962," United States Library of Congress, accessed September 4, 2016, http://www.loc.gov/exhibits/archives/x2jfk.html.

8. Blight and Welch, *On the Brink*, 112, 438.

9. Ibid., 112, 438, 464, 499.

10. Ibid., 87, 210, 438, 500.

11. "The Cuban Missile Crisis," Arms Control Association, accessed February 8, 2017, https://www.armscontrol.org/act/2002_11/cubanmissile.

NOTES

CHAPTER 29: THE SIX-DAY WAR

1. "Establishment of the UNEF," website of the United Nations, accessed September 28, 2016, http://www.un.org/en/peacekeeping/missions/past/unef1backgr2.html.
2. George Gawrych, *The Albatross of Decisive Victory: War and Policy Between Egypt and Israel in the 1967 and 1973 Arab-Israeli Wars* (Westport, CT: Greenwood, 2000), 5.
3. Jeremy Bowen, *Six Days: How the 1967 War Shaped the Middle East* (London: Simon and Schuster, 2003), 99–111.
4. "Yom Kippur War," History.com, accessed February 8, 2017, http://www.history.com/topics/yom-kippur-war.
5. Israel Ministry of Foreign Affairs, "The Six-Day War (June 1967)," Israel Ministry of Foreign Affairs, accessed February 8, 2017, http://www.mfa.gov.il/mfa/aboutisrael/history/pages/the%20six-day%20war%20-%20june%201967.aspx.
6. Bowen, *Six Days*, 395–96.
7. Ibid., 60–64.
8. Camille Mansour, *Beyond Alliance: Israel and US Foreign Policy* (New York: Columbia University Press, 1994), 89.
9. James Feyrer, *Distance, Trade, and Income: The 1967 to 1975 Closing of the Suez Canal as a Natural Experiment* (Hanover, NH: Dartmouth University, 2009), 1–3.

CHAPTER 30: THE CURIOUS CASE OF THE WATER DAM

1. Benjamin Miller, When Opponents Cooperate: Great Power Conflict and Collaboration in World Politics (Ann Arbor: University of Michigan Press: 2002), 113.
2. Rakesh Krishnan Simha, "Vietnam War: The Critical Role of Russian Weapons," *Russia & India Report*, April 30, 2015, http://in.rbth.com/blogs/2015/04/30/vietnam_war_the_critical_role_of_russian_weapons_42917.
3. "CIA Admits Role in 1953 Iranian Coup," *Guardian* (UK), August 19, 2013, https://www.theguardian.com/world/2013/aug/19/cia-admits-role-1953-iranian-coup; This Day in History, "CIA-Assisted Coup Overthrows Government of Iran," History.com, accessed February 9, 2017, http://www.history.com/this-day-in-history/cia-assisted-coup-overthrows-government-of-iran.
4. Ibid.
5. "Context of '1976: Cheney, Rumsfeld Lobby for Nuclear Power Plant in Iran'," Historycommons.org, http://www.historycommons.org/context.jsp?item=a76dickrummyiran.

CHAPTER 32: MOVING TO SWITZERLAND

1. Steve Inskeep, "Born in the USA: How America Created Iran's Nuclear Program," NPR, September 18, 2015, http://www.npr.org/sections/parallels/2015/09/18/440567960/born-in-the-u-s-a-how-america-created-irans-nuclear-program.
2. Raphael Ahren, "Did Israel, Under the Shah, Help Start Iran's Nuclear Program?" *Times of Israel*, November 1, 2013, http://www.timesofisrael.com/a-generation-ago-israelis-found-paradise-in-iran/.

CHAPTER 36: THE YOM KIPPUR WAR

1. James Feyrer, *Distance, Trade, and Income: The 1967 to 1975 Closing of the Suez Canal as a Natural Experiment* (Hanover, NH: Dartmouth University, 2009), 1–3.

303

2. Chaim Herzog, *The Arab-Israeli Wars* (New York: Random House, 1982), 227–31.

3. Abraham Rabinovich, *The Yom Kippur War: The Epic Encounter That Transformed the Middle East* (New York: Schocken Books, 2005), 8, 22r23, 74, 83.

4. Ibid., 14.

5. Ibid., 20, 44, 72.

6. Ibid., 57.

7. Israel Ministry of Foreign Affairs, "The Yom Kippur War (October 1973)," Israel Ministry of Foreign Affairs, accessed September 16, 2016, http://mfa.gov.il/MFA/AboutIsrael/History/Pages/The percent20Yom percent20Kippur percent20War percent20- percent20October percent201973.aspx. No longer accessible

8. Rabinovich, The Yom Kippur War, 454.

9. Note: the term "waiting for the balloon to go up" dates to World War I, when balloons were used as signals to go over the top of the trenches for an assault. The term has come to mean, in military parlance, the beginning of any armed conflict.

10. Israel Ministry of Foreign Affairs, "The Yom Kippur War (October 1973)." Yom Kippur started at sundown on October 5. Traditional Jewish days run sundown to sundown.

11. Russell, Wendy Thomas, "Your Holiday Cheat Sheet to Yom Kippur," *PBS News Hour*, updated September 24, 2015, http://www.pbs.org/newshour/updates/cheat-sheet-yom-kippur.

12. Rabinovich, *The Yom Kippur War*, 451, 476, 487, 492.

13. Rabinovich, *The Yom Kippur War*, 513.

14. Israel Ministry of Foreign Affairs, "The Yom Kippur War (October 1973)."

CHAPTER 37: THE WORLD'S GREATEST HOT PLATE

1. Ben B. Fisher, *A Cold War Conundrum: The 1983 Soviet War Scare*, NSA Archive, p. 35, http://nsarchive.gwu.edu/NSAEBB/NSAEBB426/docs/4.A%20Cold%20War%20Conundrum-September%201997.pdf.

CHAPTER 39: THE EVIL EMPIRE

1. Nate Jones, Able Archer 83: The Secret History of the NATO Exercise That Almost Triggered Nuclear War (New York: New Press, 2016), 45.

CHAPTER 40: ABLE ARCHER

1. Nate Jones, ed., "The 1983 War Scare: 'The Last Paroxysm' of the Cold War Part II," the National Security Archive, posted May 21, 2013, http://nsarchive.gwu.edu/NSAEBB/NSAEBB427/.

2. Fischer, "A Cold War Conundrum."

3. "Able Archer 1983: The Brink of Apocalypse," YouTube video, 1:15:52, documentary focusing on the exercises that almost led to a third world war between NATO and the Warsaw Pact, posted by "MrTredBear," August 14, 2013, https://www.youtube.com/watch?v=7ciy5R-tLiE.

4. Fischer, "A Cold War Conundrum."

5. Vernon L. Pedersen. "Reagan Engaged," a review of Beth A. Fischer, *The Reagan Reversal: Foreign Policy and the End of the Cold War*, H-Pol, H-Net Reviews, May, 1998, http://www.h-net.org/reviews/showrev.php?id=1984.

6. Fischer, "A Cold War Conundrum."

7. Jones, *Able Archer 83*, 48.

8. Ibid.
9. There's a great book written by Beth Fischer called *The Reagan Reversal* (University of Missouri, 1997) that details what happened immediately after Able Archer 83.
10. Pederson, "Reagan Engaged."
11. "A Cold War Conundrum," 2.
12. "Biography: Mikhail Gorbachev," *American Experience* website, accessed February 10, 2017, http://www.pbs.org/wgbh/americanexperience/features/biography/reagan-gorbachev/.
13. Stanley Meisler, "Reagan Recants 'Evil Empire' Description," *Los Angeles Times*, June 1, 1988, http://articles.latimes.com/1988-06-01/news/mn-3667_1_evil-empire.
14. "The Nobel Peace Prize 1990: Mikhail Sergeyevich Gorbachev," NobelPrize.org, accessed February 10, 2017, https://www.nobelprize.org/nobel_prizes/peace/laureates/1990/.

CHAPTER 41: THE DEADLY DIAGNOSIS

1. Brian Kannard, *Steinbeck: Citizen Spy* (Nashville: Grave Distractions, 2003).
2. L. A. Potter, "Letter from President Lyndon B. Johnson to John Steinbeck." *Social Education* (2003): 196–99.

CHAPTER 45: THE FIFTEEN-YEAR REFUSAL

1. Joshua Mills, "I.B.M. to Sell Its Military Unit to Loral," *New York Times*, December 14, 1993, http://www.nytimes.com/1993/12/14/business/ibm-to-sell-its-military-unit-to-loral.html.
2. Louis V., Gerstner Jr., *Who Says Elephants Can't Dance?: Leading a Great Enterprise through Dramatic Change* (New York: HarperBusiness: 2003), 67.

CHAPTER 46: GAME ON

1. Paul Lasewicz, e-mail to Olivia Fermi, May 6, 2011.

INDEX

A

ABB Group, 181

Able Archer 83, 236–37, 239–40, 246, 305n9

"Able Archer 1983" (BBC documentary), 238–39

acquired savant syndrome. *See* sudden savant syndrome

advanced radar, 30, 49–50

Agnew, Spiro, 197

aircraft carriers, 55–56, 221

Air Force, 134, 137–38, 139, 161, 162, 182

Alameda Air Base (Naval Air Station Alameda), 135

Albee, Edward, 245

Allegheny Ballistics Laboratory, 79

Allies, 71

Amdahl, Gene, 247

American International School of Zurich (AISZ), 190

Americans killed by U-boat

1939–41, 47

1942–44, 71

Anderson, Paul, 255

Andropov, Yuri, 231, 232, 243

Apollo I, 165, 263

ASEA (General Swedish Electric Company), 181, 183

Atanasoff, John, 3, 33, 43–49, 65, 66, 68, 77, 79

B

balloons, 13, 48, 74, 75, 90, 304n9

Bay of Pigs invasion, 134, 159

Berry, Clifford, 44

Biddle, Berk (Biddle & Crowther), 252

Bohr, Niels, 51

bomb. *See* atomic bomb

Bowen, Harold G., Sr., 37

Brezhnev, Leonid (general secretary of the Central Committee), 213–14, 215, 228. *See also* appendix (277–97)

Briggs, Lymann, 62, 63

Brown, Harold, 137–38, 139, 161, 182, 220

Brown Boveri Company, 181, 183, 188

Building IBM (Pugh), 265

Bush, Vannevar, 30, 36–37, 38–39, 63, 240

atomic bomb

cost of the, 64–65

source of funds for the, 65

timeline of development of the, 63–64

timeline leading up to the, 62–63

Atlantic Monthly, 36

Atlas, Titan, and Thor rocket families, 134

Atomic Energy Organization of Iran (AEOI), 181

Axene, Dave, 208–9, 220, 263

Axene, Dawn (née Clauson), 109, 117, 120, 151, 170, 183, 208, 220, 256, 263, 274, 275

C

Carson, Rachel, 85

Carter, Jimmy, 182, 220, 221

Casey, William, 239, 240

Castro, Fidel, 160, 161, 164

cavity magnetron, 38

Chaffee, Roger (astronaut), 165

China, 59

Churchill, Winston, 37–38

Clauson, Bill, 25, 80, 81, 82, 106, 109, 112, 117, 122, 129, 138, 147, 151, 158, 165, 183, 184, 185, 189, 220, 230, 247, 255, 259, 263, 266, 270, 274

Clauson, Caitlyn, 15, 256, 257

Clauson, Celeste, 5, 10–13, 15–17, 102, 111, 112, 114, 216, 217–19, 222, 252, 254, 256, 257, 271, 272

Clauson, Chris, 15, 111–12, 256, 257

Clauson, Dawn (Mrs. Dave Axene), 109, 117, 120, 151, 170, 183, 208, 220, 256, 263, 274, 275

Clauson, Dolores, 21, 22, 77, 234

Clauson, Dorothy (née Greene), 21, 22–23, 24, 27, 234

Clauson, Eldon, 20–21, 25–27, 42, 49, 77, 80, 88, 92, 99, 201–2, 234

Clauson, Joey, 15, 256, 257

Clauson, Mae, 97, 201–2

Clauson, Marilyn (née Malmquist) (author's mother), 1, 4, 11, 27, 30, 39, 41, 42–43, 49, 50, 66, 69, 73, 77, 79–80, 81–82, 84, 85, 89, 96, 98, 99, 104, 109, 110, 115–16, 117, 119, 120, 122, 126–30, 134, 138, 140, 145, 151, 154, 169–70, 175, 176, 179, 180, 183–84, 185, 188, 192–93, 198, 200, 201, 204, 207, 208, 217, 220, 223, 224–25, 227, 233, 243–44, 248, 252–53, 256, 258, 267, 269–71, 272–75

Clauson, Nedra (Mrs. Dirk Simon), 8, 122, 151, 175, 183, 187, 188, 192, 208, 243, 244, 249, 257, 263, 273–75

Coe, Conway P., 37, 50

Cold War, 3, 4, 6, 19, 21, 72, 80, 84, 117, 121, 131, 137, 142, 160–61, 166–68, 188, 203, 210, 226, 229, 233, 240–42, 247, 249, 255, 261, 264, 265, 275, 276

Committee on the Present Danger, 150

Compton, Karl T., 30, 37, 50

Conant, James B., 37, 50, 71

Congress (of the United States), 29, 37, 39, 56, 162, 213

Cuban missile crisis, 3, 159–64

cyclotron, 51, 64, 72

D

Dam, Kenneth, 239

Day After, The (film), 234, 238

Day of Deceit: The Truth About FDR and Pearl Harbor (Stinnett), 58, 60

deaths (number)
  of Americans by German U-boat 1939–41, 47
  of Americans by German U-boat 1942–44, 71
  caused by "Little Boy" and "Fat Man" (1945), 124
  of Israelis in Yom Kippur War, 212

DEFCON (DEFense readiness CONdition), 162. 214, 236, 239, 243

Department of Defense, 2

Department of State. *See* State Department

Dobrynin, Anatoly, 161

Duchess of Richmond (Canadian liner), 38

Dunwell, Stephen W., 149

E

Egypt, 166–68, 170–71, 172, 181, 199, 210–12, 213–14. *See also* appendix (277–97)

Einstein, Albert, 3, 51, 62, 90–91, 102, 104–5, 195, 266

Eisenhower, Dwight, 35, 39, 132, 133, 171

Elliot, George, 54–55

England, 38, 39, 43, 63, 68, 71, 73, 78, 95, 205, 220, 223–24, 227, 230, 244, 259, 260

"evil empire." *See* chapter 39, "The Evil Empire" (229–35); 239, 241, 242; *see also* Soviet Union

Export Control Act, 59

F

Fat Man (bomb), 124

FDR. *See* Roosevelt, Franklin D.

Fermi, Enrico, 3, 13, 62, 74–75, 90, 116, 265

Fermi, Olivia, 265
First War Powers Act (1941), 56
Fischer, Beth, 305n9
Ford, Gerald, 172
Frisch–Peierls memorandum, 63
fusion bomb versus fission bomb, 105

G

Gaither Report, 133
game theory, 90, 103
Gates, Bill, 125
George V of England (king), 95
Gerig, Roland, 108
Germany, 29, 35, 38, 51, 62, 72, 80, 90, 103, 104,
    181, 214, 220
Gerstner, Louis V., Jr., 261
glasnost, 242
Gorbachev, Mikhail, 241–42, 243
Gordievsky, Oleg Antonovich, 239
Grace, Princess of Monaco, 197
Great Depression, 7, 28, 29, 97
Greene, Nathanael, 23
Grissom, Gus, 165
Gromyko, Andrei, 162
Groves, Leslie, 53

H

Hanford Nuclear Reservation, 65
Heisenberg, Werner, 51
Hindenburg disaster, 74
Hiroshima, 72, 123–24
Hitler, Adolf, 43, 103, 104, 241
Holt, Archly, 31–32, 33, 50
Hoover, Herbert, 59
Hurd, Cuthbert, 64, 117–18, 119, 121, 265
Hursley Lab, 223, 226, 227

I

IBM, 1–2, 6, 39, 64, 73, 83, 117–23, 126–27,
    130, 133, 134, 142, 149–50, 182, 183, 188,
    196, 201, 208, 219–20, 226–27, 236, 244,
    246–48, 258, 259, 261–62, 264–67, 270,
    272, 274–76
    ACS (Advanced Control Systems) project, 149

Applied Sciences Department, 64, 118, 121,
    265
Federal Systems Group, 2, 6, 133, 134, 261,
    265
IBM 701 Defense Calculator, 103, 120–22,
    132
IBM 704 Electronic Data Processing Machine,
    121, 123, 127, 128, 129, 130, 132
IBM 7030 Stretch, 149–50, 247, 259
IBM System/360, 130, 150, 242, 259
Military Products Group, 83, 119, 120, 121,
    133
Poughkeepsie, 120, 121, 122, 123, 265
Iggy Pop, 257
Institute for Advanced Study (Princeton), 90,
    91, 103
Invasion of Grenada, 235
Iowa State College, 33, 34, 36, 42, 43, 44, 46–47,
    48, 63, 68, 78, 266
Iran, 73, 161, 171–73, 175, 179, 180–82, 189, 196,
    197, 199, 209, 214–16, 230, 245, 246, 248,
    266, 270, 278
Iran–Contra hearings, 248
Iraq, 166
Israel, 166–67, 171, 172, 180, 181, 187, 190, 199,
    210, 211–16, 270–71. *See also* appendix
    (277–97)
Italy, 134, 159, 163, 192

J

Japan, 50, 53, 56, 58–60, 72, 103, 161, 231, 238
Jewett, Frank B., 37, 50
Johnson, Lyndon, 182
Johnson & Johnson (J&J), 8, 10, 12, 72, 251,
    252, 267
Jones, Nate, 240
Jordan, 166
June War. *See* Six-Day War
Jupiter missile, 134
K
Kahn, Herman (*On Thermonuclear War*), 150
Kennedy, John F., 134, 150, 160–64
Kennedy, Robert, 161
Khrushchev, Nikita, 161, 162, 163, 275
Khrushchev, Sergei, 275

Kimmel, Husband E. (rear admiral), 61
Kissinger, Henry, 73, 212–14. *See also* appendix (277–97)
Korean War, 120, 121
K-25, 59, 61, 64, 65

L

Lakehurst Maxfield Field. *See* Naval Air Engineering Station Lakehurst
Lasewicz, Paul, 265
Lawrence, Ernest, 51, 52, 64, 72
Lawrence Livermore National Laboratory (aka Livermore Lab; Rad Lab), 47, 51, 52, 75, 123, 130, 136, 137, 138, 139, 142, 149, 182
Lebanon, 166
LeMay, Curtis, 161, 163
Lindberg, Dale, 20–21, 79
Little Boy (bomb), 123–24
Lockard, Joseph, 54–55
Loomis, Alfred, 51–53, 92
Loomis, F. W., 53
Loomis, Henry (Alfred's son), 52
Loomis, Henry Patterson (Alfred's father), 52
Loral Corporation, 261
Los Alamos Laboratory (aka Project Y), 65, 83, 92, 123, 124, 132

M

Mailes, 181
Malmquist, Albin, 79, 84, 85, 86, 89, 91, 93–100, 115, 233, 234
Malmquist, John Lars, 95
Malmquist Marilyn (Mrs. Wallace Clauson) (author's mother), 1, 4, 11, 27, 30, 39, 41, 42–43, 49, 50, 66, 69, 73, 77, 79–80, 81–82, 84, 85, 89, 96, 98, 99, 104, 109, 110, 115–16, 117, 119, 120, 122, 126–30, 134, 138, 140, 145, 151, 154, 169–70, 175, 176, 179, 180, 183–84, 185, 188, 192–93, 198, 200, 201, 204, 207, 208, 217, 220, 223, 224–25, 227, 233, 243–44, 248, 252–53, 256, 258, 267, 269–71, 272–75
Malmquist, Marjorie, 42, 96, 99, 116, 169–70
Malmquist, Sadie (née Johnson), 95, 99, 115, 233

Manhattan Project, 30, 53, 64, 65, 103, 197
Mason, Dave, 191–92
Massachusetts Institute of Technology (MIT), 30, 31, 36, 37, 38, 43, 50, 129
MAUD Committee, 38, 63
May, Ernest R., 117
McCain, John, 171
McCovey, Willie, 70
McDonnell Aircraft Corporation, 120
McFarlane, Robert "Bud," 234, 239, 240
McNamara, Robert, 161, 164
Meitner, Lise, 104–5
Michaels, Lee, 191
"military industrial complex," 35, 39, 133
MIT (Massachusetts Institute of Technology), 30, 31, 36, 37, 38, 43, 50, 129
Mohammad Reza Shah, 172, 179, 181, 196–97, 266, 270, 275
Moore, Rob, 144
Mosaddeq, Mohammad, 171, 172
Mossad, 211

N

Nagasaki, 72, 105, 124
NASA, 36, 132–34, 149, 165
Nasser, Gamal Abdel, 166, 167, 170
National Academy of Sciences (NAS), 29, 30–31, 32, 33, 37, 50
National Advisory Committee for Aeronautics (NACA), 36
National Defense Research Committee. *See* NDRC
National Military Command Center. *See correspondence in appendix* (278–97)
NATO, 162, 167, 200, 214, 223, 229, 236–39, 278
Naturwissenschaften (magazine), 105
Naval Air Corp, 66, 68
Naval Air Engineering Station Lakehurst, 14, 73–74
Naval Air Station Alameda (Alameda Air Base in text), 135
Naval Air Station Jacksonville, 66, 67, 69
Naval Ordnance Lab, 44, 48, 68, 79
Nazis, 71

NDRC (National Defense Research Committee), 30, 32, 33, 35–39, 43, 44, 46, 47, 48, 50, 52, 53, 62, 63, 65, 66, 68, 71, 78, 83, 90, 92, 120, 245, 267

New York Times, 124

1949 Armistice Agreements, 166

1967 Arab–Israeli War. *See* Six-Day War

1973 Arab–Israeli War. *See* Yom Kippur War

1983 Beirut barracks bombings, 235

Nixon, Richard, 73, 163, 213–15. *See also* appendix (277–97)

Non-Proliferation Treaty (NPT), 171, 172, 181, 182

NORAD, 129

North, Oliver, 248

North Atlantic Treaty Organization. *See* NATO

NSC-68, 117

Nuclear Research Center (TNRC), Tehran, 181, 182

Nuclear Weapon Archive, 132

O

Oak Ridge Gaseous Diffusion Plant, 58, 61, 64, 265

October War. *See* Yom Kippur War

Office of Scientific Research and Development (OSRD), 39, 50, 63, 64, 65, 71, 83, 91, 92

Ooms, Casper W., 50

Operation Hardtack, 132

Operation Urgent Fury. *See* Invasion of Grenada

Osbourne, Ozzy, 257

P–Q

Padgett, Jason, 24–25

Pahlavi, Mohammad Reza Shah, 172, 179, 181, 196–97, 266, 270, 275

Patton, George S. (general), 72

PC World, 150

Pearl Harbor, 50, 53, 55–56, 58–61, 64, 65, 72, 83 losses at, 55

Pearl Harbor Radar, 52, 53, 60

percent of the American population against getting into World War II (1940), 58

Pershing, John J. (general), 94, 95

Pershing II IRBMs (intermediate-range ballistic missiles), 220, 230, 233

Persian Gulf War, 36

Petrov, Stanislav, 232–33

Philco Corporation, 66, 67–68, 77

Pioneer Press (St. Paul), 84

PLO, 187

Poland, 29

Polaris missiles, 47, 132

Princeton University, 13, 48, 68, 78, 90, 91, 101, 103, 104, 264

Project Pluto, 136, 138

Project Y. *See* Los Alamos Laboratory

Pugh, Emerson, 265

R

radar. *See* chapter 13, "The Rise of Radar" (71–75) defined, 38

Radar Committee, 37, 78

Radio Moscow, 163

Rad Lab (Lawrence Livermore Lab, Livermore, CA) (aka Livermore Lab), 47, 51, 52, 75, 123, 130, 136, 137, 138, 139, 142, 149, 182

Rad Lab (Radiation Laboratory at MIT), 38, 43

Ramadan War. *See* Yom Kippur War

ramjet engines, 136–37

Raytheon, 36, 133

Reagan, Ronald, 220, 221, 229, 230, 232, 234–35, 237, 238, 239–42

Reagan Reversal, The (Fischer), 305n9

"Report of the National Defense Research Committee for the First Year of Operation June 27, 1940–June 28, 1941," 35–36

Roosevelt, Franklin D. (FDR), 29, 30, 35, 37, 39, 43, 56, 58–60, 62, 63, 64, 72

Roosevelt, Theodore, 171

Rumsfeld, Donald, 172, 181, 291

Russia, 61–62, 124, 137, 161, 166, 167, 170, 172, 190, 211, 213–15, 220, 230–32, 237, 239, 241, 243, 245. *See also* Soviet Union

Russians, 46, 93, 109, 131, 133, 159, 171, 203, 211, 232, 235, 239–41

S

Sachs, Alexander, 62

Sadat, Anwar, 211, 212–13, 278, 280

Sasser, Martin, 128

Schlesinger, Arthur, 213

SCR-535 radar equipment, 66, 67, 71, 300ch11n18

Selassie, Haile, 197

Shah, the (Mohammad Reza Shah), 172, 179, 181, 196–97, 266, 270, 275

Sharon, Ariel, 213

Short, Walter (general), 54, 61

Shultz, George P., 240

Siemen, Herr, 188

Simon, Dirk, 263

Simon, Nedra (née Clauson), 8, 122, 151, 175, 183, 187, 188, 192, 208, 243, 244, 249, 257, 263, 273–75

Six-Day War. *See* chapter 29, "The Six-Day War" (165–68); *see also* 170, 180 210, 216

Soviets, 47–48, 72, 80, 83, 117, 130, 160, 162, 163, 166–68, 181, 199, 210, 211–14, 216, 220, 221, 229–32, 235, 237–38, 240, 241. *See also* appendix (277–97)

Soviet Union (USSR), 3, 72, 80, 83, 117, 129, 133, 160, 166, 180, 229, 232, 237, 238, 239, 241–42, 245. *See also* appendix (277–97); Russia

Stirm, Ron, 257

Sputnik, 129, 131

SR-71 Blackbird, 137

Star Wars. *See* Strategic Defense Initiative

State Department, 245. *See also* Department of State correspondence in appendix (277–97)

Steinbeck, John, 245

Stimson, Henry, 51–52, 53, 59–60, 64

Stinnett, Robert, 58 60

Strategic Defense Initiative (Star Wars), 221, 229

Strategic Missiles Evaluation Group. *See* Teapot Committee

Strong, George V., 37

sudden savant syndrome, 24

Suez Canal, 166, 167, 168, 210–11, 212, 213, 280

Suez Crisis of 1956, 166

surface-to-air missiles (SAMs), 170–71, 181, 213

Syria, 166, 167, 181, 210, 212

Syrians, 211–12

Szilard, Leo, 62

T

Taft, William Howard, 59

TASS (Soviet news agency), 162

Teapot Committee, 75, 78

Teller, Edward, 124

Thatcher, Margaret, 235

thermonuclear weapon/device, examples of a, 125

Third Arab–Israeli War. *See* Six-Day War

Tito, Marshall, 197

Tolman, Richard C., 37, 50

Travis, Robert (general), 135

Treffert, Darold, 24

Truman, Harry S., 117

tuning (defined), 68

Turkey, 134, 159, 160, 163

Tyler, Kermit (lieutenant), 55, 61

U

U-boats, 30, 43, 47, 49, 71

UK, 166, 222–23, 226, 230

United Nations (UN), 166, 213, 216, 277

United States Department of Energy Nevada Test Site (NTS), 136

United States National Security Council, 117, 232

University of Minnesota, 36, 78, 79, 81, 83–84

uranium, 38, 58, 59, 61, 63–65, 80, 124, 172, 181

Uranium Committee, 30, 37, 63, 64

U.S. Department of Defense, 2

U.S. Navy, 44, 50, 52, 53, 55, 65–69, 71, 74, 76–79, 83, 90, 133, 158, 162

USS *Liberty*, 167

V

Vance, Cyrus, 182, 201

Vietnam conflict, planes lost during the, 171

von Neumann, John, 3, 48, 61, 68, 78, 89–91, 92, 102–4, 105, 116, 120–21, 122, 138, 264, 266

W–X

"waiting for the balloon to go up," 304n9

war budget, 56, 65

Washington, George, 23, 212

Washington Post, 52

Watson, Edwin "Pa," 62

Watson, Thomas J., Jr., 121

Watson, Thomas J., Sr., 121
Weinberger, Caspar, 240
White, Ed (astronaut), 165
Who Says Elephants Can't Dance? (Gerstner), 261
Williams, Walt (coach), 145–46
Women's Peace Camp, 230
World War I (aka First World War), 36, 94, 95, 96, 98–99, 304n9
World War II (aka Second World War), 1, 29, 36, 39, 50, 56, 58, 65, 67, 77, 161, 166, 167

Y
YMCA, 14, 15, 48, 74, 75
Yom Kippur, 212
Yom Kippur War. See chapter 36, "The Yom Kippur War" (210–17); *See also* appendix (277–97)

Z
Zurich, 73, 173–76, 178, 180, 183, 186–88, 190, 193, 194, 197, 201, 203, 204, 206, 207, 248, 275
Zwingli, Huldrych, 194, 195